The Hope at Hand

National and World Revival for the 21st Century

David Bryant

Baker Books

A Division of Baker Book House Co
Grand Rapids, Michigan 49516

Published by Baker Books
a division of Baker Book House Company
P.O. Box 6287, Grand Rapids, MI 49516-6287

Third printing, April 1996

Printed in the United States of America

Library of Congress Cataloging-in-Publication Data

Bryant, David, 1945-
    The hope at hand: national and world revival for the twenty-first century /
David Bryant.
       p. cm.
    Includes bibliographical references.
    ISBN 0-8010-1099-3
    1. Evangelistic work. 2. Evangelistic work United States. 3. Prayer. 4. Twenty-first century—Forecasts. I. Title.
    BV3790.B764 1995
    269'.2—dc20 94-32755

The Hope at Hand

David Bryant will bring you to the edge of your seat in anticipation of the next great spiritual awakening. Evidence abounds that true global revival is on its way—no doubt the greatest in all of human history—and Bryant documents precisely how. Get ready to rejoice!

Dick Eastman, international president,
Every Home for Christ

This is where God's people, united in common purpose, in prayer, and in expectation, will see the hand of God working to accomplish his purposes. Every committed Christian should read this!

E. Brandt Gustavson, president,
National Religious Broadcasters

The Hope at Hand is focused zeal for God's church. It is more than just a call for revival or a yearning for revival. It is a curriculum and preparatory guide for revival. It surges with the hope that comes through prayer.

Stephen A. Hayner, president,
InterVarsity Christian Fellowship

David Bryant challenges the Christian to put the expectation of revival on the top shelf, make it a first priority, rejoice at the hope at hand. This is clearly a watershed book to be read by all who long for his appearing.

Joe C. Aldrich, president,
Multnomah Bible College and Biblical Seminary

Are we about to see a prayer renewal of unprecedented proportions? David Bryant moves the discussion from detached speculation to passionate urgency. I recommend it highly as a tonic for prayerless complacency.

Timothy K. Jones,
co-author of *The Saints Among Us*

David Bryant is one of the Holy Spirit's "advance men" pointing the way with spiritual wisdom for people who want to be tuned to the times. His penetrative perspective is the fruit of two great sources: a life of prayer and broad experience in ministry.

Jack W. Hayford, senior pastor,
The Church On The Way

The powerful message of this book will speak to both mind and heart. I pray that God will use it as a means of encouragement for authentic revival to come to the church and a great spiritual awakening to sweep this nation—and the world.

Paul A. Cedar, president,
Evangelical Free Church of America

The mood of hopelessness, whether in the urban, suburban, or rural churches, has been challenged by David Bryant in his new book.

John E. Kyle, executive director (retired),
Mission to the World, Presbyterian Church in America

Every believer can participate as God is calling forth an unprecedented wave of concerted, united prayer that will shake the nations. David Bryant gives us the direction, instruction, and wisdom we need to know the times we live in and respond with faith.

Tom Pelton, president,
March for Jesus

The Hope at Hand is a clarion call to prayer for world revival, which throbs with excitement and anticipation. Read it, then to your knees!

Robert Coleman, professor of evangelism,
Trinity Evangelical Divinity School

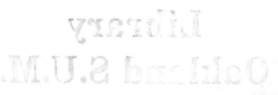

To Adam, Bethany, and Benjamin.
You have been wholly devoted to Christ from the beginning,
and to you belongs the legacy of the coming world revival.

Contents

Acknowledgments 9
Helps from Concerts of Prayer International 11

Introduction: Is There Any Hope? 13

Part One: The Rising Hope
1. The Rising Hope for World Revival 21
2. People of Hope, People of Revival 37

Part Two: The Surging Confidence
3. Confidence Builders about the Hope at Hand 59
4. Confidence Builder 1: The Decisive Person 69
5. Confidence Builder 2: The Divine Pattern 79
6. Confidence Builder 3: The Dark Prospects 91
7. Confidence Builder 4: The Disturbing Paralysis 103
8. Confidence Builder 5: The Dramatic Preparations 115
9. Confidence Builder 6: The Distinctive Praying 127
10. Confidence Builder 7: The Determined People 143

Part Three: Preparing the Way
11. Pacesetters for World Revival: Getting Started 159
    Epilogue: A Story about the Coming Revival 185

Appendices
1. From Chapter 6: The Dark Prospects 195
2. From Chapter 7: The Disturbing Paralysis 211
3. From Chapter 8: The Dramatic Preparations 219
4. From Chapter 9: The Distinctive Praying 231

Notes 245

Acknowledgments

In many ways this book is a distillation of what God has taught me the past fifteen years as I've visited with Christian leaders, united prayer movements, and ministries of renewal and mission around the world. I am indebted to them and to all they have shown me of Christ, our hope.

I want to thank the board of directors of Concerts of Prayer International for providing the spiritual covering for my ministry (including this book)—especially John Kyle, our first chairman, who mentored me and stood faithfully with me during the most formative years of this ministry.

To the staff of Concerts of Prayer International—both past and present—who labored with me, my heartfelt gratitude. You have helped create arenas throughout the body of Christ, especially in movements of united prayer, into which I can now preach the truths of this book. I want to express appreciation specifically to Barbara Moore, my administrative assistant, and to Joyce Pierce, for their many, many hours at the word processor as we worked and reworked the manuscript.

Special thanks goes to Timothy Jones, associate editor of *Christianity Today,* for his timely editorial assistance. His warm encouragements kept me on task when I might have folded in self-doubts. In the same vein, I am also grateful to Dan Van't Kerkhoff, senior editor at Baker Book House, and to his staff for their gracious and skillful support in bringing the manuscript to public light.

Finally, in addition to the dedication of the book to my children, I also want to proclaim my unceasing thanks to my dear wife, Robyne, for standing with me with such love during every facet of our ministry. Truly we are a team!

And together we offer up this book to our wonderful Redeemer, Jesus Christ—Lord of the nations and hope of the world.

Helps from Concerts of Prayer International

Small Group Study/Discussion Guide

As founder and president of Concerts of Prayer International, David Bryant has developed a multifaceted ministry designed to help promote, equip, and mobilize united prayer for revival on many levels—congregational, citywide, organizational, national, and international.

To explore how the Concerts of Prayer team and resources might serve a movement of prayer where you live, please write or call:

Concerts of Prayer International
P.O. Box 1399
Wheaton, Illinois 60189
ATTN: Steve Bell, Executive Director
Phone: 708-690-8441
FAX: 708-690-0160

Be sure to ask for our free catalog: *Concerted Prayer: Tools and Resources That Make a Difference.*

In anticipation of David Bryant's newest book, Concerts of Prayer International has prepared a twenty-two-page, eight-week small group study/discussion guide: *The Hope at Hand: Take It to Your Friends: A Small Group Study/Discussion Guide.*

Useful in Bible study groups, Sunday school classes, and other settings, this guide will make the study of the coming revival accessible to every Christian. It offers you:

11

- Discussion questions on selected readings for each week from *The Hope at Hand*.
- Life-application and church-application possibilities for the issues and insights discussed.
- Directed times of opening and closing group prayer to enable you to act on the coming revival right now, before the session is over.

With this booklet, you can help disciple others into active prayer and preparation for the hope of revival, which really is at hand! Request a copy from the offices of Concerts of Prayer International.

Introduction:
Is There Any Hope?

Almost without exception, everywhere I travel Christian leaders are telling me that the great need of their people is to be revitalized with a renewed spirit of *hope* in God. And for good reason. There are ominous signs all around us.

U.S. News and World Report, looking at "spiritual America,"[1] tells us that our nation is deeply conflicted over the role of religion in society, creating a "culture of disbelief" (to use the title of Yale professor Stephen Carter's book). Spiritual pursuits are increasingly excluded from public life, while our troubled nation is beset by violent crime, broken families, and deteriorating cities. These realities are confirmed by studies of the Index of Leading Cultural Indicators[2] (published by the Heritage Foundation), which describe a society in the midst of seeming cultural demise—the vacuum of values. Lance Morrow calls us "a country out of control: drugs, crime, and what has become a morally borderless wandering."[3]

The picture seems no more hopeful on an international level. Writing in *Atlantic Monthly,* world demographer Robert D. Kaplan forecasts a "coming world anarchy"[4] in which national borders will disintegrate under the pressures of poverty, population growth, environmental stress, lawlessness, and resulting chaos, such as ethnic wars. To this, we as Christians might add sobering statistics of what appears to be a diminishing percentage of earth's population that calls itself followers of Christ. "In a startling brief period," writes Chuck Colson, "the West has been transformed from a Christian culture—in which the majority accepted basic Christian concepts—into a post-Christian culture."[5] It is estimated that in the U.S. alone, by A.D. 2000, 37 percent (one hundred million people) will have absolutely no church background whatsoever. In addition, others document what some term an unfolding "satanic revival"[6] that is nothing less than a conspiracy from hell, exacerbating destructive global trends while at the same time reentrenching enemy strongholds against the world-wide advance of the gospel.

It should come as no surprise then, that today's "twenty-some-things"—often referred to as "baby busters"—are "world-class skeptics, cynical about mankind and pessimistic about the future." They seem to lack heroes, causes, and vision. They lack an abiding hope for themselves, for their relationships with each other, and for their relationship with God. In fact, they take their hopelessness so seriously that no previous American generation has ever experienced a suicide rate as high—more than five thousand each year.[7]

And yet . . . *and yet,* the Spirit of God is inciting hope throughout Christ's church from so many directions. Dick Eastman, international president of Every Home for Christ, says that between now and the year 2000 "more people could come to Christ than in all of recorded history."[8] He calls this the *Jericho Hour,* the church's final offensive. To use his term, the church is moving into a "season of suddenlies," where we see many obstacles of the gospel crumbling so quickly that it's almost impossible to keep up with the story of what God is doing.

Recently, for example, leaders from a number of church traditions gathered together to voice their common concern for the moral reclamation of America and to form an informal alliance to stand against the evil tide.[9] Shortly before, another coalition, Evangelicals for Social Action, drew together five hundred delegates to issue a declaration that calls for "weeping" over racism and other persistent social problems in America. At the same time, however, it calls for a rising hope that God will pour out his Spirit again to renew the church and move committed believers unitedly into both evangelism and social engagement. In addition, a new national "Reconciliation Coalition" has taken off, sponsoring interracial, multiethnic gatherings of evangelical Christian leaders to deal with past offenses and discriminations against one another, in order to bring healing to the body of Christ and to prepare the way for revival in the church.

Of course we already see great hope in pools of renewal emerging in parts of the church. Take, for example, the Charismatic movement, focusing increased confidence in extraordinary gifts of God's grace; or the across-the-board reconstitution of Christ-centered worship within various Christian traditions worldwide; or the Christian men's movement (Promise Keepers) that recently brought together hundreds of thousands of men across the country to pray, to worship God, and to commit themselves to be instruments of revival in our nation.

One of the most encouraging developments in this decade is global missionary cooperation toward the possibility of total world evangelization around the year 2000. Whether or not this can actually be accomplished, there is an air of hope that such vision breathes into all of us, which, when combined with other pools of renewal, gives us reason to reject any competing spirit of despair.

For my part, however, the activity that really sets me to cheering—and about which I write the most in this book—is the unrelenting development of revival prayer throughout the Christian community. *It truly is the most hopeful sign of our times.*

Illustrations of this are legion. For example, we've just concluded an international event called "A Day to Change the World" when an estimated thirty million Christians prayed in unison over a twenty-four-hour period for the closure of the Great Commission by the year 2000. Marches for Jesus, involving millions, occurred in every time zone in thousands of locations in more than one hundred nations. Across the globe there were all-night prayer vigils, hundreds of concerts of prayer, prayer walks, and prayer journeys. Thousands of children were mobilized and trained to love and pray for the lost children of their generation. What a creative initiative of the Holy Spirit this was!

One special dimension of this prayer movement can be seen in God's work among pastors. In just a few days I am scheduled to address six thousand pastors in Manila from every province of the Philippines, many of them heavily subsidized because they would be too poor to attend the Philippine Prayer Congress on their own resources. All of them are committed to mobilizing united prayer for revival throughout their land. And just today, there fell into my hands a document entitled "A Solemn Covenant for Christian Leaders in the Southeast." One hundred pastors from different states in that part of our

15

nation spent four days secluded in prayer for revival (quite a breakthrough for busy clergy!). At the conclusion they entered into a written covenant, confessing both the vision they are praying toward and their agreement to keep on praying together until God answers. Part of it reads,

> We repent of holding to a form of religion that denies the power of it. We repent of racism, of religious pride, of hypocrisy, of status quo mediocrity; of materialism and selfish madness and lusts of all varieties; of busyness and of prayerlessness.
>
> We are, hereby, called to devote ourselves to the Lord Jesus Christ in brokenness, repentance and obedience. We will pray until revival comes to the Southeast. We will promote this call as broadly as possible throughout the Body of Christ. We realize this call is costly and we resolve in advance to pay the price.
>
> We are full of hope and confidence that Jesus is coming in revival to the Southeast, bringing glory back to himself through the Church.

Does this reflect the longings and hopes in your own heart? It does for me and for thousands of leaders I have talked with around the globe. This is also the kind of hope we know our people desperately need.

Renowned British historian Paul Johnson in his widely respected 870-page-treatise *Modern Times* surveys the major crosscurrents in world history from the 1920s into the 1990s. His sweeping, incisive interpretation of this century concludes by asking whether the primary evil forces that made possible modern events of catastrophic proportions—bringing to a violent end over one hundred million people—can be overcome. Such forces include the rise of moral relativism, the decline of personal responsibility, the repudiation of Judeo-Christian values, and the "arrogant belief that men and women could solve all the mysteries of the universe by their own unaided intellects." His answer to his own question is found in the final sentence of the book: "On that would depend the chances of the twenty-first century becoming, by contrast, an age of hope for mankind."[10]

The thesis of my book is that the twenty-first century will be an age of great hope because it will be an age of world revival in the church. This revival will be of such magnitude that it will significantly push back the demons of which John writes in Revelation, while at the same time

16

awakening multitudes of earth's peoples to the supremacy and sufficiency of Christ.

In part 1, I want to explore with you a fresh new perspective on what true biblical revival involves, and document for you how many Christians are standing on tip-toe in anticipation that a massive revival is close at hand. In part 2, I focus on the issue of confidence—confidence in the character and ways of God in revival, and seven good reasons why we can turn from any spirit of tentativeness about a coming national and world revival. Finally, in part 3, I detail practical ways we can pray and prepare for revival, and bring others into the action with us. (Incidentally, on page 11 there is information about a small group study/discussion guide for this book, to help you go through it with some friends.)

Yes, this book is about hope. Because I'm not simply talking about a revival *in* the twenty-first century. I'm talking about a revival *for* the twenty-first century. I'm talking about a revival already bearing down on top of us. Read. Rejoice. Pursue. Receive.

Part 1

The Rising Hope

1

The Rising Hope for World Revival

Focused on the Future

In a *Time* essay on the coming millennium, William A. Henry reflects: "The future. Have any two words excited more hope, prompted more dreams and visions? Has anything contributed more to the wellspring of all progress—the relentless variety of human curiosity and invention—than the belief that the future can and must be different, bigger, better?"[1] Earthlings may have never been as focused on the future as we are today. Speculation abounds on what the twenty-first century holds for all of us.

Two American universities, the University of Houston and the University of Hawaii, offer degrees with an emphasis on future studies. Hundreds of consultants, think tanks, and government leaders study the future full-time. Even major corporations are beginning to take this field seriously. "The rise of global business competition, the fall of Communism and perhaps the approach of the millennium have all combined to make the present seem more uncertain and the study of the future more appealing."[2] Recently two thousand members of the World Future Society gathered for their seventh general assembly in Washington, D.C., in a growing effort to help businesses and governments be ready for some of the possibilities that lie ahead.

Everywhere today there's a growing sense we are on the threshold of something extraordinary, something (in Henry's words) "different, bigger, better." A recent *Time*/CNN survey found that 62 percent of Americans believe that compared to the twentieth century, the twenty-first century holds far more hope for all of us (despite the conviction that we will still wrestle with things like poverty, disease, and environmental disasters). Some, intrigued with technology, are dubbed "cyberpunks." They're preoccupied with things like brain implantation, "cyberspace" (data highways), and "virtual reality." Others, like today's baby boomers, focus on the future with optimistic determination to come out winners; they are bullish on the future if they are anything.

Of course this is not to say there is not also a fundamental uncertainty about the twenty-first century. Many are scrambling to paint for us their own hopeful scenarios. In the special issue of *Time* dealing entirely with "Beyond the Year 2000: What to Expect in the New Millennium," Lance Morrow writes, "The 1990s have become a transforming boundary between one age and another, between a scheme of things that has disintegrated and another that is taking shape. A millennium is coming, a cosmic divide."[3] One example: The battle to save the planet may replace twentieth-century battles over Fascism and Communism, as an organizing theme for international relations.

As we move into the third millennium, most do so with great expectations. And we will enter it in a way no other generation has ever crossed a time line, observing it simultaneously as one electronic global village. Already reservations for New Year's Eve 1999 have begun to pour in to hotels and establishments around the world. The Millennium Society has booked the Queen Elizabeth II to transport three thousand people to celebrate our entrance into A.D. 2000 at the great Pyramid of Cheops. Others rising up with end-of-the-world predictions feel even more celebratory. Currently six hundred different groups have formulated a host of dramatic projections on how the year 2000 will mark the opening of a perfect, utopian age. When do we break out the fireworks and let the party begin?

Preparing for Spiritual Renaissance

Respond we must. *How do we prepare for A.D. 2000 and beyond?* Among the many options presented, none are being stressed more strongly at the moment than what futurologists say is the single greatest hope for human survival: what happens to the human *spirit*. Increasingly, hope for the human race is ultimately pinned on a spiritual and moral renaissance more than anything else. In fact, in *Megatrends 2000* John Naisbitt predicts a simultaneous series of worldwide revivals, not only within Christianity but within other faiths such as Islam and Hinduism, as well as the acceleration of the New Age movement itself.[4]

Revivals? The International Social Survey Programs concurs in recently published results from polling nineteen thousand people in more than a dozen countries. It found that in the West there is a resurgence in religious beliefs in the former Communist block, as well as the return to religion of baby boomers in the United States. All of this is called by the survey "signs of an international religious revival." Their findings show that "religious devotion in countries such as the United States, Ireland and Poland may be higher than ever."[5] For example, the unexpected events in Eastern Europe have reversed predictions that there would be an inevitable decline in religious belief in the modern age.

Yes, many futurologists currently sense a genuine cry for revival and the reclaiming of the transcendent. Many Americans confess the unnerving reality of a spiritual free fall in Western culture and the impending possibility of a genuine moral collapse. According to Gallup, two out of three Americans believe the United States is in a serious, long-term decline, not only economically but, more importantly, morally and spiritually. Many Americans are asking, "What are we building for ourselves and leaving for our children in the twenty-first century?" And 68 percent say they are dissatisfied with the religious values they are passing on.

In the face of this, increasing numbers are on a God-hunt—looking for more—more faith and more spiritual reality. Another survey documents that three out of five Americans hold greater interest in spiritual things than they did five years ago. There seems to be a quiet but persistent shift from a modern secular era to what one sociologist has called "a post-modern era," which views reality much more in terms of the supernatural. Again Gallup finds one-third of Americans have reported having "a religious insight or awakening that has changed the direction of my life." Gallup calls this one of the most significant survey results they have ever uncovered. Fifty-five percent of Americans believe dealing with the transcendent will play a much greater role in their lives as they enter the new millennium. That's why University of Chicago church historian Martin Marty is calling the current revival of prayer and longing for spirituality "the event of our era."

Many are feeling "as if the hand of God were turning a page in human fate." That's what Henry Gruenwald tells us in "The Year 2000: Is It the End—or Just the Beginning?" Not only have we witnessed the end of Communism and the end of nationalism, but we are also witnessing the end or at least decline of an age of unbelief and the beginning of what might be called a new age of faith. Gruenwald observes that one of the most remarkable reasons for this has been the massive impact of dehumanizing forces from technological progress to physical violence throughout this century. Now he and others are predicting a reaction against this phenomenon. They predict that once again we will make our view of man depend primarily upon our view of God.

This reemerging, irrepressible religious impulse (what some are terming "the revenge of the sacred") is taking many forms: the spread of Islamic fundamentalism, the rise of fanatical Hinduism, New Age movements, as well as the growth of evangelical churches throughout the Third World. Prognosticators suggest we are heading into a century that really will be a *new age of faith*—"heading into an age when faith will again be taken seriously, when it will again play a major part in our existence."[6] The question to ask is this: Is God preparing to turn this spiritual restlessness in a most unexpected direction—toward biblical revival?

At a Crossroads: What May We Hope?

The existential philosopher Immanuel Kant boiled mankind's search for truth down to three major questions: 1. What can I know? 2. What ought I to do? 3. What may I hope?[7] It is to this third question that we now turn, for out of it flow answers to the first two.

What may we hope—especially as we look toward the opening of the third millennium? As we seek to answer that question, it would be good to keep in mind the warning of Jack Hayford. Sometimes we fall short of the answers God wants us to give because of an "unperceived smugness that drugs the soul with the notion that our *present* boundaries of understanding God are the *permanent* boundaries of His readiness to reveal Himself to us."[8] Which boundaries operate in your life?

As you will soon discover, *I believe the boundaries we should set are for nothing less than a coming revival, both for our nation and for the church worldwide.* I've learned in my extensive travels over these past years—into all parts of this nation, among many denominational and ethnic expressions of the church, and throughout the body of Christ worldwide—that I am not alone in my convictions. Proverbs 13:12 says, "Hope deferred makes the heart sick." Even so, I have met hundreds of leaders who are as heartsick as I am. They are filled with expectations for world revival—with persistent yearnings for this and nothing less. They can't rest. It has become for them a magnificent obsession! Take for example the leaders of national youth ministries who met the other day to prepare for a convention of ten thousand youth pastors. These pastors will come from many denominations to talk about the imminent revival among high school students in our nation and how to prepare youth ministries to handle it. The excitement was palpable.

Writing in *Christianity Today*, Timothy Jones explores many divergent streams of spiritual renewal and formation throughout the body of Christ in our nation under the title "Great Awakenings: Americans Are Becoming Fascinated with Prayer and Spirituality. Is It Time to Rejoice?" He discusses the signs of increasing spiritual hunger. Acknowledging that we live in a time of renewed spiritual ferment, which calls us to a systematic, biblical approach to the spiritual life as we strive for matters of unity in prayer, he raises the question "But is it revival? The ultimate significance of renewals and spiritual movements becomes clear only with a long view. Still, there is the question: What is God up to?" And he concludes with this: "Will today's spiritual enthusiasm lead to some profound awakening?"[9] Good question! In other words, what may we hope? Is it to be world revival?

As one social commentator put it humorously: "Mankind stands at a crossroads. One road leads to hopelessness and despair. The other road leads to total destruction. Let us pray that we will have the wisdom to choose correctly!"[10] Yes, it would seem at times as if only two roads are before us: hopelessness or destruction. Even the most cursory preview of the twenty-first century convicts us that we desperately need divine intervention. But that's what revival is all about. Revival offers us a third road—the road of hope. In fact, we could reword the end of the satirist's proverb to read: "Let us choose to have the wisdom to pray correctly," that is, to seek the God who deserves awe and offers us salvation. Because our hope is in him. This is the road that leads toward victory.

As various Christian leaders have increasingly pointed out to me, God seems to be insistent on helping us to find this third road. A denominational president remarked to me, "God is pushing his church toward revival, and into prayer for revival, from *all* sides." Historically, we know that whenever every other option outside of revival has been exhausted, revival begins to take a renewed and compelling focus in the life of the church. This appears to be happening again. The vision for revival is ascending within the church as the great new hope of our times.

A growing number of books on the topic say so. For example: *The Coming Great Awakening: New Hope for the Nineties* (David McKenna); *Revive Us Again! Realistic Thinking on Revival* (edited by Matthew David); *The Spark That Ignites: God's Promise to Revive the Church through You* (Robert Coleman); *Preparing for Revival* (Brian Mills); *Revival Fire* (Wesley Duewel).[11] Here are some other voices speaking of this hope.

Voices of Hope

- At the outset of the last quarter of the twentieth century, looking toward this very moment, Billy Graham in his final address at the Lausanne Congress on World Evangelization (that drew together some three thousand leaders from over 150 nations, committed to completing the Great Commission) expressed his hope: "I believe there are two streams in prophetic Scripture. One leads us to understand that as we approach the latter days and the second coming of Christ, things will become worse and worse. The Day of the Lord is near in the valley of decision." (He is speaking of God's judgments.) "But I believe as we approach the latter days it could be a time also of great revival . . . a rain of blessings, showers falling from heaven upon all the continents before the coming of our Lord."[12] In a recent press conference at a similar gathering in the U.S., Graham went so far as to declare: "I believe we've already entered revival. May none of us miss it."

- With equal enthusiasm, Paul Cedar, president of the Evangelical Free Church of America, speaks without apology: "Without a doubt, the major opportunity before us is the potential of an historic revival akin to the first and second great awakenings which took place in the early history of the United States. The need for such a revival is obvious. The encouraging 'signs' of an impending awakening is the grass roots prayer movement God is raising up throughout this nation among pastors, denominations, congregations, families and individuals. In addition, there is an unusual openness among church leaders for cooperation in great movements of prayer and evangelistic outreach in the decade of the 90s."[13]

- Don Argue, president of an Assemblies of God college and recent president of the National Association of Evangelicals, joins the chorus: "The answer from all quarters is unanimous. We need to pray corporately for a national revival. I firmly believe God wants to send another spiritual awakening to America. But first we need to enlarge our prayer focus."[14]

- Bill Bright, founder of Campus Crusade for Christ and New Life 2000 (bringing the gospel right now to millions of unreached peoples worldwide), states that never in all of his years of ministry has he seen so many people praying for personal, nationwide, and worldwide revival. "Wherever I go I sense a God-given conviction that revival is desperately needed. Lately I have sensed that the Body of Christ is on the verge of the greatest spiritual break-through in the history of Christianity."[15]

- John Perkins is founder of Voice of Calvary Ministries. Grappling with the desperate need of the church to confront racism and bring about reconciliation within our nation, this key African American church leader declares, "There is an awakening taking place. It is as if the sleeping giant known as the church is beginning to emerge from a long nap—awakening to its commission to be God's reconciling force on the earth. In pockets of hope around the nation, hard answers are being found to the tough questions of race."[16] One "pocket of hope" can be found in a group of pastors in Harlem who are praying for God to raise up "fifty thousand righteous men" to walk the streets of Harlem and take back the neighborhoods for Jesus Christ. Committed to praying persistently until it happens, they know that it will be nothing less than wholesale revival not only for Harlem but for the whole city.

- Those within the more organized renewal movements of our day, such as the Charismatic movement, have reached the conclusion that there is so much more God is waiting to do for his church beyond what they themselves have yet experienced. Mario Murillo, writing in *Charisma*, claims that the Charismatic renewal is in desperate need of "fresh fire." "*We must experience a new Pentecost. We must stop our frenzied round of activities and form upper rooms to pray and wait on God for a fresh outpouring of His Spirit. Seek Jesus—nothing more, nothing less, nothing else. Call upon the God who answers by fire. Soon you'll be engulfed and your fears will be ashes. Then the ensuing sense of God's purpose and power will astound you.*"[17]

- Many are convinced that the whole of western culture has no other hope but revival in the church. Christian philosopher Os Guinness has articulated this need in two recent books, *No God but God: Breaking with the Idols of Our Age* and *The American Hour: A Time of Reckoning and the Once and Future Role of Faith*. In the latter, as he looks toward the twenty-first century, Guinness ends with a discussion of our nation's prospects. One prospect is that America will become increasingly secular, deeply liberal, and prosperous. But the other is that "there will be a massive revitalization of American life, including both its ideals and institutions, *through a movement of decisive spiritual revival and reformation*."[18] His own expectation? It is that America will respond—that God will move in reformation and revival, mobilizing sufficient numbers so as to revitalize the whole of American society. And yet Guinness cautions that any kind of an American spiritual renaissance will take place only by the sovereign intervention of Almighty God.

- James Dobson, the most frequently heard Christian broadcaster today, after outlining a number of illustrations on the disintegration of our society in an article entitled "Morality Under Fire,"[19]

28

arrives at the same conclusion: "What can we do? What should be our response? First, *we must continue to pray for worldwide revival that will reawaken millions of people spiritually.* This is not mere pious sentiment. Every great revival has been accompanied by social reform. . . . We seek the Lord in earnest prayer that He would once again grant revival to his church in the U.S. and around the world."

- A similar theme resounds from the pen of Carl F. H. Henry, evangelical statesman and theologian, when he predicts, "Slick promotion and management techniques aren't the answer. *Without genuine revival the church's vision is inevitably blurred and its hope is misplaced.*"[20] This parallels the convictions of Jim Wallis, editor of *Sojourners*: "For some of us who see the danger of these times, there is also vision to see the opportunity for a true spiritual revival. Because the present crisis has so much to do with our basic spiritual values, *the possibility of revival is great.*"[21]

- Perhaps William Abrahams in his book *The Coming Great Revival* captures the current mood best when he writes, "*The present moment is a time for celebration and hope.* Those evangelicals who know the full riches of their history and the winds of the spirit should entertain hopes of better things to come. Expressing it most boldly they should be anticipating a coming great revival.

  "*The signs of that revival are already clear.* Among a host of groups within and without the mainline churches there is an urge for renewal that shows no indications of abating. There's a vast army of new Christians hungry for initiation into a modern version of the Christian faith that will integrate deep piety, social action and classical theology in a penetrating expression of the Christian Gospel. . . ."[22]

- But this sense of impending world revival may be more strongly felt by Christian leaders in the Two-Thirds World. In my travels throughout that part of the church, I have discovered a great hope for global awakening to Christ. So has Roger Greenway.[23] *Missions Now: This Generation* describes what he calls a "third wave," in the Two-Thirds World, of spiritually renewed Christians. He foresees them sweeping through the church to act on deep concerns about lost people and poor people, and striving for revival everywhere the church needs God-given revitalization.

29

- He is joined in this perspective by one of the leading pastors in Latin America, Omar Cabrera. Cabrera believes that "the best is yet to come" for the church in Argentina. The church there has been experiencing a degree of spiritual awakening, but it's only beginning to understand what to do with it. The more fully the church understands the comprehensive nature of its mission, says Cabrera, the more thoroughly he believes that *the real revival is coming.*
- In Bangkok, the pastor of Thailand's largest and fastest-growing church is full of similar hope. Kriengsak Chareonwongsak says, *"I see a great harvest coming."* With this Kim Joon-gon, a respected leader in the churches throughout Asia, concurs: "The next ten years is a time of spiritual emergency. It is a time of opportunity. The Lord Jesus has the keys to open what no one can shut. I believe in the next ten years, history's greatest revival will take place in our area."[24]
- The declaration drafted in 1993 by the Jamaican Association of Evangelicals and affirmed by evangelical Christian leaders of nine countries in the Caribbean reads in part: "We commit ourselves to be used by the Lord to bring about revival in our region, not as a catchword but as a reality, in light of A.D. 2000—revitalizing, reawakening, renewing and rekindling the evangelical church."[25]

The Most Hopeful Voices of All

Chaplain of the U.S. Senate, Dr. Richard Halverson, commented a decade ago that even though God is sovereign in the works of revival, there are still conditions that we must meet—prayer is preeminent among them. He wrote: "I think all the conditions have been met [for national revival] except one—the desire on the part of God's people for an awakening that will issue in righteousness, in selflessness, and in authentic piety."[26] How radically this trend has reversed itself since he penned those words. If Halverson is right, we can now say that *all* conditions for revival are being met because the final one is coming to the fore: *desire*—expressed by increased repentance and prayer. And these are the most hopeful voices of all.

Maybe some historical perspective would be helpful here. The evangelical scholar J. Edwin Orr summarized into one simple statement his sixty years of historical study on great prayer movements preceding major spiritual awakenings: *"Whenever God is ready to do something new with his people, he always sets them to praying."*[27] If that has been foundational to God's agenda in any generation, how can we conclude otherwise than that a world revival is coming? Look at the current growth of united prayer focused on that extraordinary work of the Spirit throughout the body of Christ. This is the most hopeful sign of our times!

For example, David Barrett, leading demographer of the world Christian movement today, has given us the following statistics from his extensive research: 1. Worldwide there are about 170 million Christians who are committed to praying every day for spiritual awakening and world evangelization. 2. Of these, twenty million believe that praying in that direction is their primary calling in ministry within the body of Christ (what we might otherwise term as "prayer warriors"). 3. Worldwide there are at least ten million prayer groups that have as a major focus every time they meet to pray to seek God for a coming world revival.[28] And finally, 4. worldwide there are an estimated thirteen hundred prayer mobilization networks that are seeking to stir up the church to accelerated prayer for world revival and mission.

If we know historically, as Dr. Orr suggests, this groundswell of prayer is a gift of God; if it is biblically accurate to teach that God has not only ordained the end but also the means (the end being world revival, the means being the prayers of his people); if this massive chorus of prayer is increasingly focused on nothing less than national and world revival; and if, when God stirs us up to this type of praying he does so because he is actually ready to answer us—how can we believe otherwise than that world revival is bearing down on top of us?

Just review with me the development of the prayer movement in the United States. It is now estimated that nine out of ten Americans pray frequently and earnestly, and almost all say God has answered their prayers.[29] Over the past twenty-five years we have seen significant stages unfold in this movement of prayer. In the early '70s the foundations were laid by key spokespersons who were often regarded as "voices in the wilderness" calling the church to united prayer for revival. But by 1976, with the first ever U.S. Congress on Prayer, came an emergence of united prayer in the life of the church that has not been silent since. Throughout the 1980s prayer momentum grew with the emergence of citywide prayer movements, with the strong leadership of pastors in churches and cities, and finally with the formation of coalitions at the national level to foster and encourage concerted prayer for revival.

All of this came to dramatic focus in 1993 at the National Consultation on United Prayer. This gathering of three hundred leaders, from 166 denominations and Christian ministries, representing nearly half of the Protestant churches in America, and coming from thirty-five states, convened for twenty-four hours beginning on the inauguration day of a new presidential administration. The purpose of the consultation was clearly similar: *to inaugurate a new era of spiritual leadership in the body of Christ, calling the church to united prayer for revival until revival comes.* During the course of the event most of the time was spent in prayer over the nation. But at one point a committee of twelve was set aside representing the diversity of the gathering. Sequestered with three hundred written recommendations from the delegates, they were to compose a simple call to prayer that would reflect the consensus of this broad-based gathering and their constituencies, regarding what God was "up to" in preparing his church for revival through prayer. They returned with a document that has been widely circulated since (see page 33).

Without question, this is a prayer movement that is already having dramatic impact. It is doing so in ways that are providing preliminary demonstrations of true biblical revival. Church historian Richard Lovelace, giving an overview of historic cycles of renewal and revival, summarizes what he has observed since his attendance at the International Prayer Assembly (IPA) for world evangelization (a historic first) in 1984. Noting that united prayer is key to past spiritual awakenings and that evangelical Christians are experiencing an acceleration of revival prayer today that may be unprecedented, he surveys a decade of prayer following the IPA. Marveling at the collapse of atheistic Communism throughout the world, he calls it a historical change as significant as the Reformation or Constantine's conversion.

God heard generalized prayers for revival and this was one result. This historic shift is not simply a political victory for the West; it is a defeat of a demonic power structure which has defied God and persecuted

National Call to United Prayer
Issued by the National Consultation
on United Prayer

January 21, 1993

Colorado Springs, Colorado

THE CALL

We recognize our absolute dependence on God and our desperate need for divine intervention.

We believe God is urging us to call all Christians of America to unite in humility and repentance across ethnic and church boundaries to pray persistently for a moral and spiritual awakening in the Body of Christ.

We believe this will greatly advance His Kingdom in our nation and worldwide.

THE COVENANT

We covenant to obey this call by taking the following actions:

- We will promote this call as broadly as possible.
- Individually, we will commune with God and pray with faith daily.
- We will encourage and participate regularly in corporate, believing prayer.
- We will fast as God prompts us.
- Feeling incomplete without embracing God's family from all races, we will seek reconciliation and participation with all our brothers and sisters.
- We will pray until God sovereignly acts.

Christians for seventy years. It is practically a planetary exorcism . . . throughout the former Communist world, there is now a spiritual hunger that puts the West to shame. . . . The worldwide renewal team we are playing on is large and diverse. What might we expect if all sectors of the professing church were awakened and unified?[30]

Once again recall the well-reasoned conclusion of Dr. Orr. I'd like to paraphrase it this way: Whenever God is ready to give a world revival, he will set his people to praying for it worldwide. Is this not what we see? And if so, can revival be far behind?

Here Comes Your Pizza!

What all these voices are suggesting mirrors the words of John Naisbitt in *Megatrends*. He calls this moment a "time of parentheses," a time "between eras," "yeasty" and "filled with opportunities."[31] To be sure, it is a special moment, not only for human endeavors and hopes but for God's purposes above all other things. Today's megatrends convince me increasingly that this is God's hour, ordained by him to leverage his work among the nations with extraordinary influence. I see nothing less than a true spiritual awakening to Christ, accelerating his mission for the twenty-first century.

In the face of all of this, I've reached one simple conclusion: We have no other choice but to keep on praying. Something wonderful is coming! It is evident that God intends this movement of prayer, with all that accompanies it, to become the fountainhead of a national and world revival that will itself be our usher into the twenty-first century.

I must be honest with you, however. I do struggle with a degree of impatience! "Hope deferred" tends to keep one restless and hungry for more. My daily experience is similar to one I had a short while ago while traveling the interstate between Chicago and Minneapolis. At one point in the Wisconsin countryside I saw coming southbound on I-90 what turned out to be a car caravan of one hundred newly painted Domino Pizza delivery cars. Evidently they were being dispersed to franchises across the Midwest. Every one of them had the same simple sentence painted in bold black letters across the front of the hood: "Here comes your pizza." I wondered, *Could it be?*

Other cars followed—two, five, ten, fifteen, twenty-five—each telling me, "Here comes your pizza." These were followed by car number fifty, then sixty, then seventy-five, all proclaiming that there was pizza coming and that it was just for me! By the time the caravan vanished in my rearview mirror, I found myself saying, "All right, already—where's my pizza?" In fact, I was so enticed by the mouth-watering thought of devouring a piece of sausage pizza that I escaped from the interstate at the very next exit in search of a pizza establishment.

In the same way, day by day, prayer by prayer, leader by leader, report by report, movement by movement, I feel as if the Spirit of God is saying to us, "Here comes your revival! Here comes world revival!" It *is* coming, and it is nearer than when we first believed. As God increasingly impresses upon us that world revival is truly at hand, it will make us even more hungry for it. In fact we'll find ourselves with greater desires for a spiritual awakening than when we first began to pray for it. The praying makes us hungry!

But we can be hungry *with confidence. The hope is at hand.* In the next chapters I want to begin telling you what I believe this revival will look like, why I am confident that it's coming, and why *you* can be confident as well.

2

People of Hope, People of Revival

Do You Hear the People Sing?

Recently our family moved from the Midwest into metropolitan New York City. (Quite an experience!) Since then my wife and I have attended a couple of Broadway stage productions. In fact in the midst of writing this book I took a break one afternoon to attend a matinee of *Les Misérables,* possibly the most popular musical of all time. It couldn't have been better timed for me.

Based on the novel by Victor Hugo, *Les Misérables* is the story of a struggle for hope, so common to every generation. The musical focuses especially on a group of students who become revolutionaries in the Paris of the 1830s, striving for a government that could bring hope and healing to the masses. The story line caught my attention immediately because *hope* is what this book is all about.

I was deeply intrigued by a chorus sung by the students as they formed a street barricade to do battle with oppressive authorities. Their desire was to establish a new day of justice and freedom for the urchin, the beggar, the peasant. Reprised as the grand finale, the song transformed into a vision of utopian proportions.

But "Do You Hear the People Sing?" is much more. It is a heart-felt cry I've often heard elsewhere—the yearnings of many to find a hope worth living and dying for. Sitting in the darkened theater that day, I could imagine them singing about a greater hope, the one God is pouring into his church right now—a hope, as we've just seen, that increasing numbers believe is at hand. See if you can catch the application:

> Do you hear the people sing
>> lost in the valley of the night?
> It is the music of the people
>> who are climbing to the light.
>
> For the wretched of the earth
>> there is a flame that never dies;
> Even the darkest night will end
>> and the sun will rise.
>
> They will live again in freedom
>> in the garden of the Lord;
> They will walk behind the plowshares
>> they will put away the sword.
> The chains will be broken
>> and all men will have their reward.
>
> *Chorus:*
>
> *Will you join in our crusade?*
>> *Who will be strong and stand with me?*
> *Somewhere beyond the barricade is there a world you long to see?*
> *Do you hear the people sing?*
>> *Say, do you hear the distant drums?*
> *It is the future that they bring when tomorrow comes.*[1]

I returned to my office to work on this book with even greater enthusiasm. For I do hear singing: I am aware of distant drums. I have met multitudes of Christians who are ready: ready to be strong; ready to stand before the Lord in prayer; ready to prepare to receive the future that God's tomorrow is bringing.

This book is their book—it belongs to such a people of hope. Theirs is a hope worth longing for, worth crusading for, and first and foremost worth praying for. That hope is nothing less than a coming world revival. As we saw in chapter 1, many in the church are confidently marching toward that hope at this very hour. Now I want to explore with you what the hope of revival looks like.

How Big Is Your Hope?

First, let's think a little more about hope itself. What are *you* waiting for? What does tomorrow look like for you? How big is your hope?

Thankfully, the Bible gives us the answer, because the Bible is pre-eminently a book about hope. Evangelical futurologist Tom Sine calls it a *wild hope*. It's the affirmation that almighty God is at work within history—within my own history—to bring forth a future by which all things will be made new. In fact, Christ summons us to become "col-laborators—literally, co-laborers with him—in birthing this new order in our lives, in our communities, and in the larger world."[2] Such a biblical hope provides the unshakable foundation from which we can face and engage the mounting challenges all around us, both inside and outside the Christian community.

Here's how Scripture describes it: We have a hope that is "stored up for you in heaven and that you have already heard about in the word of truth, the gospel that has come to you. All over the world this gospel is bearing fruit and growing, just as it has been doing among you" (Col. 1:5–6). Christians are not to be dissuaded from "the hope held out in the gospel. This is the gospel that you have heard and that has been proclaimed to every creature under heaven" (v. 23). Through this gospel, we have been "born again to a living hope, through the resurrection of Jesus Christ" (1 Peter 1:3 NASB), and are therefore urged to "set your hope fully on the grace to be given you when Jesus Christ is revealed" (v. 13). In fact Hebrews 11:1 tells us that in daily disci-pleship, saving faith is the "assurance of things hoped for, the con-viction of things not seen" (NASB). Without hope, we can't have faith. And without faith, we can't go forward in the things of God (v. 6). No wonder Paul prays: "May the God of hope fill you with all joy and peace in believing, so that you may abound in hope by the power of the Holy Spirit," (Rom. 15:13 KJV), while telling Timothy that, bot-tom line, Christ Jesus . . . is our hope (1 Tim. 1:1 NASB). He is both Alpha and Omega, John learns—the God "who is, and who was, and who is to come" (Rev. 1:8).

Let's return to Colossians. Consumed with Christ as the church's everlasting future and wanting others to be the same, Paul summa-rizes his entire life mission in one verse—Colossians 1:27: "To them God has chosen to make known among the Gentiles the glorious riches of this mystery, which is Christ in you, the hope of glory." Or as the J. B. Phillips translation puts it: "They are those to whom God has planned to give a vision of the full wonder and splendor of His secret plan for the nations. And the secret is simply this: Christ *in you*! Yes, Christ is *in you*, bringing with Him the hope of all the glorious things to come."

Actually this one verse, in the context of the verses on either side of it, may be the best one in all of Scripture to help us understand why a vigorous, "wild hope" is the bloodstream of the church. It tells us that:

1. Hope is *personal*. Christ himself is the hope. There's no hope outside of him. It's as big as he is.
2. Hope is *immediate*. The Christ who is our hope is "in us," or better translated "in the *midst* of" us. He is among his people to be all the things Colossians describes as his character and his ways.
3. Thus hope is primarily *corporate*. When Paul says Christ is in the midst of "you," the Greek word is plural. He is this for all of God's people, in all ages and at all times.
4. This hope has a *missionary* dimension. It isn't just for our sake alone. It is to be proclaimed and manifested through us for the sake of the nations.
5. The hope God gives us is *profound*. It is a "mystery," Paul says. Only now is the full scope of what we have in Christ being unveiled before our eyes and before heaven and earth. But there is still much more to come. Our hope is inexhaustible.
6. Our hope in Christ deals with *ultimate* issues. It is the "hope of glory"—it is the hope of the full revelation of all the glorious things that God has prepared for us (both now and through all eternity) in the person of his dear Son.
7. And that's why, for Paul, hope has become his *message* and his *ministry* (Col. 1:24, 28–29). He wants to bring this hope to every person, both by preaching the message of hope ("We proclaim him" NASB), by discipleship ("That we may present every man complete in Christ" NASB), and by prayer. The latter thrust is obvious in the opening of chapter 2, as he discusses his wrestling for those who have not yet even seen his face, that they may know the hope of this mystery in all of its fullness. We learn that

this wrestling refers to prayer in chapter 4, when he talks about Epaphroditus wrestling for them in *prayer* to know the whole will of God (that is, all Christ is for us as our hope).

The Big Hope: A 1:27 Revival

Now how do these thoughts from Colossians 1:27 relate to the theme of this book? What are its implications for a coming world revival? The answer is simple, but compelling. *This passage, in context, defines the heart of revival.* The manifestation of such a hope has been the chief characteristic of every historic revival. And so the reactivation of these truths in any generation must always result in that which could be called spiritual renewal, awakening, revival. In turn, we become a people of revival because we have become, once again, a people of hope.

Certainly, J. I. Packer is right in observing that spiritual renewal, or revival, is not a way out. "It is not compensation for lack of something else. It is not escapism where we sing choruses and have lively worship. It is not a blind way of looking at the world so that we don't see its suffering. It is not a prescription for instant maturity."[3] On the contrary, revival comes to the church when we are again thoroughly possessed with the hope held out to us in the gospel—the hope embodied in the one toward whom the gospel points. When we are once again saturated with Christ's energizing presence—his presence with us and ahead of us—the church is propelled, in hope, to nothing less than advancing his global cause among the nations.

Well, there's good news in the land. Once again God is raising up a multitude of believers who, like Paul, are willing to pay the price. By preaching, by discipling, by praying, they are prepared to help the church encounter the full panorama of who Christ is, of what he is doing, and of where he is headed. And to the degree that they succeed—to the degree God restores in us an "abounding hope by the power of the Holy Spirit" (Rom. 15:13) and does so for the church worldwide—*to that degree we will experience a true national and world revival.*

This is especially good news for those who give spiritual leadership to our churches today. Research shows us that pastors and other Christian leaders are experiencing battles and discouragements unlike any previous generation. They are often disheartened, confused, and desperate for hope. (Maybe you are one of them.) And yet, no matter how badly beat-up they may feel, there is also a groundswell of joyful anticipation among many of them. For example, I recently attended a half-day prayer gathering of one thousand pastors in Los Angeles. We were praying for revival when one of the pastors spontaneously moved toward a floor mike to lead us all. His grey hair and his words suggested that he had been in ministry nearly fifty years. And, as he prayed, he began to weep. He asked God to forgive him for the years he had wasted competing with other pastors and he praised God for the new beginning he had found through the quarterly city-wide prayer gatherings. He prayed with brokenness, but he also prayed with a great big hope, for he truly sensed that revival is coming. Furthermore, he was now linked up with others who were asking God for the very same spiritual awakening. The prayer he was praying belonged to all of us—his brokenness was our brokenness, his hope was our hope. There was hardly a dry eye in the room.

Similar experiences have been shared by thousands of pastors across America through what is known as Pastors' Prayer Summits. Over the past few months, summits have been held in scores of cities here, as well as in fifteen foreign countries. These four-day prayer gatherings are interdenominational retreats, where leaders' lives are transformed and rejuvenated. Why are they so popular? Executive director Terry Dirks says quite simply it is because of "a desperation for God that exists among pastors today. Pastors have done the best that man can do and are hungry for a true, holy, heaven-sent revival."[4] Yes, there *is* good news in the land!

A Long-Term Hope . . . Personal and Growing

I believe—with unshakable conviction—that we are on the threshold of the greatest revival in the history of the church. This is what *I* hope. I have no doubts that it *is* coming. In fact I can "see" it as if it were already completed. I can't explain this sense of things. I realize it sounds quite subjective—and to a degree it is. Some might call my hope a "prophetic insight," while others would simply call it a hunch. I only know that I believe God is not only able and willing to once again give revival to his church worldwide, but I believe he is ready to do so at this very moment. As this book will document, I am not alone in my convictions.

Calling others to live a life of anticipation is not a new mission for me, however. It has been a basic platform both in my writing and preaching for many years. To be sure, I feel it more strongly and see it more clearly than ever before. In recent years anticipation has been intensifying for me into an abiding *expectation.*

For example, in my 1979 book *In the Gap: What It Means to Be a World Christian,* I expressed my growing conviction that the end of time and the ends of the earth were working together. *In the Gap* called Christians to a new sense of urgency, to work at closing the gap that remains between the church and the unevangelized peoples of the world, with special concentration on those who are currently beyond the reach of the gospel (what I called the widest end of the gap).

That's why I devoted a whole chapter to the thesis that for Christians to fully participate in Christ's global cause, there would need to be a worldwide spiritual awakening in the church. I wrote, "Many missions strategists today believe we are on the crest of another great awakening, called by some the 'sunrise of missions.'" I noted the convictions of a few missions statesmen of the day, like J. Christy Wilson who said, "I believe we've entered the fourth great awakening—it has already started—and it may be the last one. Because in this awakening God can complete his plan for the nations."[5] (Many others today agree with that perspective, as chapter 1 began to highlight.)

In 1984 I published my next book, *With Concerts of Prayer: Christians Join for Spiritual Awakening and World Evangelization.*[6] Once again I returned to the theme of standing in the gap (based on Ezek. 22). But now I emphasized the phrase in verse 30 that literally tells us we are to stand there "before [God's] face," a biblical phrase referring to the ministry of prayer and intercession. I surveyed how the missionary movement historically, especially over the last three hundred years, has been propelled by movements of united prayer, often called concerts of prayer (the word *concert* meaning they were united, together, of one heart and mind). I projected that the primary step we as world Christians must take if we were to see world revival of a depth that ensures wide-scale harvest in world evangelization was to band to-

43

gether in ongoing movements of united prayer—in our churches, within our cities, and throughout nations.

With Concerts of Prayer was published the same year that the International Prayer Assembly for World Evangelization (for which I worked on the program committee) was convened. It was a historic first. Two thousand delegates from over seventy nations gathered together for the express purpose of seeking God for a global prayer movement for world revival and designing strategies for citywide and nationwide prayer mobilization. Since then there has been an unprecedented groundswell in movements of prayer across the globe—with an accompanying spirit of both urgency and anticipation. What we see today goes far beyond anything I projected in 1984.

In fact I believe we are in the midst of a prayer movement that is in many senses *the first phase* of the coming world revival. As we began to explore in chapter 1, God is sustaining prayer initiatives on all levels and on all sides, through a plethora of prayer ministries across the body of Christ. Today many leaders (not just prayer leaders) are calling for and supporting concerted prayer.

Furthermore this movement *of* prayer, developing for so many years, is now being transformed into a movement *by* prayer. The actual movement itself is becoming more comprehensive in its drive toward unity, revival, and evangelism. United prayer has assumed a role as both fountainhead and leading edge of the broader thrust.

This prayer initiative, like a bicycle, is upright and moving. What it needs is to be properly directed and kept on course. The questions before us all are: What is the vision and hope toward which all of us are praying? What is God getting ready to actually *do* in answer to our prayers? What *is* our hope?

Toward a Coming World Revival

Which brings me to the writing of this third book. If the operative word for *In the Gap* is *in*, and for *With Concerts of Prayer* is *with*, then the operative word for *The Hope at Hand* should be *toward*. We're standing *in* the gap *with* concerted prayer as we (along with many church leaders) look *toward* the hope of national and world revival for the twenty-first century.

And what is this coming world revival all about? Let me use this chapter to explore a basic understanding of this exciting subject. Much of the rest of the book expands on the fresh perspectives I give you here.

First, by *revival* I mean far more than you might assume. Despite many (often legitimate) misconceptions, revival is in fact a strong biblical concept. Psalm 85:6 says, "Will you not revive us again, that your people may rejoice in you?" True, some contemporary uses of it may seem to smack of superficial emotionalism or conjure up images of programmatic manipulations of Christian zeal. That's unfortunate but true. To counter these prejudices I've added two qualifiers that I always link with the term: *coming* and *world.* You see, I'm talking about a "coming world revival" with personal, national, and global ramifications.

By *world* I mean two things. The revival at hand is for the body of Christ worldwide, not simply for one person or one region or one Christian tradition alone, nor simply for a momentary period of congregational refreshment and renewal. Nothing less than a wholesale, spiritual awakening for the global body of Christ will do—for any of us anywhere—at this critical moment in history, as I will document in later chapters. In addition, the revival God wants to give his church is not for our sake alone but for the sake of many, many others—even for the blessing of all the peoples of the earth. God's promises of revival always have Christ's global cause in view.

By *coming* I mean it's on its way! Revival is at hand. Part 2 of this book documents the reasons to have confidence about the timing. But I mean more. Revival is coming from outside our resources, our ingenuity, and our control. It is something God must do for us, something God is bringing to us out of grace, an extraordinary work of the Spirit that invades the church to reenergize us with God's eternal purposes in Christ Jesus.

Insight from Orr and Packer

Now back to the word *revival* itself. Who can define in such a short space one of the major themes of church history? One man tried to do so. As mentioned in chapter 1, historian J. Edwin Orr spent sixty

years of his life studying the great epochs of evangelical awakenings over the past 350 years. Orr observed that the dominant marks
of every evangelical awakening are the same phenomena found
throughout Acts. He distilled his decades of research into the following definition:

> An Evangelical Awakening is a movement of the Holy Spirit bringing about
> a revival of New Testament Christianity in the church of Christ and in
> its related community. Such an awakening may change in a significant
> way an individual; or it may affect a larger group of believers; or it may
> move a congregation or the churches in a city or district, or the whole
> body of believers throughout a country or continent; or indeed the
> larger body of believers throughout the world. The out-pouring of the
> Spirit affects the reviving of the church, the awakening of the masses,
> and the movement of uninstructed peoples toward the Christian faith;
> the revived church, by many or by few, is moved to engage in evange-
> lism, in teaching, and in social action.[7]

With this perspective, theologian J. I. Packer concurs. In *A Quest
for Godliness* Packer studies the history of the Puritan movement,
defining it precisely as a model revival movement for over two cen-
turies. Attempting to distill the Puritan understanding of revival,
Packer betrays his own convictions. He writes:

> Revival, I define, as a work of God by his Spirit through his Word
> bringing the spiritually dead to living faith in Christ and renewing
> the inner life of Christians who have grown slack and sleepy. In re-
> vival God makes old things new, giving new power to law and gospel
> and new spiritual awareness to those whose hearts and conscious-
> ness have been blind, hard and cold. Revival thus animates or re-
> animates churches and Christian groups to make a spiritual and
> moral impact on communities. It comprises an initial *reviving,* fol-
> lowed by a maintained state of *revivedness* for as long as the visita-
> tion lasts.[8]

Taking the early chapters of Acts as a paradigm (just as Orr did)
and folding into that the rest of New Testament teaching (which Packer
suggests is all a product of revival conditions), he lists some of the
great marks of revival:

- An awesome sense of the presence of God
- A profound awareness of sin, leading to both repentance and the full embrace of the glorified Christ
- A release of the church to witness to the power and glory of Christ, in the same freedom that the Spirit has brought to the church through revival
- An overflowing joy in the Lord, a love for all Christians, and a fear of doing anything to violate either

But revival must also be seen from God's side. Packer suggests that from that vantage point the marks of revival include the following:

- An intensifying and speeding up of the work of grace throughout a community and throughout nations
- Multitudes brought under conviction by the gospel and transformed by the Spirit in short order
- Many converted and folded into the life of the church[9]

Packer goes on to conclude (and throughout the rest of his book amasses supporting evidence from the history of the Puritan movement alone):

> It is true, of course, that there can be personal revival without any community movement, and that there can be no community movement save as individuals are revived. None the less, if we follow Acts as our paradigm we shall define revival as an essentially corporate phenomenon in which God sovereignly shows his hand, visits his people, extends his Kingdom, and glorifies his name.[10]

An Approximation of the Consummation

Let me attempt to bring all of this down to one basic definition of revival. A Puritan that Packer highlights can help us. Maybe the most perceptive of all writers on the topic of revival, Jonathan Edwards was a New England pastor and scholar of the early to mid 1700s. In Packer's chapter "Jonathan Edwards and Revival," he observes that for Edwards, revivals held a central place in the revealed purposes of God, since the objective God had in creation itself was to prepare a kingdom for his Son, which Christ would inherit for all ages to come. Edwards saw all of God's providential activity, from Calvary forward, flowing out of Christ's ascension, and moving without hesitation to the final consummation of all things. God's sovereign initiative is to fulfill everything for which Christ suffered. From that theological non-negotiable, Edwards's perspective (and that of many others like Orr and Packer) *held revival to be the most strategic activity of God between the ascension and the end,* when Christ will dominate the whole universe. In fact, *revival is God's way of shepherding history toward that great climax.* Packer quotes Edwards:

> A universal dominion is pledged to Christ, and in the interim before the final consummation, the Father implements this pledge in part by successive outpourings of the Spirit, which prove the reality of Christ's Kingdom to a skeptical world and serve to extend its bounds among Christ's erst-while enemies.[11]

Sharing the same perspective, I have coined a definition for revival that has been quite helpful to many in understanding this distinctive activity of God's Spirit: Any revival, in its comprehensive sense, is an *approximation of the consummation.* That's why nothing can be more hope-filled than a vision for revival.

Here's what I mean. The Bible teaches that at the end of history the whole universe will experience the consummation, when Christ returns to sum up everything under himself, things in heaven and things on earth (Eph. 1:9–10). Christ will be manifested as Lord and take his rightful place as the center focus of the whole cosmos. That epoch, described in hundreds of verses throughout the Scriptures, might properly be called the *Final Revival.*

That being so, it follows that every other revival must take its cue from this final revival. If (based on biblical, historical analyses) it can be shown that every previous revival is about God giving so much more of Christ to his church than had been experienced in that generation; and if it can be shown that revival is about God's divine intervention on behalf of a people who are hopeless without it; and if Christ himself sums up all of the hopes that revival holds out to the church and to the nations in any generation (as we saw in Col. 1:27), then to that degree revival can be properly termed an *approximation* of the consummation. Revival—at the end or now—is about God wonderfully unveiling his Son before the world—either in consummation or in approximations of the consummation. The central themes of the final revival (or consummation) are activated *in principle* through Christ in every other revival. This becomes quite apparent when you study the definitions of revival spelled out by such scholars as Edwards, Orr, and Packer.

Nothing Else Matters

Recently in Washington, D.C., working with the National Prayer Committee to sponsor events surrounding our National Day of Prayer, six of us met with the President to pray with him and for him. The focus of our praying was biblically grounded and Christ-centered, and consisted of prayer not only for the President himself, but also for spiritual and moral awakening throughout America. It was a deeply moving time for all of us.

Later in the day, as we returned to our National Prayer Committee meetings, one of the members (reflecting on all that had just happened) made this statement: "If revival does not come, nothing else matters. If revival *does* come, nothing else matters!" What seemed to be a contradiction in terms became immediately apparent to us. In a real sense, revival is the only hope for our nation and for this whole generation. If it doesn't come, then most of our other strivings will ultimately be in vain. If the church is enveloped in revival, however, then we will be receiving from the Holy Spirit virtually everything that matters to see Christ sufficiently exalted in our land and among many peoples. How could we allow ourselves to talk this way? The answer is simple: It's because we understood the *comprehensive* nature of a God-given revival and all that God ordains for it to accomplish. From that perspective, truly little else matters. We knew it the day we prayed in the White House. We know it every time we gather to pray in our churches.

By the phrase "an approximation of the consummation" I mean that in revival we experience 1. the *first fruits* of the consummation as we are more fully consumed with the very same Christ whose glory will one day cover the earth as the waters cover the sea (in chapter 5, I will describe this in terms of the *seven phases* of revival), 2. a corporate encounter with Christ through *intermediate expressions* of the final revival (in later chapters I will use the words *focus, fullness, fulfillment* to analyze these expressions); and 3. *preliminary but substantial demonstrations* of what God will do among the nations at the end of all things, both in terms of justice and redemption.

What we're saying is that *qualitatively,* if not quantitatively, every revival is very similar to the final revival. It is a microcosm of what will one day be accomplished universally, a dress rehearsal of that climactic epoch. It is not only to be regarded as a dramatic foreshadowing of Christ's final manifestation to his people and to all creation (and it is that), but also as a sovereign work of God that is preparatory for it.

Bottom line, what this means is every revival—including the coming national and world revival for the twenty-first century—is best understood by a *forward* look more than a backward one. In our prayers we anticipate what is ultimately to happen rather than simply longing to return to something that once was. Since God's kingdom drama for ages to come defines, in principle, what God is willing to do now, it should also define the scope of our expectations for revival now. For example, every aspect of John's description of the heavenly city (Rev. 21–22) is capable of an approximate realization within history. That's why Jesus borrows from these images as he calls the seven churches of Asia to pursue him for corporate revival right where they live (Rev. 1–3). For Jesus, each revival entails an increased and intensified outbreaking of a life that will one day be definitive for the new heaven, the new earth, and the New Jerusalem.

For you see, revival does not simply shape the future. To be sure it does help to do that as it unleashes the church to press Christ's global cause on all fronts. But there's more to it than that. Revival is also a *receiving* of the future, of that which is the end—the omega—of all things. In revival, Christ comes fresh to his church, to conquer us in new ways that are truly precursors of the day when he will bring all things—the church, the nations, history itself—under his feet.

The Outpoured Spirit: The Presence of the Future

The key to this approximation, of course, is the Holy Spirit. Why is the Holy Spirit and his ministry always identified as the central explanation in historic accounts of revivals? Why, as Iain Murray observes in *Revival and Revivalism*, did the leaders of the First and Second Great Awakenings speak of revival preeminently as "the outpouring of the Holy Spirit"? A clear answer emerges from several New Testament passages. One of his chief ministries is to give us approximations of the consummation. The Spirit actually makes the ascended, universal Lord present in our midst as he represents Christ to us. In this way the Spirit forever keeps the consummation within our reach. He makes it *christologically* near to us. Scripture tells us the Spirit is God's deposit, guaranteeing for us all that is to come (Eph. 1:13–14). His ministry is to take the things of Christ and reveal them to us, as he shows us what is to come (John 16:13). It is the Spirit who stirs the church to always pray, "Come, Lord Jesus" (Rev. 22:20). In seasons of revival, God intensifies and accelerates the Spirit's primary mission.

Take, for example, Peter's perspective on the Spirit's outpouring at Pentecost (Acts 2). He saw it as a cataclysmic event, the inauguration of God's victory procession among the nations. And that's what he preached. Peter's interpretation was based, in part, on the prophecy of Joel. Joel foresaw the launching of the consummation in a way that would shake the powers of heaven because the Spirit would rain down on the saints to inhabit all of them. For the early church the revival at Pentecost was viewed as an invasion of Christ by the Holy Spirit in such a powerful manifestation of his all-consuming presence that the church was permanently wedded to the future. In Philip Yancey's image, the Holy Spirit was not given to believers to be a lantern to help them pick their way over treacherous terrain at midnight. Rather, he was welcomed as the glow of a dawn that was about to break, shining on believers' faces even now.

Whatever eschatological schemes each of us may hold to (and there are a number of legitimate possibilities), we can all agree about this: The biblical promises and prophecies have been consummated *in principle* in who Christ himself is. Even now, he is freely exercising by his Spirit his rightful prerogatives as king, in continuity with what he will be and do at the end. By what he accomplished on the cross, by his resurrection victory over death and the demonic, and by his ascending with all authority to the Father's right hand, the future, for all practical purposes, has already been decided. The final revival has been confirmed in who he is at this very hour.

In other words Christ is himself what the future of the human race is all about. He is (in the words of George Eldon Ladd) the "presence of the future."[12] In power, the Spirit brings this home to the church in our daily life together (Eph. 3:14–21). Remember? "Christ *in you* bringing with him the hope of all the glorious things to come" (Col. 1:27 PHILLIPS).

Where Jesus is and wherever he is actively manifesting his grace and glory, that's where all of our hope is to be found. Right there. He is the summation of the consummation. Right now. Whatever he will ultimately be Lord of, he is, in truth, Lord of even now. In Christ we no longer need to look for the future through prophetic telescopes—we can actually see it directly in him, up close and personal.

He not only makes possible the final triumphs of God's lavish grace and firm justice; he also makes them a fact. We can touch and feel the future now. And this becomes doubly dymanic for us, in powerfully fresh ways, in those epochal moments when Christ manifests himself among us in revival.

An Apocalyptic Feel

Think of it this way: Expect every revival and every promise of revival to have an *apocalyptic* feel about it. What do I mean? Well, from the Greek we know that *apocalypse* literally refers to an *unveiling* that takes place in rather dramatic terms. This can refer not only to the day of judgment but to any time God intensifies the manifestation of his Son to the world. And that's what revival is all about! It is a more comprehensive unveiling of King Jesus to his church, with dramatic repercussions. Shaken from our apathy and fears, we are launched afresh into kingdom work on all fronts. That's why we call it a spiritual awakening. We're waking up to all Christ wants to be for his church. It's like the beginning of a brand new day.

As renewal scholar Donald Mostrom writes in *Christians Facing the Future*:

> All of us need to be aware of how Christ is moving in the midst of his Church toward the end of all things, and equally aware of our deep and immediate intimacy with him. The one who dwells in the midst of his Church is bringing closure to our present age. We cannot help

but have a strong sense of living at the edge of the final consummation . . . and we cannot live close to him without a strong sense of what
is surely coming and how near it is. We breathe the very air of the impending Kingdom![13]

Such a vision has dominated every previous spiritual awakening to
Christ. No wonder the last paragraph of the Bible offers an overarching prayer for the whole church, in every place and in every age—the
distillation of all the prayers for revival that have ever been prayed:
Come! Come, Lord Jesus. Such a vision must also be the drumbeat of
national and world revival in our generation.

As the church focuses its prayers today on this coming revival, we
pray not simply with a spirit of hopefulness. We pray with a living
hope, and that hope is Christ himself. We pray with our eyes toward
that final revival when there will be a simultaneous realization of Christ's
prayers for every other revival, of all that his grace has longed to do,
and of all the blessings that prior spiritual awakenings have actually
set in motion. What will happen in the final revival is simply this: God
will culminate, execute, and then supremely extend whatever any previous generation may have approximated in both personal and corporate revival.

And so I too pray, day by day, with growing intensity and expectation, for the whole counsel of God to be fulfilled (would you join me?).
*Come, Lord Jesus! To your seeking church, come. In fresh manifestations of
your glory, come. With hope for our times, come. In genuine world revival,
come. For the sake of my own nation, come. Among all the nations, come.
And finally—hallelujah!—In the consummation itself, come. Come. Come.*

It's at Hand

Actually our preoccupation with such a wild hope should breathe the
same air of impendingness that Jesus propagated at the opening of his
ministry (which was a ministry of revival if there ever was one!). We
read in Mark 1:15 four urgent declarations that are laws for revival in
any age.

1. *The time is fulfilled.* In this phrase Jesus gathers up all the
promises of Scripture regarding everything God wants to do through

his Messiah to fully revive, restore, and redeploy his people to fulfill his purposes. He calls us to a new hope.

2. *The kingdom is at hand.* Next Jesus announces that God alone can activate these promises for his people. His sovereign reign in our lives and among the nations is the only hope for us and for the whole earth.

3. *Repent.* Here Jesus sums up the response required of everyone who senses the impendingness of an extraordinary new work of God— most immediately, the work of revival. We must renounce our best efforts to do God's work in our own strength. In addition we are to turn from all sin that would hinder our full involvement in what God is getting ready to do. We must embrace what is coming, or rather, who is coming. We must turn toward the God of the future and the future that God is bringing.

4. *Believe this good news.* Coupled with the call to repentance is the proactive response of believing and seizing this great hope for ourselves, of staking our whole lives on it, and of pursuing its implications with all of our hearts. And certainly prayer is chief among the responses God anticipates.

These four declarations can transform any people into a people of hope, a people of revival.

But note especially his use of the phrase *at hand.* Scholars suggest this defines awesome expectation of the consummation—a sense that a brand new work of God is on top of his people, like rain clouds hovering overhead just waiting to release a drenching downpour. In this phrase Christ proclaims there is so much more God is ready to do for us than we have yet experienced and that he is ready to do it soon, even now. God is poised to intervene in sovereign kingly power to do for our generation what we can never do for ourselves.

Paul put it so graphically: "Wake up, O sleeper, rise from the dead, and Christ will shine on you" (Eph. 5:14), echoing the words of Isaiah: "Arise, shine, for your light has come, and the glory of the Lord rises upon you" (Isa. 60:1). What a hope this is!

You and I must hold to these same convictions as we look toward national and world revival for the twenty-first century. Revival is bearing down on us with the feel of something akin to the consummation. This is the hope at hand—a hope, as we've seen, that is rising irresistibly right now throughout the body of Christ.

Our Lives Depend on It

Two days before I began writing this book Robyne and I were on our way to a regular weekly prayer gathering for revival. As we drove along talking about nothing important, a sentence formed in my mind that had never been there before. I had the strongest sense that the Spirit of God had given it shape. It seemed to breathe into me marching orders for my work on this project. But I consider it more than that. I've come to understand it as marching orders for my own ministry for the rest of my life. The sentence was "Write as if your life depended on it—because it does!"

I knew instantly how to interpret that. For I'm convinced there is nothing more important to which I must give my life, for the rest of my life, than to understand more thoroughly the hope of world revival and to help infuse the church with this message, particularly within some of the great movements of united prayer that God is raising up at this hour.

And so, I also write as if *your* life depends on it. The hope of which I speak must become a passion for our churches and for a whole generation. We must become a people filled with such a hope—a people who live for revival. In no other hour of church history has this been so crucial (as we are about to see). God help us to gain a new appreciation for what biblical revival is and a renewed enthusiasm for what the future holds for us in it. And God help us to be so filled with confidence in who he is and what he is up to at this moment that we will pray and prepare with confidence, too. Confidence is what the next eight chapters are all about.

Part 2
The Surging Confidence

3 Confidence Builders about the Hope at Hand

Against the Wall or Up on the Wall?

Consistently, preceding eras of spiritual awakening, God's people have been characterized as full of anticipation, waiting in a state of expectation, convinced that everything is now ready, that revival is at hand.

In other words when God moves his people toward revival, we find them growing as a people who pray and prepare for it together—with confidence. As a friend put it: "Whenever God's people feel like they're up against the wall, God's answer comes through those with enough confidence to get up *on* the wall." Isaiah 62:6–7 calls such people "watchmen on your walls," believers who can see ahead of time the big picture of what is coming. They see God restoring his people and making them his praise before the earth. With such an outlook they have no choice but to "give yourselves no rest, and give God no rest" until he does exactly what he has promised to do.

God the Holy Spirit is rapidly raising up a multitude of such watchmen. In fact one denomination is assisting churches from many traditions within individual cities to form "watchmen on the wall" (as they call it) whereby every hour of every day is adopted by various congregations within the city, so that intercessors are meeting and praying there constantly for revival. Recall in the first chapter, how at the National Consultation on United Prayer hundreds of ministry leaders rallied each other and their constituencies to be watchmen, using words like "We recognize our need for divine intervention. . . . We believe God is urging us to call all Christians of America to pray persistently for a moral and spiritual awakening. . . . We will promote this call as broadly as possible. . . . We will participate in corporate, believing prayer. . . . We will pray until God sovereignly acts." They were calling the church to prayer for revival, not tentatively but with confidence—as they stood on the wall.

Frankly I marvel at where God has brought the prayer movement in this nation and across the world over the past fifteen years. During that brief time frame we've seen it transition in the United States from a phase of national consciousness, where there was a growing understanding of the need for world revival, into a phase of national consensus, where we have become more and more agreed on the shape of a world revival, to the place where we're now entering into a phase of national conviction. There's a groundswell of conviction that world revival is, in fact, our only hope. Nothing could be more encouraging than this trend. What we're witnessing is growth in confidence—from consciousness, to consensus, to conviction.

History documents that such confident agreement among Christians about revival always puts the church at the threshold of revival. In his doctoral thesis, "The Concert of Prayer: Back to the Future,"[1] Bob Bakke argues that one of the most consistent characteristics of prayer movements over the past three hundred years has been the high level of confidence, stimulating agreement among the pray-ers, that has prepared the church to receive a fresh outpouring of the Holy Spirit.

Finney and Spurgeon Agree?

Charles Finney in his classic *Lectures on Revival,* published in 1834, drew some valuable conclusions based on his own experiences of the outworkings of the Second Great Awakening. Even though some of Finney's ministry perspectives have proven to be controversial, his understanding on this one issue of confident agreement in prayer is well worth considering. In Lecture 16 he writes:

> We must concur in *expecting* the blessing prayed for. . . . We must *absolutely believe* that the blessing of revival will come, or we will not bring ourselves within the promise. . . . We must agree in feeling the

necessity of revival, and its importance. . . . We must be agreed also on the *necessity of divine agency* to produce a revival. It is not enough that we all hold this in theory and pray for it in words. We must fully understand and deeply feel this necessity. We must realize our entire dependence on the Spirit of God, or the whole will fail.[2]

Coming from another theological perspective, a contemporary of Finney's, the great British pastor/preacher Charles Haddon Spurgeon, concurs on the importance of confidence. In one of the greatest prayers ever recorded for spiritual awakening—a bold, aggressive prayer from which all other revival praying could benefit—he writes:

O God, send us the Holy Spirit! Give us both the breath of spiritual life and the fire of unconquerable zeal. You are our God. Answer us by fire, we pray to you! Answer us both by wind and fire, and then we will see you to be God indeed. The Kingdom comes not, and the work is flagging. Oh, that you would send the wind and the fire! *And you will do this when we are all of one accord, all believing, all expecting, all prepared by prayer.*

Lord, bring us to this waiting state! God, send us a season of glorious disorder. Oh, for a sweep of the wind that will set the seas in motion, and make our ironclad brethren now lying so quietly at anchor, to roll from stem to stern.

Oh, for the fire to fall again—fire which shall affect the most stolid. Oh for such fire, that first sat upon the disciples, and then fell on all around. Oh God, You are ready to work with us today even as You did then. Do not hold back, we beseech You, but work at once.

Break down every barrier that hinders the incoming of Your might! Give us now both hearts of flame and tongues of fire to preach Your reconciling word, for Jesus' sake. Amen![3]

Finney and Spurgeon are speaking the same language! Revival comes as God's people are so full of confidence that they unite not only in their praying but in their shared expectations that God will, in fact, give them exactly what they ask from him. As Spurgeon puts it, they are so charged with God-given confidence that it could be said they have entered together into a "waiting state." They have moved beyond simple desperation for revival or even anticipation of it. Theirs is a full *expectation* that revival is on top of them. They know God will do this when, in Spurgeon's terms, "we are all of one accord, all believing, all expecting, all prepared by prayer."

The Tentative Spirit

Confidence is often not one of our daily experiences, however, especially when it comes to the prospects of a national or world revival. Many of us struggle with what might be termed a "tentative spirit." Synonyms for tentative include *hesitant, uncertain, not fully worked out, conditional, skeptical, suspicious, distrustful, indecisive.* Similar to the state motto of Missouri, "Show Me," our response to revival sometimes is "I'll believe it when I see it."

As I've met with thousands of pastors across this nation, it is clear by their own confession this is one of the greatest struggles they have. A recent survey backs this up, uncovering that as many as 40 percent of our nation's pastors are seriously considering leaving the ministry.[4] In other words they have faced seemingly intractable challenges within their churches. They have experienced so many "disappointments with God"—meaning they have trusted God in so many areas where they *thought* he was willing to act and have not seen the evidence that he has—that their confidence toward God has been seriously undermined. Furthermore they lack any significant degree of hope that God might be willing to do something as great as revival in their own lives and churches, let alone a world revival. As a metropolitan pastor of a large church said to me recently, "Many pastors in my city have gone beyond desperation. They have moved into hardness." What he meant was, they have sought God so desperately over their situations with such intensity and for so long that they have actually become embittered and hardened against God himself and against his promises. For them it is simply an issue of emotional survival.

A pastor in another city, whose bookshelves were once lined with volumes on revival, spent years studying and praying for revival with seemingly little results. Finally he quit the ministry altogether, disillusioned, confused, tentative. The day he and I talked he was just reentering the pastorate, after a lengthy sabbatical, with renewed vision for revival. He said, "The risk we take as we seek and prepare for revival is that without sufficient internalized support for the vision when we pray for revival, *we can actually pray ourselves into unbelief.*" Avoiding that trap is what the middle section of this book is about.

The trap has already been set for many of us. One of our foremost evangelical urbanologists, Ray Bakke, has concluded out of years of urban consultations in some three hundred cities worldwide that of the ten major barriers hindering the advance of the gospel in our cities, nine of them are *inside* the church not outside the church. Of those nine barriers, the greatest may be a "spirit of hopelessness." It is the sense that nothing can be changed, that the desperate condition of the city is too overwhelming for the meager resources of the church—the tentative spirit.[5]

In *The Seventh Enemy*, former Oxford don and environmentalist Ronald Hagens talks about this as a part of the universal struggle for our generation.[6] Of all the appalling threats overhanging the human race as we close this century, the greatest enemy may be the seventh: apathy. Hagens describes apathy as a feeling of tentativeness rising out of suspicion that nothing can be done, that nothing can be changed. It's what Latin-American missiologist Ed Silvoso refers to when he defines "spiritual strongholds" within the church (2 Cor. 10:5–8). He calls them "a mindset impregnated with hopelessness that causes the believer to accept as unchangeable something that he or she knows is contrary to the will of God."[7]

Surely this tentativeness—hopelessness, apathy, unbelief—is the most prominent stronghold raised against revival. And with this lack of confidence comes the second stronghold: *lack of agreement.* For without confidence there cannot be agreement. Without agreement there cannot be effective prayer. Without prayer that focuses our total dependence on God for the fulfillment of his promises to us in revival, revival will not come.

In some sense we may actually be confronting a spirit of *practical agnosticism.* It may take two forms:

1. The *pessimist* who says, "Everything is in such a hopeless con-dition right now, and the church is so spiritually depleted that absolutely nothing can be changed. We've prayed for revival, but we've not seen it come. We've tried to work toward revival, but nothing seems to have happened. It may be a long time be-

fore God is agreeable to the idea and willing to rearrange things to make revival possible. If God wants to give revival, fine. But it is totally out of our hands and beyond our ability to do anything about it. We must leave it immersed in the mysteries of God. What will be will be."

2. The *pragmatist* who says, "Revival is not practical, it's not down-to-earth enough. It is nothing more than a fantasy, an escapist's dream. Revival is simply the church's misplaced desire to find a quick fix for our problems. We need to face our challenges in more concrete, specific, and manageable ways. We need to take it one step at a time. This is not the moment to challenge people to wait for the dramatic. We must get them into the action. The needs are great. Let's roll up our sleeves and get to work."

Have you ever experienced either of these reactions to others' claims of a coming revival?

Seven Confidence Builders

The next seven chapters are an antidote to practical agnosticism. They can break a hardened spirit and help a person get back up on the wall. They explore seven confidence-building reasons to grow strong in our faith about a coming world revival. Their purpose is to help us counter various reactions of tentativeness—in ourselves or in the church at large—by showing that God is not only willing and able (for the sake of the pessimist) but also ready and committed (for the sake of the pragmatist) to bring about a spiritual awakening to Christ for the twenty-first century.

These seven confidence builders will help us come together in greater unity around the issue of revival—that it is, what it is, and that it is at hand. They will act as counselors to lead us into the "waiting state" of which Spurgeon speaks where we are all "of one accord, all believing, all expecting, all prepared by prayer."

Here are seven signposts of the road ahead:

- Confidence Builder 1: *The Decisive Person*
- Confidence Builder 2: *The Divine Pattern*

- Confidence Builder 3: *The Dark Prospects*
- Confidence Builder 4: *The Disturbing Paralysis*
- Confidence Builder 5: *The Dramatic Preparations*
- Confidence Builder 6: *The Distinctive Praying*
- Confidence Builder 7: *The Determined People*

The upcoming chapters will also offer these benefits:

1. The seven reasons we explore form a "curriculum" on revival. Each reason gives you categories for thinking about revival and for interpreting the ways of God in revival both in the Scriptures and in our own generation. In turn, you can continue to flesh out this curriculum on your own as revival comes.
2. These seven areas also help you to better prepare for revival. They give you new directions to move both as an individual and with others in equipping yourself to seek and prepare for the full work of the coming revival. For example each area provides wonderful fuel to help you fire up a meaningful prayer meeting for revival. (Such applications will be most evident in chapter 11.)
3. You can share these seven confidence-building perspectives with others to incite them to join with you in full agreement and expectation, by prayer and preparation, for a coming revival.
4. Studying these seven areas will reinforce your expectations about the full scope of revival—that it is to be nothing less than "an approximation of the consummation." The scope of these confidence-building reasons will make you aware of the great things God intends to do in revival, giving you renewed determination to settle for nothing less for our generation. God may use these chapters to awaken a greater desire for revival in you than you've ever had before. I certainly hope so! Because the hope is at hand.

Prisoners of Hope

At a prayer conference in Washington, D.C., Senate Chaplain Richard Halverson challenged the hundreds from all over the nation gathered to pray for revival by asking us, "How much have you prayed for the second coming of Christ and the consummation of history?" As he pointed out, to pray for revival and not to pray for Christ's return is a contradiction. Because the two work together, they draw from each other; they inform and shape each other. The longing that we have for national revival, he said, should be of a similar nature as our longing for the New Jerusalem. And vice versa. To hope for one is always to hope for the other. To want one is to want the other. To be confident about one is to be confident about the other. Revival is an approximation of the consummation. And that's the kind of hope to which we can gladly—confidently—surrender.

I saw this perspective dominate a citywide revival-prayer movement in Philadelphia. It took as its motto a popular phrase from the film *Field of Dreams*. In that movie a sports fanatic builds a baseball stadium in the middle of his Iowa corn field. Why? Because he's heard a voice, a voice that repeatedly assures him that if he does so, famous baseball players of the past will reappear to play on that field for him to watch. The voice whispers to him over and over, "If you build it, they will come." With a corresponding sense of fanatical hope, Christians in Philadelphia (made up of scores of churches of all denominations and ethnic backgrounds) set before them a similar motto: "If we build it, *he* will come." By this they meant if they build the movement of prayer, uniting together as God's people to seek him for citywide revival, then Jesus would come into that arena. He would come upon the churches in great power with healing and redemption for their community and beyond.

I have met tens of thousands like them in my visits with prayer movements around the world. Multitudes of Christians would say of themselves what Bishop Desmond Tutu says of himself (praying for so many years over the tragic struggles of South Africa), that they have become "prisoners of hope."[8] (You met some of them in chapter 1.) Not prisoners of hope in some vague emotional sense. No, these are prisoners of *the* hope, the hope of genuine revival, both the immediate revival that is coming and the ultimate final revival that will one day consume the whole universe.

As President Kennedy once observed: "Some folks look at things as they are and ask 'Why?' Others look at things as they could be and ask, 'Why not?'" Prisoners of hope are people who continue to ask, "Why not?" God has given them the gift of seeing things as he wants them to be, and they are not willing to settle for anything less. As St. Augustine observes, hope has two daughters: anger and courage. Hopeful people have a holy anger with the way things are ("this is not what God designed, this is not what he desires, this is not what he deserves"). But they also have the God-given courage to be agents of change—mainly by getting up on the wall as a people of prayer.

As we turn in the next chapters to explore the impact of true revival, we do so with the question "Why not?" Why would God not want to unleash over the world such a revival—such an approximation of the consummation—for the twenty-first century? Why would he not want to make *you* a prisoner to the hope of such a revival—and an agent to help bring it forth?

4 Confidence Builder 1: The Decisive Person

One Increasing Purpose

The hope of national and world revival is at hand. We can be confident of this for seven good reasons. The first reason—the Decisive Person—rests on this basic thesis.

> God intends for his Son to be at the center of everything—at the end of history and at every step along the way. He has no greater desire. In whatever he does, his ultimate purpose is to sum up all heaven and earth under Jesus as Lord (Eph. 1:10). Every revival—including the final revival—is meant to accelerate, intensify, and expand this process. In revival God dramatically intervenes to restore Christ's rightful role as Redeemer King among his people and to more fully advance his kingdom among the nations. *Therefore we can pray and prepare for a coming world revival with confidence.*

It was not lost on religious commentators that when the Soviet flag was lowered over the Kremlin indicating the internal collapse of atheistic Communism, it took place on Christmas Eve of 1991. What a sign of the great biblical truth: Christ is the victor. He is decisive. Everything stands or falls with its response to him. "The expectation of the renewal of all things in Christ is also the vision in which the whole church lives; it is the hope that lies behind everything we do as Christians. Evil is *not* ultimate. The last word is Jesus Christ."[1]

In Christ we not only see who God is and where he is headed, but in Christ we also see how God intends to get there. In the words of Bishop Stephen Neill, God has "one increasing purpose,"[2] and it all centers on Jesus Christ. History is not moving in a vacuum. History and the expansion of Christ's kingdom are inseparably interlinked.

Thus, since revival propels the expansion of Christ's kingdom and the increase of his purpose among the nations, God's ultimate commitment to his own Son is sufficient reason for us to seek and prepare for revival now, with confidence.

Confidence and the Ascension

To fully grasp the decisive nature of Christ and the implications of this truth for coming revival, we turn to the *ascension*, possibly the most neglected doctrine of Scripture today. By the ascension we see Jesus installed as Messiah to rule over the earth right now. All authority in heaven and earth has been given to him. The ascension signals that God is even now bringing all things under Jesus as Lord (Eph. 1), reconciling heaven and earth through his blood (Col. 1). As John Calvin and other reformers taught, Christ ascended to rule heaven and earth with a more *immediate* power than he ever had in the days of his flesh. As we learn from Psalm 110, Christ does not need to be physically present to conquer his enemies and extend his salvation with invincible power.

At this very moment Christ is about the business of bringing unconditional surrender among all the nations. According to Revelation 6, Christ is not only the heir but also the executor of creation. It is his estate. Right now he is asserting his right over everything that belongs to him.

Therefore there is always great potential in any generation for the advance of God's purposes throughout the earth. Not one corner is left out of the exercise of Christ's lordship. No human enterprise is irrelevant to his concern or lies outside his authority. No human structure and ultimately no peoples of the earth can indefinitely remain indifferent to his reign.

Now please be patient with me here. I realize this is a challenge for all of us, to plumb some of the depths of what God is up to in our midst. What I'm saying is that the redemptive strategy in God's "one increasing purpose" is to achieve glory for his Son from the greatest number of people, to the fullest scope and deepest level possible. *And often that requires revival.*

The key phrase Jesus used to describe the decisiveness of his reign was "the kingdom of God." And what does this mean? David Mains is right in concluding that our Lord was talking about any situation in which Christ is recognized as king, his will is obeyed, and obedient subjects reap the benefits of his reign.[3] This is true in the consummation. It is also experienced in countless situations prior to the consummation, and sometimes, with great intensity! Revival!

We began to look at revival from this perspective in chapter 2. Now I want to explore it with you in greater detail. Let's find why this understanding of who Christ is in the purposes of God should deliver us from all tentativeness in our prayers and preparations for revival.

For you see, to whatever degree Christ is Lord ultimately, he is Lord now. Revival simply intensifies that lordship. That's why we can expect revival. To whatever degree Christ is to be the perfection and fulfillment of all things, he is to be that in substantial ways even now. Revival simply accelerates that work. So, we can expect revival. To whatever degree God is committed to the consummation, he is equally prepared to give any generation approximations of that consummation. Revival simply unleashes that. So, we can expect revival.

The question of God's predisposition toward revival is already decided—in Christ. There is no plan B. This is God's longing for any generation. He is not only willing and able but also ready and committed to do this on behalf of those who seek him for it.

Confidence and the Cross

Multidenominational, multiracial prayer movements for revival were the hallmark of the spiritual battle for South Africa during the 1980s and before. It all culminated in 1994 when thirty thousand people assembled in a stadium in Durban on the eve of the first multiracial national elections, to pray that God would spare their nation a bloodbath and would rain down righteousness and healing on their land.

71

It was no coincidence that as they prayed, leaders of the Zulu nation and the African National Congress successfully deliberated in the same stadium. Civil war was avoided at the eleventh hour. Michael Cassidy, an Anglican clergyman and leader of African Enterprise, who organized the prayer rally (and many other similar gatherings over the years), said of that one day's event, "We believed, as we prepared for the Jesus Peace Rally and as we participated in it, that if we were obedient to God, came together, and humbled ourselves prayerfully and penitentially before him, that he would bring forth the political miracle that we so longed to see. God has heard our prayers."

Truly, this was a foretaste of the larger work God wants us to have in the coming world revival. It all happens when we, like they, are willing to put ourselves under the cross. Under the cross we find our greatest confidence about revival.

Look at it this way: Just as Christ is decisive in everything that touches human experience, including revival, so without a doubt, *the cross marks the most decisive moment in his reign.* The cross is the crossroads of all history, of all human destinies, both of individuals and of nations. At the cross Christ challenges all of the false hopes to which the world might cling. The cross exposes them, rebukes them, and replaces them with the greater hope of God's inexhaustible grace. The cross acts as a hinge to swing open the floodgates of God's saving bounty upon the human race both now and in the consummation itself. At the cross God has already rendered cosmic judgment. Christ was judged for the sins of all humankind, and in his blood God brought down his verdict forever on the world, the flesh, and the devil. The cross was also the starting point of the new creation, when Christ broke the power of death by coming off the cross to rise from the grave.

The manifestation of Christ in Revelation 5, for example, is of a Lamb reigning as a Lion. The Son slain is victorious—he prevails from the cross and by the cross. So how can the Father turn away our cries for a revival that extends Christ's reign, when (as Wesley would say) his wounds forever plead for this?

In every real sense, therefore, revival is secured for us by the cross. Everything that revival brings has been bought and paid for at the cross.

72

Does revival bring unity? Then revival requires the cross (Col. 1:20). Does revival restore holiness? Then revival requires the cross (Col. 1:22). In revival does God open up to us a fullness of life in Christ (Col. 2:9, 10) and a newness of life (Col. 2:13), while defeating the powers of darkness (Col. 2:15)? Then the cross is decisive at every step.

There Is Always So Much More

The cross guarantees that with God, Christians can expect so much more, as God comes to a people under the cross—repentant and broken, but filled with confident hope—and reawakens them to the glory of the reigning Christ among them.

That's what Henri Nouwen suggests in *With Open Hands*. He says there are three components of hope to which Christ invites us: 1. We must constantly expect something new from God. 2. We must look ahead for that which has not yet appeared. 3. We must be ready to accept the risks of daring to stay open to whatever lies ahead.[4] In other words, God's purposes revolving around the cross are so comprehensive that we must always pray and prepare for more with confidence. Greater blessings are coming!

In eighteenth-century preaching and writing on revival, leaders never gave way to the feeling that the condition of the world was so desperate that the only hope left was to "hold the fort" until Jesus comes back. Instead, "in their mind, to have done so would have been to fall into unbelief in regard to the promised results of His first coming. If what was predicted seemed impossible, the remedy was to contemplate more closely the authority and glory which now belongs to the Head of the church."[5]

In other words they constantly prayed for and anticipated revival. They did so simply because they saw in the crucified and ascended Jesus that God always has so much more for his people even prior to (though pointing toward) the second coming of Christ. They also recognized there are times in God's economy when all of his abundance in Jesus may converge with new intensity upon the church. It is experienced as Christ *decisively* inserting himself once again into the center of our consciousness, vindicating himself as our hope of glory, and all of this for the sake of nations still in darkness.

Revival Is Christ

From whatever angle we view it, therefore, revival is fundamentally one thing: *Revival is Christ.* That's because God can do nothing greater for his church than to reawaken us to the sufficiency, supremacy, and destiny of the Lord Jesus Christ. This is as it should be. God does not possess anything for his people, now or forever, beyond who Christ is and what his kingdom is all about. Jesus exhausts for us all we can ever know about God. He encompasses everything we hope to receive from God, everything we hope to become for him. He embodies every hope we share as we enter the twenty-first century. Accordingly, Jesus also exhausts every facet of the church's experience of revival—and of the coming revival.

In revival God arouses his people to a more comprehensive manifestation of his grace and glory in Jesus. We are brought to a rediscovery of the *whole* Christ. Let me pull this together by using three simple words. They describe the full impact of all true revivals in our relationship with Christ: *focus, fullness, fulfillment.* 1. In revival there is a *new focus* on Christ's person (who he is *to* us, especially his character as God's Son) and on his passion (who he is *for* us, especially in his death, resurrection, and ascension). As a result, 2. we experience together in new ways the *fullness of his life* over us (as he rules *over* us as Lord and Head of the church) and in us (as he *indwells* us with his resurrection power). 3. All of this presses us into new involvements in the *fulfillment of Christ's mission* where we live and among the nations, as he carries out his purposes (*through* us), and as he establishes his preeminence among many peoples (going *out ahead of us* to lead his global cause to victory and to bring about the consummation of all things).

To put it in a sentence:

> Revival is when God intervenes with his people at a particular moment to manifest decisively the presence of his Son in three ways: to give them a new *focus* on who Christ is to them and for them; in order that they might enter together into the *fullness* of his life over them and in them; so that they might serve together in the *fulfillment* of his mission through them and out ahead of them.

Superspective: The Manifest Presence of Christ

One of my favorite words to describe this threefold impact of revival is *superspective*. By this I mean a spiritual awakening is more than just dusting off our everyday view of Christ. Instead it's an extraordinary reintroduction to God's Son as Lord—Lord of history, of nations, of the church, of the ages, *of me*. This superspective revolutionizes how the church thinks about him, as well as about ourselves or about the world as a whole. And it revolutionizes how we think about the future, even about the twenty-first century. Clearly if there is one hallmark of the revivals documented in Scripture (and repeated the past two thousand years), it is this: In revival God *reveals* more of Christ. He gives his church vision, superspective, hope.

Puritans like Edwards had their own synonym for God-given superspective. They called it the "manifest presence of Christ."[6] Here's what they meant. There is, they said, the *essential* presence of Christ, that is, Christ is everywhere present, all the time. We are never far from him nor he from us. It's unavoidable. But they also spoke of Christ's *cultivated* presence, the sense of his fellowship that comes to believers as they walk faithfully with him day by day. We cultivate a deeper knowledge of the Lord, and in that sense he seems to become much more present with us as time goes by.

But when the Puritans talked about revival, they coined another term: the *manifest* presence. By this they meant those times when God reveals his Son to a generation of his people in such a dramatic fashion that it seems as if Christ had been hidden from them, then suddenly made manifest.

Imagine actors on a stage. Though they are just as much in the auditorium before the play begins as after it begins, they become manifest only as the curtain is drawn back to introduce act one. Once that happens, however, everything in the theater is transformed. The actors are no longer names on the playbill; they have become real people full of vivid energy, acting out their parts before your very eyes. The plot takes shape and moves towards its climax. Even so in revival God pulls the curtain back. The chief actor, Jesus Christ, appears at center stage. Hailed and studied by all, he takes up his lines and occupies the rest of the evening by the sheer force of his presence until the story is told and the audience cheers and runs on stage to join him in the drama.

75

In other words, in revival, Christ and his kingdom become the center of attention, first to the church and then to the nations among whom God's people dwell. There is such an intensified awareness of who Christ is that even skeptics must acknowledge that what is happening with the Christians is only explainable by supernatural causes. Historian R. O. Roberts put it succinctly:

> Without doubt, the greatest single aspect of every true revival is the peculiar and wonderful sense of the presence of God which is manifest. It is this mighty sense of the presence of God which draws large crowds, produces intense conviction, causes tears to flow, enables hardened sinners to right the wrongs of years past, produces seemingly instantaneous conversions, and results in spontaneous joy and enthusiasm.[7]

No wonder Scripture couches revival in the motif of *encounter*. It talks about God's visitation among his people, about God rending the heavens and coming down to his people, about how he pours out his Spirit upon his people and breaks into their midst with stunning glory. As we saw earlier, there seems to be less the promise of survival and much more the experience of *arrival*. In revival God arrives among his people—he shows up!—with a greater focus on his Son (bringing fullness and fulfillment with it). Christ invades us, as it were, to capture and conquer us afresh, to take us with him as he goes before us into our homes, into our cities, and among the nations.

Scripture often describes a people transformed by revival by saying, "The fear of the Lord was upon them all." Truly, revival is an awesome experience as we fall into the hands of the living God who is intent on consuming us with the presence of the risen Christ. Henry Blackaby boils it down to just two words. Revival is "experiencing God!"

When He Shakes His Mane

In C. S. Lewis's series *The Chronicles of Narnia*, such a revival is typified by events anticipated by a Mr. Beaver as he talks with four children who have stumbled into Narnia through a magical wardrobe. For some time, he tells them, a lion known as Aslan (the Christ-figure of this series) has been noticeably absent from his dominion. In his place the White Witch, filled with evil venom, has transformed Narnia into a place where "it is always winter but never Christmas." But as the humans talk with Aslan's faithful citizen who along with many others longs for the king's return, they are told of an ancient prophecy many believe is about to be fulfilled. Already rumors have surfaced that Aslan has returned and is on the move in the land. Filled with a contagious hope, Mr. Beaver recites for them the prophecy on which their whole future depends:

> Wrong will be right, when Aslan comes in sight,
> At the sound of his roar, sorrows will be no more,
> When he bares his teeth, winter meets its death,
> And when he shakes his mane, we shall have spring again.[8]

He goes on to tell them, "You'll understand when you see him," adding that if the evil sorcerer can stand on her two feet and look Aslan in the face, it will be the most she can do "and more than I expect of her."

In those few lines Lewis has defined for us the heart of revival. It is the revelation of the King. It is his manifest presence restored once more among his subjects: He "comes in sight, roars, bares his teeth, shakes his mane." But Lewis also gives us a hint of what the future holds for a generation that experiences such a revival: "Wrong will be right . . . we shall have spring again."

It is a national and world revival of this magnitude and more—wonderfully reflective of the Decisive Person for whose sake it is given—that many believe will be the hallmark of the twenty-first century—a hope that is at hand. They are confident of this—for more reasons than one. Let's look at confidence builder number two.

5 Confidence Builder 2: The Divine Pattern

God Has Done It Before

The hope of world revival is at hand. The second of seven good reasons to expect it is the Divine Pattern. It rests on this basic thesis:

> God is faithful and consistent in all his ways. He has been pleased to grant times of significant revival throughout the generations of his people from Genesis to the present. One day he will culminate all revivals in the final revival—the consummation of everything in Christ. Surely what God intends to accomplish for all creation and what he has, in fact, approximated repeatedly for so many previous generations, he is able, willing, and *ready* to do right now for our generation. *Therefore we can pray and prepare for it with confidence.*

How is it that the church today is eighty-three million times larger than when it first began? How is it that the outward movement of the gospel is the longest sustained human endeavor in the history of mankind? A primary answer to such questions—and one that is coupled with confidence-builder number one, the Decisive Person—is this: God has been pleased to grant to his people in one generation after another episodes of revival (both local, national, and international). They have been glorious ruptures of divine intervention to manifest to his people so much more of Christ.

Martyn Lloyd-Jones concludes that historically revival has been "God's way of keeping the church alive."[1] Church historian Richard Lovelace says that "the central theme of redemptive history is God's recovery of an apostate people." In *Incendiary Fellowship* Elton Trueblood concurs: "When a Christian expresses sadness about the church, it is always the sadness of a lover. He knows that there have been great periods, and he is not willing to settle for anything less than those in his own time."[2]

Patterns in Biblical Revivals

In my first edition of *With Concerts of Prayer*[3] I discussed various aspects of this divine pattern that I would like to summarize here, adding some additional insights I have gained since that time.

First it's a pattern that can be clearly documented from the Old Testament. Exodus, for example, gives us a prototype of spiritual awakenings. Through God's answer to the prayers of Israel, both the Jews and Egyptians were shaken by the mighty unveiling of God's power, justice, and grace.

Again, in the Book of Judges we find a four-hundred-year account of this divine pattern that goes something like this: A new generation rises up who does not know the Lord and forsakes him for other gods. God gives them over to their enemies. Their physical and spiritual lives are depleted until they awaken to their need to be restored to Jehovah. They cry out together to the Lord. He responds by raising up judges who lead the people back into his ways. As a result surrounding nations stop harassing Israel because the fear of God comes upon them.

We continue to trace this pattern into the days of Solomon, a definite high-water mark among all the revivals Israel experienced. Whole nations were drawn into it. Magnificent moments of revival also surfaced during the reign of Judah's kings, such as Hezekiah. God also stirred up the exiles to return to the land, with revival vision to rebuild the place of prayer and reestablish God's testimony among the peoples.

All the prophets talk of revival, frequently using concepts that have helped the church understand the essence of revival ever since—images such as a new day appearing, waking up, drinking of the fountain of life, being purged by God's fires, international prayer movements, the drawing in of the nations, and most importantly the comprehensive final revival linked with the coming Messiah. The last prophet Malachi insists God is preparing to awaken his people once more in such a way that the Gentiles join them to offer prayers in response to God's revealed glory.

The Psalms give us practical, personal experiences of revival as well as signposts about what revival should look like within the whole nation. The Psalms also provide some of the most powerful prayers for revival the church has ever used.

Key accounts of Old Testament revival patterns are summarized in the writings of Walter C. Kaiser Jr., especially in his book *Quest for Renewal: Personal Revival in the Old Testament.*[4] But, every promise of revival in the Old Testament finds its most graphic demonstration in the first-century church. God unleashed an unprecedented revival through the ministry of Jesus Christ. As Martyn Lloyd-Jones points out in *Joy Unspeakable*, revival was the pervasive climate of the New Testament church era, from Matthew to Revelation.

As I've described in previous chapters, when Jesus set out to preach, heal, and break demonic powers, he had his eye on all that the prophets had promised. Every hope they offered for recovery through a mighty, God-ordained revival was now "at hand" for his generation because he himself embodied the revival foretold. Out of his suffering and resurrection the awakening unfurled with greater intensity. Revival leaped beyond the disciples when the church, saturated with Christ through the Holy Spirit, began to bring the power of forgiveness and reconciliation to multitudes. And so Pentecost became another high point in the history of revivals. Everyone was filled with awe, wonders and miracles abounded. As a result many were added to the church. The manifest presence of the Lord was deeply felt by all, not only in the church but throughout the city of Jerusalem.

Ultimately, however, the church had a grander assignment than extending awakening within Jerusalem. Revival became the experience of newly planted churches throughout the Gentile world, right into Rome itself. We see this in many of Paul's written prayers, which when answered as fully as Paul intended, invariably led to revival.

In fact when Jones entitled his book *Joy Unspeakable*, he was referring to 1 Peter 1:8. His thesis: When Peter told the church in the diaspora that they were even then experiencing unspeakable joy, he was

81

able to do so because he was confident all the churches were already living in the atmosphere of true revival. Thus joy would be a natural experience for them day by day.[5]

And finally, in the Book of Revelation Christ calls many of the Asian churches, born in the initial awakening, to relight their fires and to come back to the intensity of their first love. He then proceeds to display an enlarged view of his purposes for history, showing his church the outworking of the final revival, the consummation of all things. As noted earlier, Jesus draws on many of the images from the end of the book to motivate the churches toward spiritual revitalization now.

Patterns in Church History

This strategy of revival, to no one's surprise, has continued on for two thousand years. (Duewel's *Revival Fire* and Murray's *Revival and Revivalism* are two recent books that provide exciting, insightful accounts beyond what I highlight here.)

For example, the great Monastic movements, which endured for fifteen hundred years, frequently acted as bases of both renewal and missionary operation. Breaking with the values of their cultures, these communities developed lifestyles of praise, commitment, vision, simplicity, and mission, which became a renewing force time and again. The Reformation itself was one of the greatest revivals since Pentecost and focused specifically on reforming the church's understanding of the transcendence of God and the saving work of Jesus Christ. A whole continent was set on fire as a result. Subsequently the Puritans in their writings and their praying pressed the Reformation into what church historians today call the First Great Awakening of the modern era.

One of the leaders in that Awakening was Count Nikolaus Ludwig Von Zinzendorf, who spawned a twenty-four-hour prayer watch in Germany that interceded for revival and mission for one hundred years. The Moravians, as they were called, not only sent out missionary teams to many unreached peoples worldwide, but with equal zeal they deployed "renewal teams" to preach revival and unity in Christ to churches in many parts of Europe and the Colonies, even going to Rome to preach to the pope.

This extensive eighteenth-century revival also involved people like the Wesleys, George Whitefield, and Jonathan Edwards. Richard Lovelace describes the divine pattern in Edwards's experience when he writes:

> The classical pattern generally began with concerted prayer, which led to a deepened sense of the holiness of God and depth of sin. Under Jonathan Edwards's ministry in North Hampton, the whole town went through a collective "dark night of the soul." Lay persons lay awake struggling with convictions, not of gross sins but of pride and envy. Yet during the day they were so fascinated by God that they could not conduct business. To persons in this state of spiritual openness, Edwards's preaching of Jesus Christ as justifier and sanctifier was seen to be intensely relevant and was eagerly welcomed. Once church members were awakened and thoroughly converted, they became an evangelizing team seeking out relatives, friends, and neighbors with the message of salvation. The result of an awakened church was inevitably a subsequent wave of evangelization.[6]

A Second Great Awakening is staked out by church historians from 1790 onward. Prior to this revival, leaders like William Carey, called by some the father of modern missions, formed small prayer bands that met monthly for almost eight years before they saw their revival prayers answered. Others like William Wilberforce, a member of a prayer community in the Anglican parish of Clapham near London, spearheaded efforts in slave abolition in addition to a new missionary enterprise. The presence and power of God was so evident in the church that they also led battles for judicial, penal, and industrial reform and for the spread of popular education.

A Third Great Awakening surfaced noticeably in 1857 when a Manhattan businessman, Jeremiah Lamphier, gathered together a few on Wall Street for a noontime prayer meeting for revival. By 1858 New York City alone had six thousand people involved in such daily prayer gatherings. Tens of thousands crowded into the churches for prayer in the evenings. Within a year one million converts were added to the church rolls across the United States. As Dr. Orr notes in *The Fervent Prayer*:

> The mid-century awakenings (1858–59) revived all of the existing missionary societies and enabled them to enter other fields. The practical

evangelical ecumenism of the revival was embodied in the China Inland Mission founded by Hudson Taylor in the aftermath of the British awakening. . . . As in the first half of the century, practically every missionary invasion was launched by men revived or converted in the awakenings of the churches in the sending countries.[7]

Timothy Smith proves in *Revivalism and Social Reform* that this revival also had significant impact on the social needs of that day.[8]

Historians mark another worldwide revival that began in the early 1900s, the aftermath of which is still with us in many forms, including the modern Charismatic movement. Often called the Welch Revival, because its origin seemed to have begun in Wales in the preaching of Evan Roberts, its impact extended far beyond what happened there (which included eight thousand converts in five years). Dr. Orr writes:

One of the leaders of the revival in 1905 was a young man of the ivy league who later became perhaps the world's most famous professor of missions. When he was at Yale in 1905, 25% of the student body was enrolled in prayer meetings and Bible studies. Again, the ministers of Atlantic City reported that of a population of fifty thousand in that city, they knew of only fifty adults who were unconverted. In Portland, Oregon, two hundred and forty department stores closed from eleven to two for prayer and signed an agreement among themselves so that no one would cheat and stay open.[9]

Such are some of the patterns when God gives revival.

Perhaps one of the most dramatic descriptions of true revival in any generation is the one given by James Burns in his book *The Laws of Revival,* published just shortly before the outbreak of the Fourth Great Awakening. Having spent a good deal of his life studying episodes of revival in church history, he drew the following conclusions:

The appearance of revivals owes nothing to chance; they are a witness to God's sovereignty. . . . *We are able to see a regularity in their appearance and, within certain limits, to anticipate their coming. . . . First of all,* we perceive that they come when preparations have been made, when the times are ripe. *Next,* their appearance is signaled by certain infallible signs one of which is a growing discontent in individuals' hearts with corruption and backsliding. With this comes an intense craving for something better. A growing spirit of expectation that change is coming soon develops.

At last, when contributing streams converge at a definite point there suddenly appears the messenger who speaks for God, and whose voice people instantly recognize and obey.[10]

Another similarity is what occurs when the revival movement is set in motion. When the voice of the leader is heard, vast forces, which seem to have been lying dormant, are awakened. The revival spreads like fire, and huge numbers of people are affected. Wherever it goes, and into whatever heart it enters, it creates an overwhelming realization of sin—then confession. With the forgiveness of sin comes a joy that expresses itself in song. The main effect of the revival is felt in the inner life. It awakens new spiritual emotions. It sharpens lives into subjection to the will of God. It brings the church back to simplicity, sincerity, and a renewed spiritual vitality. . . .[11]

No revival can come from below. All attempts to create a revival fail. Nor can we bring a revival down, since prayer is not the cause of revival but the human preparation for one. By prayer we prepare the soil. Is there a disposition to pray for revival? Are devout men and women everywhere becoming alarmed, not for the success of the church, but for the glory of Christ?[12]

Writing at the same time, South African theologian Andrew Murray focused the last two of his nearly 130 books on this divine pattern. In 1900 he wrote *Key to the Missionary Problem*, a treatise for world church leaders gathered at the New York International Missionary Convention, to discuss the possibilities of evangelizing the world in that generation. In the book he reviewed the divine pattern of revival and then confronted them with the fact that unless that pattern was repeated again in his generation, all of their great plans and good intentions for evangelizing the nations would ultimately fail.[13]

He took up the same thesis ten years later as he wrote a response to the International Missionary Conference in Edinborough, Scotland. *The State of the Church* reasoned that the verdict of history was clear. Unless missionary leaders dealt with the condition of the church and its desperate need for revival, calling forth united prayer to that end, their missionary enterprises would ultimately be an embarrassment to them and the name of the Lord.[14]

Murray understood the truth that what God has done repeatedly for so many previous generations, he was willing to do and must do for theirs. He urged them to seek and prepare for world revival diligently and with confidence, even proposing a worldwide week of prayer the following January.

A Pattern with Seven Phases

Let me conclude this brief overview of the divine pattern by collapsing all of my years of study on this subject into what I see to be the seven major phases of every historic revival. I realize this is a lot to digest. But really, what I've done in the end is paint a simple picture of how revival expresses itself—a picture you can use in critiquing the developments of this drama in our generation, or even within your own city or congregation. (I'm also saving you years of research with these seven points—and that's worth something!)

Each phase is a gift from God. Each phase intensifies and accelerates the work of God in revival. Each phase, if it's allowed to do so, will lead to a final experience of full-orbed revival for that particular generation. I believe phases one and two are already in motion today, which creates in us no small anticipation of what is waiting just ahead (phases three through seven) and what its dimensions will be for our generation:

1. *Realization.* A particular generation of God's people comes to the realization of their desperate need for revival. There's a growing *expectation* that God is ready to give revival, to give so much more of Christ than they have yet experienced. The realization comes through both the preaching of many who see this vision and the convincing pressure of events and circumstances within which the church finds itself. In the end it is all a gift of the Holy Spirit—a "waking up" that has already begun.

2. *Preparation.* Christians begin to persistently pray and prepare for revival. They *pray* both individually and corporately with a growing consensus of what revival should look like and that revival is near. The prayers are expressed in terms of joyful anticipation but also sober repentance. Above all, ardent requests are

made to God to fulfill his promises. Christians also commit themselves to *reorder* their lives and ministries to be ready to run with the full impact of revival when it comes. *Repentance* is a primary characteristic of how they pray and prepare. (I will discuss more on preparation in the final chapter.)

3. *Manifestation*. God answers the prayers of his people! He provides a greater revelation of his grace and glory in Jesus Christ. This brings about a corresponding *reformation* around the doctrines of Christ and his kingdom, as well as a *restoration* of devotion in the hearts of God's people toward the Lord, and a *reorientation* of the church toward the work of the kingdom and the future into which God is leading us.

4. *Consecration*. The impact of revival brings renouncing of sin, a hunger for holiness, and a zeal for the glory of God. This causes God's people to offer themselves in fresh new ways to be used of him to extend the kingdom of Christ in whatever ways he chooses as an outflow of the revival. Revival is a time of *recruitment* when God raises up and thrusts out laborers who are wholly devoted to Christ and his global cause.

5. *Revitalization*. The church experiences *renewal* through the unleashing of the fruits of the Spirit, *renaissance* through the unleashing of the gifts of the Spirit, and the ensuing *renovation* of the very programs and structures of the church to fit in with God's new day for his people. All of this brings forth a revived community that is experiencing in greater measure "the fullness of the stature of Christ" along with greater maturity in worship, discipleship, and ministry for Christ.

6. *Penetration*. The revived church begins to influence and impact the society in which it finds itself. Through its witness God gives a *reformation of society* in morality, righteousness, and justice and a renovation and rebuilding of the structures of a society to be more compassionate and just. Above all this, *evangelization unfolds* as the revived church goes forth to bear witness of Christ within every structure of society, at every level, among every people, and within every situation and need. The power of such penetration by the church rises in part from how the fear of God has come, first on God's people through revival and

then on unbelievers who sense the presence of God in the midst of a revived church. But it doesn't stop here. Finally there is expansion.

7. *Expansion.* The gospel is extended into many parts of the earth and among many peoples where the kingdom has not yet come. Out of revival there is a release of the laborers, an increased vision for reaching those who are currently beyond the reach of the gospel, and a rebellion against the strongholds of the enemy that have usurped Christ's lordship among the nations. In the end, churches are planted among peoples where Christ has never been named before, to become bases of operations for his kingdom in their own societies and beyond. Of course, all of this will trigger many evil forces against the gospel and may lead to significant persecution.

What's so exciting about this seven-phase analysis is that it connects beautifully with the three words used in chapter 4 to describe the impact of revival: focus, fullness, and fulfillment. Here's how it works.

Through the phases of realization, preparation, and manifestation, the church is given a new *focus* toward the person of Christ—all that he is to us and for us. Through consecration and revitalization the church enters afresh into the *fullness* of the life of Christ—all that he wants to be over us and in us. And finally out of the phases of penetration and expansion the church moves forward in new ways into the *fulfillment* of the mission of Christ—all that he wants to do through us and out ahead of us. We can picture it like this:

The Divine Pattern	
Focus	1. Realization
	2. Preparation
	3. Manifestation
Fullness	4. Consecration
	5. Revitalization
Fulfillment	6. Penetration
	7. Expansion

That's the divine pattern, plain and simple. In a sense, however, we'll never fully understand it until our generation has gone through it. Furthermore, as it continues to unfold for us, the expressions of each phase will be so unique to our times—unmatched by any stories of previous revivals—that even the backward look will only begin to help us grasp where we're headed. However, in principle, this is what we have to look forward to! What God has done before, he is not only able and willing but also ready to do again.

The First Law of Wing-Walking

History, observes Lance Morrow, "is filled with regenerations, with new beginnings, as one era replaces another." But because "regeneration is always cleansing but usually dangerous," it requires that we all learn how to apply the first law of wing-walking. This law cautions, "Never let go of what you've got until you've got hold of something else."[15] That's true for all of us! We are like wing-walkers. Our flight into the twenty-first century carries a certain sense of that terrifying moment of suspension in midair between two planes—that is, between two eras.

A coming era of national and world revival presents us with something fresh, something dependable to take hold of, something worth stepping on to. There need be no fear here because a look at the divine pattern indicates, in principle, precisely what we're stepping on to. We have every reason to let go of the old. We can seek and prepare confidently for what is coming with a minimum amount of terrifying midair suspense! And we'd better get started soon—because the hope is at hand!

6 Confidence Builder 3: The Dark Prospects

Apocalyptic Times

The hope of world revival is at hand. And there's a third good reason to expect it (although this chapter may initially seem to contradict it). Here's the thesis:

> God loves the world and longs to see his Son exalted among all earth's peoples. But he knows the world is currently facing extraordinary crises and challenges beyond its own resources. He also knows humankind is under the dominion of both sin and dark spiritual powers. Deliverance for the nations rests once again in God's sovereign intervention to reveal his glory, to push back the darkness, and to release his solutions in Christ in a revival equal to the desperate needs of our time. In fact, revival in the church is the only hope he currently holds out for the world he loves. *Therefore we can pray and prepare for it with confidence.*

"These are apocalyptic times," writes journalist and editor Rodney Clapp, "apocalyptic in the sense that the entire world is seen as besieged by crises so severe we are on the brink of the end. . . . We can expect apocalyptic fear to spread in the coming years. Many fear total disintegration."[1] There is no question that the megatrends of this hour on both national and global levels are leading many to feel overwhelmed. Hopes we hold for the twenty-first century may soon be suffocated by the challenges. Paul Kennedy, writing in *Preparing* for the Twenty-first Century, says, "Far from a stimulus to preventative actions, global trends are so large as to induce despair."[2]

When I teach about revival in seminar settings, I often pass out summary lists of the most disconcerting megatrends we face. (A version of such handouts appears in appendix 1.) Of course, newspaper headlines, news magazines, evening news broadcasts, and neighborhood conversations keep us constantly aware of what ails our world. I find, however, that we sometimes fail to grasp how sobering the sum total of it all should be. When Christians do open up to explore the issues further, we are often overwhelmed by unexpected dark prospects we confront. And I must confess that when that happens, it is a response I am actually grateful to see! For it is only as we come to grips with the extent of our need and extremity that we will be driven to seek, as our only hope, Christ and the revival he brings.

The Seeming Disappearance of Hope

In overwhelming times, a people of such biblical hope are desperately needed.

Bishop Lesslie Newbigin, aware of our emerging crises, commented a decade ago that we are witnessing a virtual disappearance of hope in Western culture.[3] It is being replaced by wide-spreading pessimism and fatalism about the future. For example, Doom, a nonreligious apocalyptic group, predicts the imminent end of the world unless wholesale action is concentrated on environmental and economic problems.[4] Other groups speak of the potential of an "urban apocalypse" because most Two-Thirds World cities don't have the infrastructure to sustain the level of population growth currently taking place. Chuck Colson observes that in America "our inner-cities are coming very close to anarchy."

Some foresee the time when the U.S. finally takes such a strong stand against Japan's economic encroachments that it has the feel of all-out military conflict. (See *The Coming War with Japan* by George Friedman and Meredith LeBard.[5]) On the home front a popular economist projects financial bankruptcy (*The Coming Collapse of America and How to Stop It*[6]), while in even stronger terms Larry Burkett (*The Coming Economic Earthquake*) sounds an alarm over the destruction of our economic system through personal bankruptcies, the debt of corporate businesses, and the wrenching of an aggregate national debt that is moving toward 3.5 trillion dollars by the year 2000.[7] He quotes J. Peter Grace, chairman and CEO of the W. R. Grace Company, who says, "We're on a disaster course and the time for action is right now. . . . By the year 2000, interest payments on the Federal debt will take 102% of all personal income taxes." *Time* magazine calls recent semi-apocalyptic upheavals "once in a lifetime dislocations that will take years to work out." It includes among them the job drought, defense-industry contractions, the savings and loan collapse, the real estate depression, and the health care cost explosion.

Writes Norman Robertson, chief economist at Pittsburgh's Mellon Bank, "There's going to be a lot of trauma before it's over." No one is projecting any quick fixes. Robert Stan Lacey, publisher of the newsletter *Work-place Trends,* says, "The U.S. work-place is in a profound, historic state of turmoil that for millions of individuals is approaching panic."[8]

Beyond Economic Earthquakes

If we look beyond national economic trends, how hopeful are other prospects? Unfortunately they too are not only disturbing but in many cases seem to defy any solution. For example, one theologian raises the possibility of a coming race war in which racism, urban violence, and the marginalization of African Americans may force this nation to undergo ethnic civil wars on a level we now only read about in Eastern Europe and Africa.[9]

Recently at Yale University, Senator John Carey gave his view of the dark prospects as he told the student body:

> Consider a different part of the reality of America today: a violent, drug-ridden, rat-infested reality; a reality in which the institutions of civilized social life have broken down; of disintegrating families; boarded up store fronts; schools that have become armed camps and crack houses replacing community centers as the focus of neighborhood life.
>
> I ask you to consider a reality where more than 80% of babies are born to single mothers; where young men die violently at a rate exceeding that of any American war; where only one child in three fin-

ishes high school and even then, too often, can barely read; where the spread of AIDS and homelessness rifts so visibly at the fabric of community; where far too many families are on welfare for far too long, and where far too many children carry guns instead of lunch boxes to school.[10]

One need only consider the plight of our youth in the midst of such measurable cultural disintegration to acknowledge we need answers desperately. We see the sharp increases in teenage pregnancies and drug addiction. Gripped in fear, constantly confronted with murder and mayhem in our cities, young people by the millions must begin their classes by stepping through metal detectors put in place to help minimize violence. Because many youth are raised in homes with few values and with significantly increased incidents of child abuse (physical, sexual, and emotional), it is no surprise that many are incredibly hostile and even seek to resolve their internal conflicts with the use of a firepower often greater than what the police forces have to deliver in return.

As president of the Carnegie Corporation, Dr. David Hamburg warns in *Today's Children: Creating a Future for a Generation in Crisis* that the U.S. is committing "atrocities" with its children. "We've already lost a substantial portion of the generation of kids under age sixteen. Their loss to drug abuse, crime, and teen pregnancy, but also to more subtle corrosives like malnutrition, illiteracy and poor self-esteem."[11]

Philadelphia Enquirer columnist, Claude Lewis, ponders, "Shouldn't we be depressed by what we see on the national landscape? . . . Someone informs us that a baby is 'God's opinion that the world should go on.' One has to wonder, if this is the kind of world we want to go on."[12]

Prospects for the Soul of a Nation

Some have accented our troubling national prospects with the term *culture wars*.[13] They see us caught up in a rending struggle for nothing less than the heart and soul of our nation. In *Hollywood vs. America: Popular Culture and the War on Traditional Values*, Jewish film critic Michael Medved graphically describes the "foul-mouthed, sex-soaked, violent (especially toward women), anti-family content of modern films," and sees the film industry as a "poison factory which assaults our most cherished values and corrupts our children." Further, he echoes others who suggest that Hollywood is joining universities, the news media, and many public-interest organizations to undermine the Judeo-Christian values that once informed and shaped our culture.[14]

Unquestionably there is intense discussion right now about the definitions of our values for the twenty-first century. Those on one side of the debate have every reason, humanly speaking, to feel despair. Carl F. H. Henry sees us potentially moving into the "twilight of a great civilization."[15] For example our culture has shifted from a "sanctity of life" ethic to one more focused on a "quality of life" ethic, which opens a Pandora's box on many fronts, from abortion to euthanasia. In another arena a recent Gallup study suggested that based on current changes, only about 10 percent of American families will be what we think of as "traditional" families (mother and father and children living together) by the beginning of the twenty-first century. But he goes on to say that 70 percent of Americans are equally convinced that American society is likely to collapse if the traditional unit falls apart.

The forces of relentless secularism currently appear to be striving to denounce the supernatural as irrelevant for this nation, as well as criticizing absolute beliefs as arrogant. They want to promote nonreligious and in some cases even antireligious philosophies as the new "moral cohesion" for our society.

When he received the 1993 Templeton Prize for Progress in Religion, Chuck Colson in his acceptance speech confronted this dark drift straight on:

> We are stripping religion away from public life to our great and everlasting peril. It is the most self-destructive process the nation could embark on. We are trying to erase the indispensable role of religion in informing the moral consensus by which civilized society has survived. We have embarked into a "brave new world" without moral directions, of values erased from teaching, of tolerance elevated above truth, of the expunging of the last vestiges of religious symbols in this country. What we've got is a "brooding hostility" toward religion. We're no longer neutral about religion but hostile to religion. On most every front there is an increasing secularization of America. The basic presupposition has developed that we are no longer a Judeo-Christian culture.[16]

George Hunter III documents that whereas in 1969 only 9 percent of the population had no church background, in 1989 it was 26 percent, and it is projected to be at least 37 percent by 2001.[17] And this in no way includes the millions of others who have dropped out of church because they were never meaningfully touched by the gospel while they were members. On top of all that, we also know that currently there are at least three million people who have no knowledge of Christ and no one near them, culturally speaking, to even begin to tell them. In addition, there are fifty million unchurched urban poor in our inner cities.

Clearly, the darkness overwhelming our society right now is comprised of many forces, from hostile antisupernaturalism to materialism and affluence, to injustice and racism, to lack of compassion toward the disenfranchised within our country. Carl Henry suggests that we may even now live in the half generation "before hell breaks loose" and, if its fury is contained, he says, we will be remembered, if we are remembered at all, as those who laid down their lives as the "dikes" to hold back impending doom.

In the call to be willing to be such dikes, many hear the Spirit's summons to take up the only hope we have for victory: to seek a national spiritual awakening to Christ. For out of that, God can raise up literally tens of millions to turn the tide. In fact the rapid changes, looming challenges, and desperate crises enveloping our generation require a church prepared for comprehensive action not only in holding back the doom but in advancing a fuller revelation of Christ and his kingdom as the great hope of all nations.

Darkening Prospects among the Nations

Much of the discussion in this chapter so far has focused on national prospects. But we are part of a "global village" that is also overwhelmed with a host of international challenges. All of this simply serves to compound our sense of hopelessness and doom. However, the international prospects can likewise drive us to turn to God in ever-increasing dependence, with growing conviction that only a sovereign God can endue our redemptive efforts with sufficient power and effectiveness. Again, revival is our only hope, amplified this time by a global vision. (See appendix 1 for an extensive catalog of these prospects.)

For Christians the one international issue that might push us the furthest into despair, were it not for the promise of God's reviving presence, concerns the Great Commission. The sheer immensity of what needs to be done is staggering. We sense the urgency of almost three billion to be reached with the gospel who have never heard it before. To grasp the work ahead of us, consider that three billion is the number of times your heart will beat from the day you were born to the day you reach seventy-five. That is a lot of people!

Then if we add all the other dark prospects that plague the world community, it is clear that for Christ's mission to go forward victoriously it will be very costly to us who serve him. The church needs to be equipped with a new level of spiritual power for bold action on a host of challenges that impinge directly on fulfilling Christ's global cause. We can only hope to push back the night among earth's peoples if God intensifies a manifestation of Christ and his kingdom through us such as no generation has ever experienced before—or ever needed to.

And yet beyond the tangible dark prospects, there are the more hidden, subtle spiritual forces we must confront as well. The Bible describes two mysteries at work in the world: godliness and iniquity. Evil is growing concurrently with good. Our generation, facing obstacles never imagined by any previous age, finds itself thoroughly embroiled in a whirlpool at the convergence of these two diametrically opposed powers—Christ against demonic forces. Both history and Scripture bear witness: Until the final day of judgment, every bit of progress in the gospel, on all fronts, will be paired with times of retrogression and suffering as Satan deploys his subversive legions to attempt to overwhelm the cause of Christ.

Every "harvest field" was previously a "battle field." As we anticipate the advance of the gospel, we can anticipate intense encounters with Satan, with ensuing resistance and counterattacks. The charts in appendix 1 point out graphically that if we take Christ's world mission seriously, we face in the twenty-first century a conflagration with the demonic of such a magnitude in its consequences that nothing short of revival will ever see us through it.

As noted earlier, J. Edwin Orr observed that all revival is a time of "warfare of the Spirit against the devil."[18] In revival, satanic forces perceive the intensification of the presence of the Conqueror moving among the nations. Satan understands this much about true revival: If given its fullest expression, it will always entail successive dethronements of his kingdom here and worldwide. And so the nearer we come to revival (or rather, the closer revival comes to us), the more intensified will be the resistance of "anti-forces" of darkness against whom that revival is so specifically targeted. Attempting new breakthroughs in world evangelization and engaging all the dark prospects arrayed against our generation, we will be involved in unprecedented spiritual warfare. Demonic territorial counterattacks and preemptive confrontations by the powers of darkness will be normal occurrences.

Now What?

Billy Graham, visiting in the aftermath of hurricane Andrew's devastation in South Florida, tells of Christians working night and day to help the survivors get water and food. One of them noticed a sign on the roof of a devastated house that read, "Okay, God. You've got our attention. Now what?" Graham drew a parallel: "I see storms of apocalyptic proportions on the horizon. God is beginning to get our attention. Now what?" The thesis of this chapter is that the only hope for our nation and for the peoples of the world is a God-given revival in the church. *That* is what!

A recent survey taken by the National Association of Evangelicals (NAE) asked the opinion of Christian leaders regarding the greatest concerns facing this society, for which we are in desperate need of answers from God. They listed in the following order: moral decline, deficit, abortion, family breakdown, health care, domestic economy, drug and alcohol abuse.[19] Many believe biblical revival is the only solid, practical answer to every one of these. Not surprisingly, shortly after the survey, the NAE turned over a portion of their fiftieth anniversary conference to pray concertedly for the only hope we have as a nation: corporate revival in the church.

It is not that revival is a magical panacea. Rather, as we've already learned, revival in its true biblical sense is nothing less than "the manifest presence of Christ," first to his people and then through them to society and to nations. The deliverance of our country depends above everything else on God's willingness to intervene sovereignly with his church in a manner equal to the desperate needs of the times. And that intervention must be nothing short of an "approximation of the consummation." Only a church wholly revived—with a greater focus on Christ, leading into a fullness of his life together and on to the fulfillment of his global cause—can be victorious. Only such a church can successfully confront and transform the dark prospects that this generation faces, whether political, technological, economic, social, or religious.

Further, out of his great love for earth's unreached—love that cost his Son the cross—God is not only willing but ready to act. He longs to give the world through a revived church what it desperately must have to see these dark prospects turned into arenas of convincing victories. He knows that the only future for such a world, living as it is in "apocalyptic times," is an apocalyptic-type foretaste of what awaits the nations in the final revival.

For example, consider what might ultimately be true for every one of the NAE concerns listed above when God finally consummates each area in Christ (whether public righteousness, family life, material resources, or personal well-being). The hope of revival speaks to this. God wants to approximate that work in an intermediate sense even now as his people are revived and redeployed with a new vision of Christ. The same can be said for every one of the scores of prospects listed in appendix 1. Out of God's love for the world, he desires to displace in graphic measure everything that contradicts who Jesus is, replacing it with his kingdom work.

What If?

Missiologist Bryant Myers, writing on "the changing shape of world mission" in a recent MARC newsletter sketches the hope before us. Analyzing current structures of sin around the world (organized crime, drug traffic, pornography, military spending, gambling, tax cheating, etc.), he offers this helpful insight. Over 30 percent of the gross world product is related to these "structures of sin," with a total cost every year of 5.2 trillion dollars. Only 520 billion dollars per year would be needed, however, to provide all the world's poor with adequate food, water, education, and shelter. He asks, "What effect might a worldwide revival of righteousness have on meeting the basic needs of the poor?" What effect indeed![20]

This is not to suggest that revival will bring in the New Jerusalem. Nor am I attempting to argue here for a postmillennial view of history. Not at all! I'm simply reasoning (whatever your eschatological perspectives may be) that *there is so much more* God wants to do among the nations—particularly in face of these dark prospects—than we have yet experienced. I'm suggesting that God is yearning to intervene powerfully to do something about it. And I'm suggesting the primary entry point for a marvelous new work of God's grace, truth, and justice is through a church fully revived. Such a church will be empowered to take up the work of the gospel by word and deed and enter with redemptive healing into the mainstream of the world's chaotic, unpredictable, and potentially destructive onrush into the twenty-first century.

Fresh Perspective on Dark Prospects

Not long ago Aleksandr Solzhenitsyn commented that if former generations could have looked ahead to see what is happening in our generation, they would have called it "apocalypse."[21] That being so, the apocalyptic nature of these dark prospects should also give us every reason to seek God for the apocalyptic nature of revival (I'm drawing here on the actual meaning of the Greek word itself as we saw in chapter one—a dynamic *unveiling* of Christ to his people and then to the world). Extraordinary crises require an extraordinary unveiling of Christ! God's love for the nations and the breaking of his heart over the desperate plight of earth's unreached peoples should instill in us absolute confidence. We will not find ourselves seeking and preparing for revival in vain. God knows there is no other hope. He knows these apocalyptic times require his apocalyptic visitation in a wide-ranging moral and spiritual awakening in the church. His love for the world will move him to visit his people with power once again.

Earlier in this century a great prayer leader in Norway, Olaf Hallesby, realized the same desperate need for Christians to pray for revival in his generation. What he wrote to them are words that can be written to the whole church today:

> We will want to have a part in praying for the awakening in the widest sense of the term, a world awakening. We see that that is just what the world needs now, more than anything else. Many of us are asking almost despairingly, "Where will it all end?" Where will it all end if we do not have a revival so far reaching in general that it will stem the tide of sin in all parts of the world, and open up new avenues for the Gospel in the frivolous and wicked generation which today peoples our earth?[22]

Before reading on, you might find it helpful to look over appendix 1, asking:

1. What difference would it make in any one of these issues, trends, or peoples if the church were so saturated with the presence of God that we were experiencing all that Christ is to us, for us, in us, over us, through us, and out ahead of us?
2. All things considered, is there any greater hope for reversing these dark prospects apart from world revival in the church?
3. In light of the difference we believe world revival could bring to any of these categories, how should this hope begin to change the way we actually pray for our nation, for our world, and for revival in our churches?
4. How should it change the way we prepare for revival, if we believe revival is ordained of God to impact these concerns in practical ways with the kingdom of Jesus Christ?

7 Confidence Builder 4: The Disturbing Paralysis

Where Is the Salt?

The hope of world revival is at hand. As we've seen already, there are many reasons to expect it. The fourth one may once again seem to contradict that hope, but notice how the thesis puts it:

> God loves the church and intends to bring glory to his Son among the nations primarily through his people. But he also sees that the desperate condition of the world is largely due to the church's struggles with its own spiritual powerlessness, brokenness, dullness, and sin. His love for us and his calling for us in Christ cannot leave us indefinitely in this unrevived state. Since he is committed to the welfare of Christ's body, he must deliver us. He must awaken us to a fuller manifestation of his Son. He knows such revival is the only hope for the restoration and liberation of the church. Our paralysis is not the last word. It should, like the dark prospects around us, drive us toward our hope in God. *We can pray and prepare for revival with confidence.*

In *Decisive Issues Facing Christians Today,* Anglican church leader John Stott poses a fundamental indictment of today's church. He pictures a house darkened at nightfall and says no one would blame the house for its darkness as the sun goes down. He also pictures meat that has become rotten and inedible. The meat is not to be blamed for what the bacteria has been able to do when left to breed by itself. Where is the salt? Where is the light? If society deteriorates and its standards decline, leaving people in darkness and putrification, no one should blame society, for that is what we should expect to happen if humankind is left to itself and people's sinful hearts go unchecked. Stott writes, "The question to ask is: 'Where is the church? Why are the salt and light of Jesus Christ not permeating and changing our society?'"[1]

Stott helps us see that for God to lead us forward into revival, Christians must first assume responsibility for our condition. We must confess to what I call our *disturbing paralysis* and the negative repercussions it has on Christ's global cause.

Why do I use the word *paralysis?* When part of a man's body is paralyzed, he may have wonderful ambitions, but the common frustration of a paralytic is that he is trapped by his inability to do with his body what his mind can visualize and what his heart desires. What can be said of a paralytic can also be said of the church when it is in a prerevival condition.

This becomes obvious on three levels: 1. The dark prospects in the world continue to get darker, and we feel impotent to do anything about it. 2. We are frustrated with the fruitlessness of many Christian enterprises and frequently forced to confess our barrenness in trying to be the church and do the mission of the church in the world. 3. Our best dreams elude us. The longings we hold deep inside—to know the fullness of Christ in our lives together and to accomplish great things together in the fulfillment of his global cause—remain paralyzed. It is not that we're unwilling, but rather that we are often unable.

Yet all of this points to something even more basic. Scripture bears out that when the church lacks any real sense of the presence of God, there will always be an attendant increase of paralysis in the church and of wickedness in the world. The absence of the manifest presence of Christ is like removing the police force from a city or breath from the body. Everything falls apart.

No light and no salt mean only darkness and rottenness.

Beyond Survival

Gallup polls have repeatedly shown little difference in ethical views and behavior when comparing the unchurched with the churched. And while 94 percent of Americans claim to believe in "God or some kind of unseen spirit," far fewer credit faith as an important influence in their lives. When George Gallup and Timothy Jones devised a survey to find America's truly spiritually committed, which they wrote about in *The Saints Among Us,* they found only 13 percent of our adult population could be so defined.[2]

In many cases the public image of the evangelical church is one of irrelevance and boredom coupled with periodic scintillating scandals. No wonder Billy Graham speaking at the fiftieth anniversary of the founding of the National Association of Evangelicals lamented the "shallowness, compromises, laxity, and accommodations" that he sees in many evangelical churches.

Meager impact in recent church growth efforts provides further evidence of the paralyzed state of the church. Researchers have discovered that 3,500 people leave the church every day in the United States.[3] According to studies by the Association of Church Missions Committees (ACMC), 250,000 of the 300,000 U.S. Protestant congregations are either stagnant or dying. Research on church growth in the U.S. in the 1980s uncovered disturbing statistics: 85 percent of churches were losing members during the '80s, while 14 percent grew only by transfer growth. Only 1 percent actually recorded growth by conversions.[4] According to Peter Wagner, during the 1980s not a single county in the United States had net growth in church attendance.

In other words, with all our church growth innovations we were barely able to hold our own. How could we succeed, then, to mobilize ourselves with new initiatives, to penetrate our society with righteousness and truth, or to send forth the gospel among the nations. As one church statesman put it during a discussion on CBN television, "It seems that we may end the 1990s so far out of the mainstream that we may never be able to get back in again."

On top of this is a growing sense of *hopelessness* in the church. Despite the formidable force that the Religious Right posed in the 1980s and early 1990s, there is still massive cultural drift away from Judeo-Christian ethics in the public square. Many who have been a part of the effort to transform society through political leveraging are now some of the strongest voices calling the church back to basics, back to prayer for revival, back to a focus on changing the hearts of our citizens. We cannot change the world simply with political savvy!

Syndicated columnist Cal Thomas, who once worked for Moral Majority, represents this change of perspective:

> The Christian Church has lost its moral power and has become a prisoner, rather than a leader and liberator, of the culture. The church once had power: moral power, spiritual power, the power to transform not only people's lives but also to heal society's deepest ills. That power, as the history of this and other countries has revealed, is greater than any government, no matter how much money government spends and no matter how many points of light it seeks to illuminate on its own.[5]

Others within one of the great renewal movements of our generation, the charismatic renewal, admit they also need a fresh touch from the Holy Spirit. In the *Charisma* article referred to earlier, Mario Murillo tells "Why We Need Fresh Fire": "We must experience a new Pentecost. . . . Why can't we just admit we need fresh fire? Have we lived so long without it that we dread the embarrassment of admitting our need? We are powerless, and we need a new outpouring of the Spirit."[6]

Murillo discusses what he calls the seven "fatal attractions" undermining this renewal movement such as arrogance, hoarding blessings meant for others, superficial mass production, competition, hype, and worshiping the past. His diagnosis of charismatics is equally true for most of evangelicalism!

Paralysis Worldwide

The problem of paralysis is being experienced on a global scale. Every week most Western mission agencies struggle with having numbers of qualified candidates ready to go on the mission field but unable to be sent due to the unwillingness of churches to release the necessary funding. One study found recent giving to all Christian causes is approximately twenty-five dollars of every thousand dollars that Christians spend. Some project that the average giving per church member might drop to as low as 1.94 percent of total income by the year 2002.

Looking at the global church's resources, researcher David Barrett asserts, "the world should have been evangelized a thousand times over by now" if the church had moved out in strategic ways under the power of the Holy Spirit. Instead, we find ourselves light-years away from seeing the task completed.

Christian futurologist Tom Sine, in *Wild Hope*, sees us "waking up to a worldwide Christian shortfall." He talks about the tremendous conflict the Protestant and Catholic churches in Latin America face, the challenges of hunger, famine, environmental breakdown, AIDS epidemics, mounting violence in Africa, and the tearing of the church in Asia by dichotomies of wealth and poverty, all of which hinder the church's daunting mission. He documents the decline of the church in Europe and the struggling of the church in Australia and New Zealand where it tends to embrace a culture of consumerism.[7]

This evangelical paralysis should shock us all, suggests one leader:

> During the greatest resurgence of evangelicalism in this century, belief in the Bible has declined and religious influence has been so thoroughly scrubbed from public life that any honest observer would have to re-gard this as a post-Christian culture. Gallup reports the most bewil-dering paradox: religion up, morality down.
>
> Why have evangelicals not more effectively influenced the world?
>
> We have, I fear, substituted therapy for truth, trivialized our wor-ship, and tolerated—yes even encouraged—a dangerously low and parochial view of the church. A little like Custer's lieutenants arguing over mess privileges before the Battle at Little Big Horn, we've pro-tected our enterprises but in the process lost the culture.
>
> Looking at the state of evangelicalism and the state of the culture gives little room for optimism: How can we expect others to take what we profess to believe more seriously than we ourselves apparently do?[8]

On the Verge of Collapse

Rising out of years of travel in and out of the evangelical movement, I've concluded the worst may be still ahead. What I see developing goes beyond paralysis. It is even more frightful. It is the potential for total collapse. We are increasingly overwhelmed by the immensity and com-plexity of the challenges before us. We are overloaded with a vast array of activities, causes, and enterprises that sap us of excellence and pro-ductivity. We have been oversold on many claims, procedures, and pro-grams that have disappointed us time and again. We are overextended both in the breadth of our commitments and the multiplicity of our agendas, all of which we try to sustain at the same time. We are weary from being overactive, trying to maintain all the systems we have set in motion for doing Christianly things. We lack the spiritual energy to tackle the most important activities to which Christ is calling us.

Overwhelmed, overloaded, oversold, overextended, overactive—we need revival! One leader told me, "If we don't see revival by the end of this decade, we may watch the evangelical movement simply collapse in upon itself out of sheer exhaustion from trying to do God's work in our own strength." He's right. Apart from an extraordinary infusion of Christ's power, we are no match for the gale winds against which we sail into the twenty-first century.

We're like the chameleon that wandered through a fabric store. As it walked across a green swatch of cloth, it turned green. When it walked across red, it turned red. But when it stepped onto a piece of plaid, it blew up. It couldn't be everything at once.

Pastors understand this experience. Os Guinness refers to a recent study that found a local church's requirements of its pastor had expanded from five (according to a 1934 study) to fourteen![9] Pastors are expected to perform different responsibilities well in administrative planning, facilitating worship, sensitivity to personal congregational needs, the spiritual development of congregational life, pastoral counseling, visiting the sick, supporting church stewardship programs, administrative leadership, involvement of the laity in church programs, support for the church's mission to the world, holding issues of social justice before the congregation, and helping them get involved. Obviously such a broad mandate is impossible for most pastors to accomplish. No wonder many are thoroughly depleted and exhausted. This results not only in the paralyzing of their ministries but also in rendering them incapable of equipping the church to be aggressive and effective. Their paralysis becomes the church's paralysis.

The Paralysis of Unbelief

In the end the greatest paralysis with which we wrestle is not overactivity or misplaced priorities. It is the paralysis of our unbelief. Most other forms of paralysis are wrapped up in unbelief. The paralysis of unbelief means we choose not to believe what God has said regarding his own character and regarding the ways he has chosen to advance Christ's kingdom through us among the nations. Either we choose to willfully ignore his grand intentions, or we defy those purposes and replace them with other things.

Apart from the transformation of our natures by a thorough spiritual awakening to God's grace and glory in Jesus Christ, we carry with us an affinity toward the *status quo* (instead of the kingdom of God) and toward *idolatry* (instead of the character of God). These two predispositions lie at the root of our paralysis of unbelief. In turn, they are responsible for rendering us so helpless in the cause of Christ.

Appendix 2 lists some of the critical manifestations of both predispositions—the signs of status quo thinking and the forms of idolatry in the church. Appendix 2 shows how these two predispositions are not only rooted in unbelief but also foster unbelief. You may want to look at it now. Approach both lists in the appendix asking yourself three questions:

1. What difference can we expect the coming revival to make for each form of predisposition?
2. Without revival is there any hope that we can be delivered from paralysis in the church?
3. What do these predispositions tell us about our need for repentance if revival is to come; how would such repentance be expressed both in prayer and in obedience?

Now let's briefly look at each predisposition.

Predisposition toward the Status Quo

The signs are everywhere. Today's church is paralyzed by the seeming impossibilities of the redemptive tasks before us. We sense the weight of urgency, coupled with uncertainty of how to proceed. We know that the tasks carry a sure guarantee of high cost for those who choose to go forward. In the face of this, our predisposition is not to move out. Rather it is to retreat and "hold the fort until Jesus comes."

Often we opt for a survival mentality with little expectation for either changed lives or a changed world. We may fall to smugness, setting boundaries on the ways and works of God.

Our predisposition toward the status quo arises out of our predisposition toward parochialism, our willingness to stay in religious ghettos. We have all been there. This keeps us from seeing the needs of the world or being called to seek God for increased power to address those needs.

In many senses our churches are in a state of "denial" regarding the need for revival. As long as things are more or less all right for my family and my friends and my local church functions, I may ignore the vision of what more God wants to do and must do. I may retreat into the comfort of what is, much like an alcoholic who refuses to face up to his problem though everyone else can see it. As long as he remains in denial, he cannot be helped.

For many this retreat—presumption, smugness, intentional parochialism—really comes down to an issue of self-centeredness and self-indulgence. We are complacent about God's desires to transform the status quo in revival and to unleash through us an invasion of Christ's kingdom in new ways among the nations. Why? *Because we are content to live without these things.* As A. W. Tozer writes, "Acute desire must be present or there will be no manifestation of Christ to his people. He waits to be wanted."[10] All too often, our desire is not acute because our desire is only for our own needs. "The termites of laziness, self-indulgence, narcissism, materialism, prayerlessness, and theological and biblical shallowness easily riddle the foundational planks of world missions."[11]

But when we turn the coin over, we find yet another destructive predisposition.

Predisposition toward Idolatry

Idolatry is any illusion that has caused us to put something in the place of Christ. Idolatry is giving our allegiance and affections to another. As Os Guinness points out in *No God but God,* evangelicalism is rife with idols. He warns that idolatry is more offensive to God than apostasy. Idolatry is like adultery. It is not so much an issue of ortho-

110

doxy as an issue of passion. And if our passion is for the wrong things, then we will find ourselves depleted of all spiritual power. God will never bless a people who worship the works of their own hands.

To what extent has the evangelical church been seduced by the philosophies of this age—even by the futile hopes that the world holds on to for the twenty-first century? Have we grieved and quenched the Spirit of the living God? Have we too often devoted ourselves to the enterprise rather than the Prize?

We know, for example, that currently 99 percent of all global Christian material resources are consumed by Christians for themselves. Although there has been a tremendous jump in disposable annual personal income among Americans (a $2,511 average yearly increase), only $49 of it was given to the church last year by the average church member. In fact, projections are that average Christian giving will decline throughout this decade from a high of 2.79 percent of total income to a low of 1.94 percent by the year 2002.[12]

And there are many other forms—often quite surprising to most of us—that this idolatry can take. Appendix 2 suggests a few.

In the end, our paralysis is often an indictment of how "unblessable" we are before God. It is a manifestation of God's anger with our idolatry, his predisposition to resist the proud, even to become our enemy if need be. This is what Joel, for example, shows God to be toward Judah in the locust plague he calls "God's army." God is leading it against an unrevived, idolatrous generation, and by it is paralyzing his people. Jeremiah proclaims, "The Lord is like an enemy; he has swallowed up Israel" (Lam. 2:5). And Jesus warns a seduced congregation, "I will soon come to you and will fight against them with the sword of my mouth" (Rev. 2:16).

Breaking with Satanic Strongholds

There is a final arena to be faced as we deal with our paralysis of unbelief. Satan lurks in the shadows, waiting at every point to exploit our two predispositions, to distract us from who Christ is and what he wants to accomplish in us, and to diffuse and divide every attempt we might make to rise up in faith and start again—to pick up our mats and walk.

According to a primary passage on the topic of satanic strongholds, 2 Corinthians 10, the most debilitating ones are found *inside* the church. There Satan has raised up barriers to our ability to understand the character and ways of God and to trust him accordingly. Clinton Arnold's *Powers of Darkness* pinpoints one of Satan's recent schemes in this regard: "This past decade has witnessed perhaps one of the greatest discreditings of the church in its history. Evangelical ministries have succumbed to temptations of sensual lust, pride and wealth in unparalleled proportions. In the West, the purity of the church has been disgraced."[13] If Satan is not resisted, if his subtle toying with our paralysis of faith is not understood and confronted, if such strongholds are allowed to remain, we will be rendered even more powerless in impacting this generation.

The greatest danger, however, is this. The strongholds of our twofold predisposition can ultimately lead us into hardness of heart toward the things of God. This will once and for all kill our ability to make any difference for Christ. Then Satan will have prevailed in sabotaging us.

Until recently, rampant prayerlessness in the church might have led one to believe such hardness had already set in, irrevocably. (My own informal survey over the years has supported the conclusion that the average Christian prays about five minutes a day, and the average pastor not much more.) Prayerlessness is not only a reason for impotency in the work of God, but it is often a sign of impotency—we have become too paralyzed to hope, too calloused to believe, too cold-hearted to care enough to pray.

But as described earlier, the good news is there is not only a great increase in prayer but a rising commitment in the church worldwide to ask God to deliver his church from this unbearable burden of paralysis, to seek and prepare for a coming national and world revival. (Chapter 9 discusses this in detail.)

He Must Intervene

God loves his church too much to leave us in our unrevived condition. Furthermore he loves us too much not to help us fulfill our destiny as coworkers with Christ in his global cause. He longs to visit us—to awaken us afresh to Christ.

112

So we can pray and prepare with confidence. God knows the church is in a condition that our healing, restoration, and redeployment in the mission of Christ is beyond our ability to accomplish for ourselves. *He* must intervene. *He* must bring us to repentance. *He* must reverse the predispositions within us. *He* must raise us up, set us free, and send us forth. *He* must pour out upon us a new revelation of Christ to break the paralysis of faith. "Faith comes from hearing the message, and the message is heard through the Word of Christ" (Rom. 10:17). And then he must take us on into so much more to accomplish so much more for his glory.

We can come to him with the abounding hope that permeates Scripture: "Arise, shine, for your light has come, and the glory of the Lord rises upon you. See, darkness covers the earth and thick darkness is over the peoples, but the Lord rises upon you and his glory appears over you. Nations will come to your light, and kings to the brightness of your dawn" (Isa. 60:1–3).

"This may be the great opportunity for the evangelical community," observes Carl F. H. Henry. "We may at last discover that we need each other. It may put an end to the entrepreneur rivalries and it may drive us to our knees in prayer rather than in a manifestation of evangelical triumphalism. Only God knows."

Confidence Builder 5: The Dramatic Preparations

Amazing Progress!

The hope of revival for the twenty-first century is reinforced by the dramatic preparations for it. Here's one way to say it:

> The attempts of the contemporary church to fulfill the Great Commission form nothing less than a prelude to revival. The great increase in local churches among the nations, the potential in resources and workers, the comprehensive strategies for world evangelization, the cooperation among Christians to complete the task— all this and more cry out for fulfillment through the empowerment that revival brings. Clearly God is setting the stage worldwide for a new advance of Christ's kingdom. If this is his work of preparation, he will not fail to bring it about. *We can seek revival with confidence that it is coming.*

As we've seen, God is at work throughout the earth to bring everything to consummation in Jesus Christ. So it should not surprise us that in the face of the dark prospects overshadowing this generation and despite any paralysis that temporarily renders the church ineffective in serving Christ's global cause, mission leaders worldwide testify that God is setting the stage for an extraordinary new advance of Christ's kingdom. As we're about to discover, the extent of the preparations going on in this hour to accelerate world evangelization require nothing less than an extraordinary outpouring of the Holy Spirit on the church. Only in this way can God's people adequately exploit the amazing opportunities he is setting before us.

Dramatic preparations are evidenced by the nature of current progress in world evangelization even prior to a full-orbed world revival. George Otis Jr. observes, "About 70 percent of all progress toward completing the great commission has taken place since 1900. Of that, 70 percent has occurred since World War II. And 70 percent of that has come about in the 1990s alone."[1] While church growth in the U.S. seems to have stagnated, there's an explosion of spiritual harvest around the world such as the church has never seen before. Many believe this great turning to the Lord worldwide is simply the *first-fruits*, a sign of all that God is getting ready to do through the coming world revival. They believe the reports of spiritual awakening in certain parts of the church (such as Eastern Europe, China, Indonesia, Argentina) are merely preludes of what is to come. They are God's wonderful way of preparing his church to understand what revival is and how to work with it toward his missionary cause as he unleashes full revival on the whole body of Christ.

Seen from one perspective, even the dark prospects may actually be dramatic preparations. How so? God's mercy to the nations is that he is forcing us to acknowledge our utter bankruptcy as we face the sheer magnitude of the crises before us. South Indian missionary leader Sam Kameleson calls them "creative instabilities." They move mankind toward Jesus Christ and his indestructible kingdom because they leave us with no other adequate hope but this. If, as E. Stanley Jones explains, the universal sickness is "homesickness,"[2] and if these instabilities and crises are simply intensifying that homesickness, then every single dark prospect could be interpreted as God's megaphone, his wake-up call inviting earth's peoples to turn toward home.

Can the Fire Be Far Behind?

As modern-day missiologists describe world developments and particularly the ongoing expansion of the missionary movement, some say we are on the "crest of the wave." Others speak of the "sunrise of missions," suggesting what we are seeing now is but the faint light of dawn breaking over the horizon, by comparison to all that is coming.

I describe it in terms of a fireplace. As I see it, in each of these dramatic preparations, it's as if God is building a fireplace brick by brick for the ultimate purpose of projecting the heat and light of Christ's kingdom to the ends of the earth. If God is building this fireplace, can the fire of world revival be far behind? If God is preparing at so many levels to advance his gospel worldwide—even to the fulfillment of the Great Commission—should we not expect that close at hand waits an extraordinary empowerment of the church to help us effectively enter that mission? And should we not all be praying for this with unstoppable hope?

Appendix 3 gathers together illustrations of dramatic preparations. Take a peek—you'll be amazed! God is moving so rapidly to set the stage among all nations, however, that it is virtually impossible to stay abreast. Even so, let me try to interpret the hope provided in these stories by presenting here nine arenas of dramatic preparations. You can continue to fill in your own stories under each category as God adds more bricks to his fireplace in the days to come.

When you look at appendix 3 and the nine arenas below, ask the following questions.

1. In the coming revival, how will preparations like these insure that such revival can have the greatest possible impact for Christ's global cause?
2. In what sense are such highlights clear evidence that national and world revival cannot be very far off?
3. In what practical ways should these preparations help to shape how we seek and prepare for revival, both individually and as churches?
4. How should these preparations change the way we believe and pray for revival?

Nine Arenas of Dramatic Preparations

1. Bases of Operation Are in Place

There is an unprecedented increase in the number of Christians and churches worldwide, providing the Spirit of God with new launching pads for kingdom ministries such as we've never seen before. Worldwide over eighty thousand people become Christians every day, and over two thousand new churches open their doors every week. There are currently nearly three million "worship centers" around the globe, people gathered weekly in local churches.

The potential for completing the Great Commission can be illustrated by looking simply at the five hundred thousand churches in the United States alone. If each church focused on reaching one of the approximately nine thousand unreached people groups still unpenetrated with the gospel, that would be fifty congregations for every unreached group. If we included churches worldwide, there would be over three hundred focused on each individual people group. If even 10 percent of these churches were thoroughly revived, it is reasonable to expect the completion of the Great Commission within this generation. The same kind of logic can apply to future ministries to the urban poor, to the world's universities, or to other dimensions of mission.

We also know there are over one million Christians already sprinkled among most of these unreached people groups (even if churches have not yet been planted among them). Prior to any new missionary penetration from the outside, these Christian minorities, freshly empowered out of world revival, might accomplish far more to advance the gospel among their own people than we ever dreamed possible.

Can the fire be far behind?

2. Available Workers Await Redeployment

There are at least 500 million Christians worldwide who are committed to sharing their faith with others. When we compare the present workforce with what we had at the beginning of Christianity, we see how God is poising the church for what some have termed "the final push" in world evangelization. Although the human population today is over thirty times larger (6 billion) than when the church began (181 million then), in terms of the growth of the church there are over four million times more potential workers than when the church began (500 million versus 128). The current ratio of non-Christians to Bible-believing Christians is about 6.81 to 1, the low-

118

est in history. And when we consider what the Spirit of God accomplished in that first-century revival, as recorded in Acts, and how well God has set the stage for total world evangelization in this generation, we must have hope.

One historian surveys the tremendous potential in a coming world revival this way:

> While the broad mass of the laity in American churches continue to be exhaustingly absorbed in the rat race of business life, at least a portion of their finances is being diverted to furnish a substantial economic foundation for a remarkable missionary program abroad. One cannot help but wonder what the result would be if this mass of lay people could be spiritually released from their servitude in the American success system and reoriented to channel their major energies toward building the Kingdom of God. Foreign missions would be enriched with a new flow of personnel and resources. . . .
>
> If America were . . . to be "born again" for a generation as England was "born again" during the second awakening; if America were to become a showcase of justice as well as liberty; if Christian opinion were visibly to compel the sharing of America's resources to feed and train the whole human community; if the network of multi-national corporations were tamed and brought into service as a rail service for the Gospel, as the Clapham leaders tamed the British Empire and used it for world missions; then "the Great Century" of missionary expansion, the nineteenth, would in all likelihood yield to an even greater successor.[3]

Can the fire be far behind?

3. Mission-Sending Structures Are Rapidly Multiplying

Currently there are 3,970 missions agencies worldwide, fielding 250,000 career missionaries and 180,000 short-term missions, backed by 400 missions research centers. This includes 49,000 missionaries out of 1,000 agencies in the Two-Thirds World alone. In fact, the non-Western missions movement is growing five times faster than the Western movement.

Of course none of this must ever overshadow the massive potential that exists in organized lay outreach invading the marketplaces of world societies, who through their own professional outlets can penetrate segments of the human family who have yet to be exposed to the gospel.

Can the fire be far behind?

4. Unparalleled Global Cooperation Has Arisen

There is an intentionality toward cooperation in world evangelization such as we've never seen before. This is true on both international and regional levels.

On the international level we have the formation of a number of worldwide networks that are mobilizing the resources available to the whole church to take the whole gospel to the whole need of the whole world. Groups such as the Lausanne Committee for World Evangelization, the A.D. 2000 and Beyond movement, the World Evangelical Fellowship, and the International Charismatic Committee for World Evangelization are just a few of the networks forming. There are also informal networks developing, such as among Christian relief agencies focused on specific areas of world disaster and world hunger.

Unified ministry can also be seen on regional and national levels. Recently in Nigeria, for example, over 11,000 pastors from 2,150 denominations and forty-five African countries gathered to lay the groundwork for cooperation to fully reach their continent by the twenty-first century. It was the largest such gathering of pastors in history, and it was specifically for the purpose of working toward the fulfillment of Christ's global cause in their region.

About the same time another meeting took place called the European Leadership Consultation on Evangelization, sponsored by the Lausanne Committee, and involving 160 Christian leaders from thirty-six countries in Europe. Convened at Bad Boll, Germany, they developed a written commitment (the Bad Boll Declaration) that articulates much of the vision to be found in many of today's efforts of regional and global cooperation. Their commitments include:

- To be open to God to experience more rapid and radical change than we have experienced in the past. We will express this in the

120

intensification of individual and corporate prayer and action for the healing of our nations and the advancement of the kingdom of God in our world. We will convey this conviction about a new day dawning in all the churches and fellowships from which we have come.

- To work in concert with other Christians to reach and serve all the many neighborhoods, communities, and groups in our countries
- To advocate and practice maximum cooperation among evangelical churches and organizations as critical to the essence of our call to preach the Gospel
- To mobilize local congregations and all the people in them
- To do all these things with a sense of urgency, knowing that we do not have time to do them in a leisurely way or with any perfectionist attitude. We believe that we are here for such a time as this.

Can the fire be far behind?

5. *Extensive Financial Resources Are Available*

Never before has the church enjoyed such financial resilience to press the world missionary enterprise among all earth's peoples. Worldwide, Christians have a total annual personal income of about nine trillion dollars, according to David Barrett. However, we are barely beginning to tap the potential. Christians spend only about 1.5 percent or 140 billion dollars per year on their churches and home ministries. An even more dismal 0.1 percent goes to foreign missions. Think what God could do if in world revival 500 million committed Christians would be willing to simply tithe their incomes. We would be pushing near to one trillion dollars! And even a tithe of that would unleash 100 billion dollars towards ministry to the nations. Why has God put such massive resources in the hands of his people at this hour? Certainly not just for our benefit!

Can the fire be far behind?

6. Wide Open Doors Stand before Us

Much of the world's population is accessible as never before to Christian witnesses coming in some capacity from the outside. In fact, right now there are far more doors open than there are laborers or resources released to enter in. Further, research indicates more individuals and more segments of populations are receptive to Christ now than at any time in the last two thousand years. This has been the discovery of a recent thrust into the former Soviet Union and among peoples of Eastern Europe by a multi-organizational cooperative effort called CoMission. They are currently seeking to mobilize hundreds of lay couples who would be willing to spend two years sharing the gospel with thousands of former Communists.

One way God is opening doors is through the process of worldwide urbanization. It is projected that by the twenty-first century 80 percent of the world will be living in major cities. "The emergence of a worldwide urban culture is setting the stage for the world's first truly global awakening," writes John Dawson. "From China to Brazil, cities are becoming more and more uniform in culture. . . . this global unification of mission fields, especially among youth, represents a significant new development."[4] Ray Bakke concurs: "Today at their own expense vast numbers of people are flocking into every city of the world. The potential for a twenty-first century Pentecost is unmistakable."[5]

Can the fire be far behind?

7. Technological Sophistication Is at Our Disposal

In addition to urbanization we are experiencing the globalization of the world in a way that enhances global access to earth's peoples. The church is poised to capitalize on this unprecedented proliferation in methods and sophisticated technology, such as the use of mass media, computers, anthropological and linguistic sciences, and high-level management sophistication. Of course, Christian mission is ultimately incarnational. Servants of Christ must lay down their lives daily among the people of the earth if they are to truly disciple them according to Jesus' standards in Matthew 28:18–20.

But never in the history of humankind has it been as possible to communicate the gospel to the whole earth as it is today. Surely God intends for us to exploit these advantages for his glory. Over the past ten years, for example, with one simple tool, *The Jesus Film*, millions of people in almost all major languages have been confronted with Christ as portrayed in the Gospel of Luke, with hundreds of thousands coming into the kingdom as a result. And now teams of missionaries are following up many of these conversions, establishing discipleship groups and house churches.

There are a legion of other tools just waiting to be taken up in similarly creative ways.

Can the fire be far behind?

8. Commitment to Evangelism Is More Radical Than Ever

The commitment to evangelism is seen in the phenomenon of martyrdom. The church has always been a suffering church, but more so today than ever. According to David Barrett, in the 1980s 270,000 died every year as Christian martyrs. By 1990 the number was 325,800. And it is projected that there will be 500,000 martyrs annually by the turn of the century.[6] If "the blood of the martyrs is the seed of the church," then the Spirit of God must be sowing for a magnificent harvest.

In addition, world missionary leaders are taking a much stronger stance on the need to engage Satan and his dark hosts as we seek to reach the billions locked away in sophisticated religious systems under deep-seated demonic bondage. Perhaps never before has the global church been so ready to unflinchingly engage the principalities and powers and to do so despite the cost. Currently networks are forming worldwide that bring together scores of ministries recently raised up for the specific focus of what some call "spiritual mapping" and "spiritual warfare." Much healthy discussion is underway as we seek theological and tactical balance in this approach. But there is a holy determination to uncover the biblical realities of satanic work among unreached peoples and to dislodge these forces of darkness by Christ's direct intervention through a revived missionary movement. All of this exploration appears preparatory for the strategic battles up ahead as the gospel is powerfully unleashed out of a twenty-first century revival.

Can the fire be far behind?

9. Pools of Renewal Are Poised to Become Rivers

Pools of renewal are made up of those who are drawn together with like heart and passion to seek God's face in prayer for world revival and to work together in holy, obedient preparation to serve wherever revival takes them. (I discuss them in more detail in chapter 10.)

These pools are found not only within individual local churches, but even in whole denominations. They are also identifiable in a most exciting form in the united prayer movements emerging in many cities. God is even now digging trenches between the pools (often through these movements of united prayer or through coalitions for evangelistic activity) to bring them together to create grand reservoirs of renewal. In turn, they will become mighty rivers of renewal, empowering all kinds of cooperative efforts in world outreach.

For example, countless pools have been dug worldwide by the Pentecostal/Charismatic movement. The last decade has witnessed a rapid increase in this renewal as it has spread throughout all 156 major ecclesiastical families or traditions of the Christian world. It is estimated that there are 372 million Christians now identified with this movement and with its strong emphasis on recapturing both spiritual gifts for building up the body and spiritual power for witness to the world.

Digging pools at a whole different level, most predominantly within the Catholic church, are the "base ecclesiastical communities." Base communities are small groups focused on the fundamentals of Christian prayer and witness. They began among the poor in Latin America but have spread throughout Africa, the Philippines, and other parts of Asia. Each community consists of ten to twelve families. They meet once a week primarily for prayer, first for themselves, then for their families, and finally for their cities. David Barrett estimates there will be one million base communities worldwide by the year 2000, enabling the poor to be world evangelizers in their own right.[7] Richard Lovelace remarks that the base-community renewal movement "may be more pervasive worldwide than the Charismatic renewal."[8]

Wherever they come from and whatever they are called, two fascinating characteristics about today's pools of renewal make them unique. As opposed to previous "great awakenings," they are pervasive throughout all parts of the body of Christ. Secondly, they are focused preeminently on renewal in the body for outward advance on all fronts of Christ's global cause. In other words there appears to be a shared expectation that world revival is coming to bring closure to world evangelization and the consummation of all things. Never to this degree has this characteristic so dominated prayer movements of the past.

Come, for Everything Is Now Ready

Who has dug these pools of renewal? Can the river be far behind? Who is shaking the church out of apathy and hopelessness? Can the earthquake be far behind? Who has put all these bricks into place? Can the fire be far behind? "Being confident of this, that he who began a good work in you will carry it on to competion . . ." (Phil. 1:6).

The implications of such preparations are simply staggering. What if, in fact, among the over one billion Christians, God is preparing to raise up a revived church galvanized for biblical action on a whole spectrum of global issues? (Even 20 or 30 percent would be an awesome army!) What if massive revival would come to the church to such a degree that there would be an unbreakable solidarity among Christians in all parts of the body to labor together for the fulfillment of the Great Commission among the remaining three billion unreached people of the world?

What a panorama of challenge and hope this puts before us! Have we any other alternative but to join in a movement that prays and prepares for nothing less than national and world revival, and to do so with confidence? Hear the Father say, in the words of Jesus' parable, "Come, for everything is now ready" (Luke 14:17). The hope is at hand.

9 Confidence Builder 6: The Distinctive Praying

Rising Like a Mighty River

The hope of world revival is seen in how people pray. That's the thesis of the next confidence builder:

> God is stirring up his people to pray specifically, increasingly, and persistently for world revival. He is doing this by giving believers everywhere a common vision for the need for revival, a broad-based agreement on what the coming revival will look like, and a growing conviction that revival is at hand for those who seek it together. If God is stirring up the church to pray with this distinctive focus and consensus, he will not let us pray in vain. He has promised to hear and answer us fully. *We can prepare for the answers with confidence.*

In *With Concerts of Prayer* I told a parable about a cadre of people gathered at a partially opened door, knocking together for entrance. The sounds of their knuckles on wood grabs the attention of others, desperate for liberation, who come to join them at the threshold.[1] Interestingly when I wrote this little story in 1984, I did so to illustrate what I saw to be the initial phases of an emerging God-ordained prayer movement toward world revival (the other side of the door). But today we are way beyond initial phases. The doorway is jam-packed! As one denominational leader put it, "It is as if God is pushing his church toward revival and prayer from all sides." Appendix 4 documents this with scores of inspiring accounts from around the world.

Even secular publications like *Newsweek* notice the increase in prayer: "Talking to God: In America, as the prophet Amos put it, those conversations are rising like a mighty river. . . . This week, if you believe at all in opinion surveys, more of us will pray than will go to work, exercise, or have sexual relations. . . . In an allegedly rootless, materialistic, self-centered America, there is also a hunger for a personal experience of God that prayer seeks to satisfy."[2]

George Gallup in a major study on the impact of prayer in the United States concludes: "In previous surveys, we have discovered that high on the list of things people want from their churches, whether evangelical or not, is teaching about prayer. We do need to get people in touch with God and teach them how to pray, through prayer and Bible study groups, among other means. To pray in a group is uniquely powerful."[3]

A Global Phenomenon

Recent statistics back up this interpretation. I've already cited that worldwide approximately 170 million Christians are committed to pray every day for revival and evangelization, with twenty million claiming this as their primary calling in the body of Christ. Ten million prayer groups make revival prayer one of their primary agendas, while hundreds of prayer networks are committed to mobilizing such prayer within denominations, cities, and whole nations.

The vitality of this global prayer movement was dynamically unveiled at the International Prayer Assembly for World Evangelization in 1984. A first-of-its-kind gathering, it involved two thousand prayer mobilizers from seventy nations who concluded their week of strategizing on prayer movements by issuing an "International Call to Prayer" (part of which is quoted in the accompanying box). Nine years later in 1993, another gathering with more national import took place in the United States—the National Consultation on United Prayer—inaugurating a "new era of spiritual leadership" in our land, bringing to our nation a special "National Call to United Prayer" (reproduced in chapter 2).

128

A Call to Prayer

*From the International Prayer Assembly on World
Evangelization, 1984*

God has impressed on us an urgent desire to call for an international prayer movement for spiritual awakening and world evangelization. . . . Only the omnipotent Holy Spirit, applying the fruits of the finished work of Christ through a church constantly awakened through prayer, can deliver the lost from the power of Satan (Acts 26:17–18), as the Lord adds daily those who are being saved (Acts 2:47). The awakening of the church is thus essential to the completion of world evangelization. . . . The means of grace can only be empowered for us today through fervent and persistent prayer to the Father in the Name of the crucified and risen Christ. . . . Explicit agreement and visible union of God's people in extraordinary prayer for the awakening of the church and world evangelization is essential for the extension of the Kingdom of Christ through the preaching of the Gospel. We re joice that in the last few years, in many parts of the world, the Holy Spirit has instilled a growing dependence on God, leading to increased unity in prayer within the Body of Christ, transcending denominational, national, ethnic and cultural divisions. . . . We are constrained to call the Body of Christ worldwide to mobilize intercession for spiritual awakening in the church and for world evangelization.

In the years between those two major events, I observed significant, identifiable developments in the prayer movement, both nationally and internationally, including the increase of prayer mobilizers bent on drawing the church together in prayer within whole cities. We have seen the emergence of community-wide pastors' prayer gatherings for revival, matched by new thrusts in revival prayer within the ranks of denominations and Christian organizations.

This movement is finding expression in whole new ways within local churches as well. Recently the Christian Reformed Church published *The Praying Church Sourcebook* based on extensive research on congregational prayer growth within many church traditions.[4] They uncovered a variety of increased prayer activities in churches throughout our nation including: more prayer in worship services, schools of prayer, family prayer altars, prayer telephone ministry, prayer emphasis weeks, prayer chains, prayer triplets, prayer vigils, church prayer support groups, evangelism prayer groups, prayer groups for world missions, pastors' prayer-support groups, concerts of prayer, personal and churchwide prayer retreats, prayer ministry teams, prayer healing services, twenty-four-hour prayer rooms, businessmen's prayer gatherings, women's prayer fellowships, seniors' prayer groups, children's prayer gatherings, solemn assemblies—to name only a few!

To this could be added other current prayer expressions, often involving churches working together. Some of these include prayer concerts (citywide mass prayer rallies focused on revival in participating churches and in their cities, as well as on world evangelization); prayer walks (interceding for neighborhoods as Christians walk the streets in teams); prayer marches (interceding for whole cities as churches march together through the center city with songs and prayers); and prayer journeys (teams of intercessors going out among the nations to pray in the midst of specific, unreached people groups).[5]

We may be standing in the vortex of the most significant prayer movement in the history of the church. Appendix 4 is only a sampling of all God is doing. No generation has ever seen such an acceleration and intensification of prayer worldwide.

Recently we conducted a statewide Concert of Prayer in Iowa. Billboards were placed across the state inviting people to the rally. I saw one billboard beside another that advertised a painting company. Its motto (in big, bold, red letters) was "You've got to be kidding." Together the two signs read, "Come to the statewide Concert of Prayer rally for revival" followed by "You've got to be kidding!" Over the years that has been my recurring response as I have witnessed the spectacular emergence of this diverse prayer movement. Something extraordinary is taking place right before our very eyes. I keep saying to myself, "You've got to be kidding!"

An Unprecedented Movement of Prayer

Of course, this movement has not sprung into life overnight. There are important roots to be aware of. Countless individuals and groups across the world have been praying for a prayer awakening for many years. I have met with some prayer bands that have been seeking God for this for forty years.

Now, however, that an increasing number of church leaders have served this effort in the past decade, we are seeing tremendous multiplication of local and national prayer ministries and coalitions of prayer trainers to nurture the movement. In addition, there have been the increasing and faithful prayers of thousands of pastors who now realize, as the pastor of the largest church in America titles his recent book, that they are "too busy *not* to pray."

Here are evidences of the unprecedented nature of this movement (and appendix 4 has illustrations of each):

1. The Prayer Movement Is Unprecedented in Numbers

In America over the last few months alone, tens of thousands have been united in citywide prayer rallies in communities large and small. Hundreds of thousands have joined together in prayer from coast to coast through the broadcast of world-revival prayer meetings by radio, led by local and national leaders. Pastors meet regularly by the hundreds in prayer groups nationwide, seeking God for renewal in their own lives and within their churches. Recently in one city, two hundred pastors came together for four days of prayer over this city and returned the final night to lead a prayer rally of nearly fifteen thousand in the local stadium. In other cities the numbers turning out for prayer rallies have been so large we have actually experienced full-fledged traffic jams, even turning hundreds away. All of this for a prayer meeting!

What is happening here is happening in even greater measure in other nations, as evidenced in appendix 4. For example, recently in one month alone nearly thirty million Christians in more than one hundred nations joined in thirty days of prayer to cry out to God for a spiritual awakening that would bring the gospel to all the unreached peoples throughout most of the Muslim, Hindu, and Chinese world. Some called it the largest prayer meeting in history.

2. The Prayer Movement Is Unprecedented in Its Breadth

Crossing many borders within the body of Christ, the prayer movement is multidenominational (involving people of all spectrums of the church) and coalesces Christians from many different ethnic and social backgrounds, united in prayer toward the same vision. It is breaking down walls that many Christians have raised in our major urban centers, particularly racial barriers.

And it is bringing together Christians of all ages. Youth, however, may be leading the way. This is true not only of teenagers (and there are hundreds of thousands in America who have recently shown consistent interest in praying unitedly for revival) but also of young children. An international conference on prayer is planning an entire track for children to attend as participating pray-ers.

In Boston a prayer rally took place that involved eight hundred Christians from seventy-five churches throughout the center city. It was conducted by different races in four different languages to fairly represent the diversity of the Christians involved. Interestingly it took place in historic Park Street Church, which itself was planted out of a multidenominational concert of prayer in the early 1800s.

The breadth of this movement can also be seen in how it involves whole denominations. Some denominations have set goals to mobilize as many as three million intercessors in this decade (such as the Assemblies of God in Brazil). Others are scheduling national denominational meetings exclusively focused on fostering concerted prayer for revival within their congregations, even passing official resolutions that commission the pastors to make this top priority.

And believers across hundreds of cities worldwide are involved in national days of prayer, prayer rallies, prayer conferences, and media events—all of which is under the guidance of local spiritual leaders.

Whether it be bands of multiracial prayer groups in South Africa, concerts of prayer planted among unevangelized Mongolians and in officially closed Muslim countries, one hundred thousand high school students praying in the Olympic Stadium in Seoul, or international prayer mobilization efforts such as those fostered by the World Evangelical Fellowship, the A.D. 2000 and Beyond movement, and the Lausanne Committee for World Evangelization—the breadth of revival prayer is global.

3. The Prayer Movement Is Unprecedented in Strategy

The growing understanding among prayer leaders worldwide is that the movement of prayer is not intended simply to undergird our personal and denominational ambitions for God. Rather there seems to be a paradigm shift. The movement is perceived increasingly as uniting the church in prayer as the fountainhead of everything else that will happen in national and world revival. This is why we find united prayer development to be the first order of business in many national and global plans for world evangelization by the year 2000. There is the growing conviction that everything we do (whether evangelism, social action, or ministries of compassion and justice) must be built on concerted prayer.

Let me give you a personal example. In a radical divergence from his seminary lectures of many years, Peter Wagner has expanded his understanding of church growth principles to include the missions dimensions of prayer. In doing so he has become an articulate "dean" for an emerging school of thought on the subject. Recent titles include: *Warfare Prayer, Prayer Shield, Wrestling with Dark Angels, Breaking Strongholds in Your City,* and *Your Church Can Pray!*[6] Not all agree with all he teaches, particularly relating to spiritual warfare and "prayer mapping." But he is stirring up healthy discussion on a broad range of prayer topics relating to world evangelization throughout much of the church. And he's doing so because of his personal soul-wrenching conversion on the issue. Now, he says, God will not let him turn back.

There is also an increasing attempt to link prayer movements with citywide evangelistic efforts. Billy Graham, Luis Palau, and others have made increasing attempts to insure that crusades inaugurate or strengthen ongoing prayer movements for spiritual awakening long after the crusades are over. In Atlanta, GAP (Greater Atlanta Pray) is helping to mobilize three hundred churches into united prayer for revival and evangelistic outreach over much of this decade, including outreach during the Summer Olympics. The same can be seen internationally. The All-Japan Evangelistic Prayer Bands have as their goal to mobilize one hundred thousand Christians in prayer and personal evangelism to reach the one hundred million unevangelized Japanese. The All-Japan Revival Prayer Movement has set its sights on even larger numbers after a recent rally of one hundred thousand in the Osaka baseball stadium.

In many parts of the prayer movement, the church is focused on united prayer to bring about reconciliation within the church community. Increasingly it is through the prayer movement that races and denominations are beginning to "cover each other in love," to build bridges of trust, acceptance, and understanding, and to stand together with a common focus for the reaching of their cities. As a result, in a number of citywide prayer movements there are reports of changes in the "climate" of their cities, and the body of Christ is discovering new ways to minister together to moral and spiritual crises in approaches that bring long-term healing for their cities.

In some cities God has enabled prayer leaders to develop multifaceted prayer movements, which are therefore potentially multifaceted in their impact on the city. One of the most significant urban prayer strategies today is the one unfolding in New York City. This movement expresses itself in the following ways:

- Regular, citywide prayer rallies, prayer marches, and prayer vigils
- Pastors' prayer gatherings and prayer retreats
- Training of congregational prayer leaders
- Churches "adopting" one another and praying for revival for one another
- Local concerts of prayer within individual churches

- Radio broadcasts that facilitate bringing the metropolitan area together in prayer
- United, daily "prayer watches," involving hundreds of churches who raise up intercessory teams for each day of the year to pray for the overriding concerns of world revival
- Commitment by a multitude of smaller prayer groups to become a part of a "prayer net" in which they integrate at least ten minutes of prayer for world revival every time they meet
- Regular written communications on prayer concerns for world revival as well as reports on the prayer movement locally and worldwide
- Businessmen praying for revival as they conduct preaching missions in the Financial District (their motto: "Pray boldly, preach boldly," from Acts 4:31)
- Prayer conventions directly related to evangelistic outreaches (like the Billy Graham rally with 250,000) and social ministries (like the 1,000 parents who spent a Saturday afternoon interceding for the city's teens and their schools)
- Volunteer prayer coordinators for the citywide movement meet with their counterparts from many other cities nationally to pray for and learn from one another

The great hope we have in the linking of strategic prayer and outreach struck me as I polled the executives of one hundred mission societies (a number of which were founded within the past twenty years). I asked them, "How many of your agencies actually began in a movement of united prayer? I don't mean that after they began they went out looking for prayer support. Rather, how many at the outset started with a company of praying people concerned for Christ's global cause, to whom God finally gave vision and resources that ultimately took the shape of the mission society you serve today?" Immediately almost every hand went up (and those who didn't raise their hands, I suspected, were unaware of their history!). Is it any wonder that in the past decade more and more mission-focused consultations are setting up twenty-four-hour prayer watches to "cover" their planning deliberations? Never before has there been such a widespread consensus that prayer is our number one strategy.

4. The Prayer Movement Is Unprecedented in Leadership

In previous historical awakenings, prayer movements have been served by various kinds of leaders. In the early 1700s, for example, the First Great Awakening was led primarily by the clergy. In the late 1700s, the Second Great Awakening was led by those who were mission-minded (such as William Carey and William Wilberforce). In the Third Great Awakening, with central figures such as Charles Finney and Jeremiah Lamphier, it was often what we might today call "parachurch" groups that set the pace. In what was sometimes called the "businessman's prayer revival," lay people worked together across denominational lines to mobilize tens of thousands into prayer for world revival. J. Edwin Orr documents in *Campus Aflame* that throughout most awakenings, young people banded in prayer groups on their campuses have often been at the forefront of the whole movement, catalyzing concerted prayer in the church at large.[7]

But the encouraging thing today is that leadership is coming from *all* of these levels. It can be seen in the over thirteen hundred prayer-mobilization networks worldwide that collaborate in the effort. Not long ago in the U.S., within a twelve-month period, national-level leadership forums were convened for denominations, national youth ministries, missionary agencies, city prayer-movement leaders, and even directors of major Christian philanthropic foundations. The full historic spectrum was in motion: leaders from churches, missions, parachurch groups, lay groups, youth. Formal coalitions have formed as a result, such as the Denominational Prayer Leaders Network and the National Youth Leaders Prayer Forum. And in every case the goal is the same: to work together as catalysts toward united prayer for world revival.

At the local church level, thousands of pastors are currently gathering in hundreds of four-day "prayer summits" (where they give themselves to prayer only), to seek God for spiritual awakening in their own lives and communities, and returning to call their churches to follow their example.[8] And even as I write, plans are underway to bring together seventy-five thousand pastors to pray over the nation and to return to mobilize congregational and citywide prayer thrusts for revival.

At the same time, never before has such prayer leadership been as international in its expression. What is happening in the U.S. is unfolding with equal and greater force in many countries. International Intercessors, for example, has teams of trained prayer mobilizers in over seventy nations. The united prayer track of the A.D. 2000 and Beyond coalition has unearthed thousands of Christian leaders (at all levels) who are now being networked into one of the most comprehensive prayer mobilization enterprises ever.

5. The Prayer Movement Is Unprecedented in Vision

As I study what is being taught by the plethora of prayer ministries worldwide, as I listen to the focus embodied in recent calls to prayer, as I watch the direction toward which various coalitions for prayer are headed and note how God's people are praying within their congregations, in mass citywide prayer rallies, or in international prayer assemblies, I consistently hear one major concern: national and world revival.

The praying may be expressed with many creative techniques. It may involve a combination of the historic prayer approaches (discussed in depth by Richard Foster in *Prayer*).[9] The "spirit" with which people pray will surface in various ways along the historic continuum. At one end we find contemplative praying (reflection, communion, listening to God). At the other end we find what theologian Donald Bloesch calls "prophetic praying," where people sense that through their active praying God is actually bringing new things into being. (See Bloesch's *The Struggle of Prayer,* in which he documents that though both approaches have been intertwined in most great prayer efforts, historically it is prophetic praying that must be the leading edge if the prayer thrust is to remain healthy.)[10]

Even prophetic praying will vary in its expressions. It may move from times of rejoicing and celebration in the hope of what is coming, to repentance over everything in us that might hinder God from bringing revival, to resisting enemy attacks against the preparations for coming world revival, to intercession that cries out to God to fulfill his promises for revival, to commitment to God to be used in any way he pleases to bring it about. But the heart of the vision remains the same. All these forms of praying continue to give expression to one overriding concern: the unleashing of a massive global spiritual awakening to Christ that decisively advances his cause in every place.

In fact, unlike any previous prayer movements, this one carries its passion for revival as a result of a prior burden for the fulfillment of Christ's global cause. World missions is not an afterthought of the prayer movement; in many ways it is the spawning ground for it.

What Does It Mean When . . . ?

Not long ago in a midsized city in the south, one hundred churches united for a citywide prayer rally. The week before, they ran a full-page ad in the local paper that consisted basically of one question in bold print centered on the page: "*What does it mean when all of these churches unite together to pray for revival?*" Underneath the question, in smaller print, they listed the one hundred cooperating churches by name. And then at the bottom of the page the answer was given by quoting 2 Chronicles 7:14. In a sense, that's the meaning of this unprecedented global movement of prayer, wherever you find it. God is calling his church to unite, to humble themselves, to seek his face—not to coax him to revive us, no. He longs to awaken and restore his people, and through them to bring healing to their communities and to the nations.

Recall once more Dr. Orr's principle: "Whenever God is ready to begin something new with His people, He always sets them to praying." That's what it all means! This is *God's* prayer movement. He has ordained that he will be open to our cries as a part of the sovereign process toward his ordained ends of world revival (and ultimately of the final revival). The Scriptures are clear: There are some things in the church and in the world that God will not do until his people pray.

This prayer movement is a gift from God. Because of our natural aversion to prayer (our predisposition toward the status quo and toward idolatry), God himself must stir up the work of prayer in us. Just as faith is a gift of God, so prayer is a gift of God. Therefore, praying people are a gift from God, and movements of prayer are his gift too. And if God is giving this gift, he will not fail to answer the prayers that he himself has stirred up in our hearts to begin with. Truly, the prayer movement is a powerfully reassuring sign that national and world revival is at hand.

Has God Begun to Answer Yet?

But someone may ask, "Is there any evidence that God is responding to this increase in prayer? Has revival begun?"

From one perspective the response is simple: *God's current answers to our revival prayers are found in the very fact that he is increasing the movement of prayer itself.* If revival comes to those who seek it in prayer together; and if the revival God is preparing for this generation is something bigger than any one of us or any one of our churches or denominations or nations can fully contain; and if, as it comes, the impact will be on the whole mission of Jesus Christ so that this revival is something in which we all have a stake; and if it's going to take the whole body, fully revived, to fulfill God's whole vision for this whole generation worldwide—then this makes sense. One of God's major answers to our cries for spiritual awakening would need to be the acceleration of a much broader-based work of concerted prayer. Since God's seekers ultimately become his receivers, then as he works toward full-orbed revival, he must first expand the prayer movement. He must have the full attention of the church-at-large, actively seeking him for it. That way the whole church is ready to receive what he desires to give—a revival that embraces the whole church.

But there is another perspective on the question of answers to revival prayers. There are both *immediate answers* to this prayer movement as well as *ultimate answers.* The ultimate answers are obvious. They will be found in a thorough spiritual awakening to Christ in the church worldwide. This means, as we've seen, a fresh revelation of Christ to his people, an intensification of his life within his people, and the consummation of his mission through his people among the nations. Every prayer—and every act of concerted prayer—lingers before the Father until these ultimate answers are given in full. Revelation 5 guarantees this, describing prayer as "bowls of incense" that ascends before the throne and before the Lamb, with the ensuing fulfillment of the Lamb's global purposes—even to the final revival itself.

But there are also *immediate* answers, foretastes of revival that arise out of the process of the prayer movement itself, even before thorough world revival descends on the church. As I have visited united prayer initiatives in many nations, I've become aware that involvement in the *process* significantly impacts people's daily walk with Christ. It provides them a genuine touch of revival now. It is worth it for them to be involved, even if God takes years to answer their prayers with full-scale awakening. Immediate answers that come as we pray include an enlarged vision of Christ, a deepening hunger for God's glory, a more dynamic sense of being God's family together, the acceleration of congregational praise and praying, greater drive toward full consecration to the Lord, the releasing of dreams and visions for outreach, and the liberation of men and women to enter into Christ's work wholeheartedly.

But as important as anything, the process of praying inspires a new spirit of hope and celebration about all that God is getting ready to do in the future. And that, apart from anything else, has the power to start breaking the chains of paralysis discussed in chapter 7.

This came home to me one day when I was on retreat at a farm in Virginia. Aware of such a longing to know Christ more deeply, I was truly thirsting for personal renewal—literally day and night. Early one morning as I walked through the fields, I watched a cow break out of the herd and wander down a hillside to the stream below. She walked straight into the water, planted all four feet in the middle of it, lowered her massive head, and began to drink. Her neck muscles rippled with each delicious gulp. Suddenly I cried out to God, "I'm just like that cow! Jesus said in John 7 that if we were thirsty, we could come to him and drink, and out of our innermost being would flow rivers of living water. That's what I want to do. But how do I drink?"

Immediately I sensed God giving me an answer: "I know you're thirsty. I've made you thirsty. And I want to keep you that way. That's how you grow. But be assured of this: every time you gather in your little concert of prayer back home, praying for revival in my church, you are drinking, right then and there."

I've never attended a prayer meeting since then without that perspective on what's happening. The immediate answer to prayer is that then and there we are drinking more of Christ. All of this should be enough to lead us to pray with bold persistence, even for national and world revival.

Whose Prayer Movement Is It Anyway?

But even more important is the question as to whether God himself is stirring up this dynamic prayer movement. Is the distinctiveness of its focus, unprecedented breadth, and intensive *growth from God?*

My answer is, Can there be any other biblical explanation for such a phenomenon? I think not. There's absolutely nothing in this old nature of mine that would ever desire to seek God's face for revival. Every praying person you know is a miracle unfolding right before your eyes!

And if all of this is from God, would he be encouraging a prayer movement for world revival while intending in the end to frustrate us and leave us empty-handed? Of course not! So we can pray and prepare with confidence. We can praise God with the same hope voiced by the hymnist John Ellerton in the mid 1800s during the Third Great Awakening:

> We thank Thee that Thy church, unsleeping
> while earth rolls onward into light,
> through all the world her watch is keeping
> and rests not now by day or night.
>
> As o'er each continent and island
> the dawn leads on another day,
> the voice of prayer is never silent,
> nor dies the strain of praise away.
>
> So be it, Lord; Thy Throne shall never,
> like earth's proud empires, pass away;
> Thy kingdom stands, and grows forever,
> Till all Thy creatures own Thy sway.

But behind all this distinctive praying lies the seventh reason to expect revival for the twenty-first century: the rock-bottom commitment of the people who are doing the praying. I call them the "determined people"—a breed unto themselves. We meet them next.

10 Confidence Builder 7: The Determined People

An Extraordinary Story of Seekers

Having explored six of the seven confidence builders, how can we not conclude that the hope of revival is at hand? But the final reason to expect it may be more convincing than any other: the determined people. My thesis is this:

> God is galvanizing a host of people worldwide who are convinced that revival is the only hope for the church, as well as for the nations. They are confident there is so much more that God wants to do in this generation for his Son. And they are willing to pay any price to prepare the way for God to do it, first of all by repentance and prayer. Further, they are active in recruiting others to the same confident vision. As a result their numbers are increasing. Because of who they are, they form a chief sign of the nearness of an impending spiritual awakening to Christ. In fact they are the first phase of it. *Surely revival is on top of us. Of this we can be confident.*

In March of 1992 shouts, whistles, drumming, and screams of 150 pro-choice, gay, and lesbian demonstrators sought to drown out the prayers of Christians gathered inside Chicago's Armitage Baptist Church. The congregation outside the church came from ten militant organizations—including Sister Serpent (a witches group) and Queer Nation (a homosexual group). They were organized to protest the pro-life stand of the church members who gathered regularly for a weekly prayer meeting in the multi-ethnic church. Inside the building, everything proceeded as planned. A "concert of prayer" was lifted up, not only for the demonstrators outside but for revival throughout our whole nation.

The nearly two hundred members of Armitage Baptist who normally gathered for these prayer concerts were not alone, however. They were joined that night by another twelve hundred from fifty other Chicago churches who had heard about the planned demonstration and came to support the Armitage believers. In fact, there were so many praying Christians that they overflowed from the main auditorium into a second auditorium and out into the streets. Finally, seven buses from Salem Baptist Church pulled up, with the entire Salem choir who began to sing praises to the Lord on the steps of the besieged building. It wasn't long before the demonstrators fell silent and slipped into the night.

The pastor, Charles Lyons, told *National and International Religion Report,* "God's people came together and God's people prayed. And there was a sense of God in the midst of all of this." He's talking about the kind of people that I want to describe in this chapter—people who are determined, in the face of all opposition, to seek God for revival until revival comes. God's determined people.

Who are they? Actually they have always preceded great moments of renewal in the church. Jesus called them the meek and said they would inherit the earth. That's because the meek are anything but apathetic! The meek are those who seek. It is the seekers who ultimately become God's receivers. And when they receive, it is never for themselves alone but for the sake of many others.

From beginning to end, the Bible is a story about *seekers.*[1] The Bible explains how seekers are called and what they are promised. It describes the discoveries they make in the process of seeking as well as the destiny they share because they do. God wants his people to be a company of seekers because he wants to be wanted—he waits to be sought. He actually commands his people to place their hope in him, to "rejoice in the hope of the glory of God" (Rom. 5:2).

To whatever degree there is a supernatural dimension to the coming world revival (and obviously there is), to that degree there must be a body of people worldwide who are determined to seek and prepare for awakening. They must place themselves in a position to receive it and run with it as it comes. Theologian Lewis Drummond writes, "In the ecclesia [church], the faithful remnant has always been God's way of precipitating powerful movements. If we wait for everyone to be deepened and ready for blessings, we may wait forever. And if that ever did happen, we would not need an awakening; it would have already occurred."[2] Revival cannot be engineered by a committee. Revival comes only by the sovereign work of the Holy Spirit. But God brings this new day to his church through those who pursue him for it relentlessly. They are the very conduits of the revival because their hearts are set on nothing less.

Perhaps this is the greatest indication that the church is being positioned for a sovereign work of revival: the appearance once again within the church of an extraordinary kind of Christian, determined to pray and prepare until revival comes, no matter what the cost. People like Cotton Mather, who in the early 1700s not only preached on the need for revival and wrote a theology of revival but gave himself to 490 days of praying and fasting for revival until the day of his death in 1727. On that very day revival broke out in Northampton, Massachusetts, under the ministry of his son-in-law Jonathan Edwards—another determined seeker—and swept through the colonies over the ensuing decades, often through determined people banded together in concerts of prayer.

Samuel Shoemaker, who labored for spiritual renewal in the mid-twentieth century within the Episcopal Church, highlights in *With the Holy Spirit and with Fire* his experience of the critical role of determined people:

> It would be difficult to believe that God is not ready to "pour His Spirit upon all flesh," if only more of us were deeply available to Him. In one sense, the awakening is His business—in another sense, it is very much up to us. For while we cannot bring about the awakening in our own strength, we can hold it back by our own refusals. We know all too well that it is tens of thousands of people just like ourselves, partially converted, partially trained, partially mobilized, but not "given" as we might and could be, that keep God's forces in the world running at such minimal strength and at such slow pace.[3]

Seekers Are Receivers

The strategic role of seekers in revival might be illustrated with a child's brainteaser: If a tree falls in a forest, but there is no one there to hear it, does it make a noise? Of course it makes sound waves, but if there are no ear drums to translate those waves via the brain into what we term a "noise," does the tree really make that sound? Similarly if God were ready to send revival on his church worldwide, but there were not a sufficient number of believers in position to receive it because there were too few determined people prayerfully preparing for it, would revival come? I believe the testimony of Scripture and church history is it would not.

When talking about these determined people with the pastor of the largest church in the world, he reminded me of a verse that nicely describes them (obviously his church was full of them): "The kingdom of God has been forcefully advancing, and forceful men lay hold of it" (Matt. 11:12). Today's determined people are those who are privy to where God is headed in Christ, what he is preparing to do to advance his kingdom in the twenty-first century. In response to his action they have reached out to lay hold of his forceful initiative— to lay hold of him. In the process *they* are being transformed into a people of force.

Much like an acrobat who studies a swinging trapeze and launches out to seize it with all her strength so that her destiny above the center ring gets wrapped up in the destiny of the trapeze itself, so it is with determined people. By their pursuit of the hope of national and world revival (which can only come by God's sovereign intervention), their own destiny gets wrapped up in that vision. It may not be too much to say that once God has a sufficient number of determined people (people of force) awakened by him to his revival initiatives and wholeheartedly pursuing them, revival will descend upon the church without delay. The seekers will become receivers. They will lay hold of it and then run with it. They will be a mirror image of God's own forceful agenda and in turn become (as Paul would say) "fellow workers with Christ."

Who are these determined people? As I have met with thousands throughout the body of Christ, I believe one can identify them by at least five characteristics.

The Characteristics of Determined People

Extraordinary Seeing

Determined people live with what we called earlier "superspective." They have a vision so full of hope both of the final revival (the consummation) as well as the coming revival (an approximation of the consummation) that they are compelled to seek and prepare for it. In fact their focus on the final revival ennobles all of their other longings for world revival now and makes it impossible for them to settle for anything less.

What they're looking at is Christ. It's not so much that they are determined to *do* more; instead, they see that God is calling them to *seek* more. Coming to Christ for who he is and for all that his kingdom promises, they are compelled to seek God both on the basis of what they do not have as well as on the basis of God's unlimited promises for what they shall have.

Like skeptics in the days of Christopher Columbus, some Christians could be called "flatlanders."[4] They see the horizon but expect and seek nothing beyond it. Determined people, however, are "round-earthers." Because of who Jesus is, they know there has to be a whole other world of God's blessings reaching far beyond what is immediately apparent. So they live and work both in the light of what can be seen, like flatlanders, as well as what cannot yet be seen. They live daily in the reality of the issues we have studied in this book. No wonder they are so unshakable, so full of confidence!

Extraordinary Feelings

Their unshakable confidence is also molded by unrelenting yearnings for revival, yearnings that will not let them go. It's not that determined people are necessarily more spiritual than other Christians; it's just they are more *restless*. They have a sense of impending breakthroughs, a sense that God is ready to give revival now. And they are in hot pursuit. They've moved beyond desperation and even anticipation into a trembling expectation—beyond willingness for it into readiness for it. Beyond curious interest in such a work of God, into a passion for it. Extraordinary feelings indeed!

147

This passion also carries with it a sense of urgency, even emergency. They seek and prepare, knowing procrastination would be sin. Why? Because a spiritual awakening to Christ is our only hope for this generation. Engaging the Father with energetic embrace, they persistently appeal to him for world revival, thoroughly dissatisfied with everything short of it. Their pursuit reflects that of John Piper who says of himself that he is "insatiably greedy. The more you have, the more you want. The more you see, the more you want to see. The more you feel, the more you want to feel. This holy greed for joy in God wants to see and feel more and more manifestations of His glory."[5]

Another friend of mine used a most surprising phrase to describe these same feelings. He recalled his preconversion years as a heroin addict. Spending almost every waking hour either stealing money, buying drugs, shooting up, or sleeping it off, he thought of little else but heroin. His addiction was more important to him than food or housing or survival. He summarized those years as "desire in constant motion"—that is, desire for heroin. But now with his great longing for revival both in his own life and within his city of Miami, he says he has fallen back on that same phrase as the only way to describe how he feels as a Christian. By Scripture studies, in prayer and obedience, by his ministry to the poor and oppressed, by his calling others to revival prayer, his daily life has become once again one of *desire in constant motion*. It's the opposite of a feeling of resignation. It is much closer to what someone has called "rebellion against the status quo." In fact, determined people often experience an exhilaration comparable to what one might expect in the midst of a revolution.

But this should not catch us unawares. This is how it has always been, according to revival historian Richard Owen Roberts:

> When prayers and strong pleas for revival are made to God both day and night; when the children of God find they can no longer tolerate the absence of revival blessings; when extraordinary seeking of an extraordinary outpouring becomes extraordinarily earnest; and when the burden of prayer for revival becomes almost unbearable, then let praying hearts take courage, for the Spirit of God who is the spirit of revival has brought His people to this place for a purpose.[6]

148

Extraordinary Living

In the full expectation of national and world revival, determined people let the horizon of God's future shape their obedience to Christ today. As I said in chapter 3, they have become "prisoners of hope." Captive to the vision, they are determined to stay awake and not be diverted. Giving full attention to what God has promised, they make their lives as purposeful in the light of those convictions as they possibly can. They even "act as if" (a C. S. Lewis phrase for the whole Christian life) revival had already begun—obeying Christ now the way they expect to obey him then.

You might say that determined people have actually undergone a type of "second conversion." Whereas all Christians have been converted out of the world to Christ, determined people are those who have been "converted" with Christ back into the world. Their daily routines are ordered in the light of the consummation of God's plan for all nations. They can no longer act as "tourists" simply enjoying the sights and sounds of the neighborhood. Instead they are "pilgrims" on a journey toward a fuller revelation of Christ to all peoples in this generation.

They have integrated a search for world revival into their daily discipleship, wrapping their lives around that cause and nothing less. Everything about their own Christian walk supports their claim before others that they believe revival is at hand. Everything they do and say is also geared to stir up increased conviction within others that God is ready to act in revival.

Of course that's not the same as saying they believe they themselves can make revival happen. They are quite aware the hope before us is so great, it cannot be accomplished by human efforts. They also know nothing they resolve can control or force God to act and bring it to pass. Instead in everything they do and say, in every area of their lives and in every facet of the life of the church, they strive to *prepare the way* for Christ's manifest presence in full-orbed revival.

In a sense these people have become true *fanatics*, a word that comes from Latin, meaning "temple dweller." Similarly, determined people live every day dwelling on God's heart for the world, on his promises for revival, and on his readiness to act on behalf of those who seek him. They live in the presence of the Lord, in everything they do, seeking him for revival.

This decisive devotion toward Christ proclaims, "I am prepared to commit all that I know of myself, all that I know of Christ, all that I can be and do to hasten his day of revival." Determined people review each day and rejoice when they can say, "I know this day my life has helped to strategically encourage God's people toward the hope of world revival in the church, for the sake of Christ's mission among all nations."

Such extraordinary living may even begin to look like revival itself! At the very least it becomes *a dress rehearsal for revival* because to reorient our lives around the hope of revival is to flesh out in preliminary ways what we expect from the full impact of revival. "Hope hears the music of the future; faith dances to it right now," as my friend Ben Patterson puts it. As Lewis said, we "act as if."

For example, determined people

- *worship God* with a new spirit that includes a spirit of anticipation. They celebrate the greater manifestations of his glory just ahead of them even before they see it, praising the God who is, who was, and who is to come (Rev. 1:8).
- *study Scripture* with an eye to all that it highlights regarding the hope of revival and its blessings on the nations. There are hundreds of such passages.
- are compelled toward *fellowship* with other believers, striving to become a community of hope that focuses not only upon Christ and each other but also on where Christ is going out ahead of them.
- look at *material possessions* in a different light, making the accumulation of goods and the giving of resources proportionate to the hope they seek, investing in the coming revival.
- find new courage for *mission*, as the hope of revival assures them that current evangelism will create new possibilities for spiritual awakening to break through more powerfully to more people made ready by their witness. Thus, chief among their priorities will be the missionary penetration of the thousands of remaining unreached people groups worldwide.
- respond to *human needs* around them in a new way, because their hearts are fixed on the final revival as well as the coming revival. This leads them into ministries consistent with how they believe

the world will be changed as Christ is more fully manifested among them in revival. Chief among such demonstrations of compassion will be renewed identification with earth's one billion poor, who are always a priority with God when he gives revival.

Because of stresses in the Cold War in the late 1970s, President Carter ordered the U.S. Olympic Team to boycott the Summer Olympics in Moscow. As a result a number of the athletes who had spent four years in continuous preparation for the Olympics had to commit to train another four years—eight years total—until the 1984 Olympics in Los Angeles. What kept them going? The hope of being a part of the spectacular drama of the Olympics and the hope of achieving a victory rewarded with a gold medal. Determined people have a similar hope and drive as they live for Christ and prepare for revival.

Extraordinary Dying

As we've seen, the cross of Christ is the ultimate fountainhead of all revivals, including the final revival. It should be no surprise, therefore, that God calls those determined to seek revival into an experience that is a reflection of the cross itself. Missionary statesman Samuel Zwemer, said in a message entitled "The Glory of the Impossible" that "The unoccupied fields of the world must have their Calvary before they can have their Pentecost." In the same way, if the glories of national and world revival, which may currently seem impossible, are to come to us, this generation must have its Calvary before it receives its Pentecost.

This is not to say that seekers are morbid. To the contrary, they are awaiting something wonderful, and they show it, always rejoicing in the hope of God's greater glory (Rom. 5:2). But since they know it must be by God's action not theirs, they are compelled to confess their brokenness, sin, and powerlessness to bring the church into spiritual awakening. On the one hand they refuse to simply settle for the scope of God's previous activities in revival because they realize so much more of Christ is needed if his kingdom is to advance in the twenty-first century. But on the other hand, they aren't in themselves able to spawn the necessary revival for which they are so desperate. And so, since they won't go back and cannot go on, they must go down. And

151

that is the cross. They have chosen to humble themselves under God's mighty hand, to come under the "foolishness" and "weakness" of the cross by signing up to be determined seekers. Just as Jesus did on the cross, they too cry out in desperate need for God's intervention. In one sense they share Christ's sufferings as they take upon themselves the sins of the world. By this I mean they share with him his pain over the dark prospects among the nations and over the disturbing paralysis within the church and they share his willingness to pay any price to see this changed.

Further, like Jesus on the cross, they must *wait*. This may be the greatest pain of all. Waiting can feel like a "sentence of death" (2 Cor. 1:9), especially when we're waiting in heartbreaking desperation for a revival that has not yet come. We wait, "far beyond our ability to endure," placing our hope in God who raised Jesus from the dead and who is also able to deliver a whole church in answer to their prayers (2 Cor. 1:8, 9).

The Scriptures are full of God's command to his people to wait on him and to patiently watch for his extraordinary work of deliverance on their behalf. In a sense, the call to the cross in revival is a call to be "wait watchers" (not weight watchers!). Like dieters, we say *no* to the desires of the moment, refusing momentary relief through spiritual junk food, because our sights are set on giving to Christ a bride that is holy. We are willing to endure our hunger pangs today, and suffer loss today, so that we can have Christ's fullness tomorrow.

Martyn Lloyd-Jones warns, "When we get tired of praying for revival and say we must start doing something, then be careful. In holding back the answer, God is preparing us. He wants us to come to the place in which we realize we are indeed helpless and hopeless, and so become desperate and cry to Him alone."[7]

Recently I conducted a Concert of Prayer rally in an auditorium just hours before a Josh McDowell "Why Wait?" campaign. In these nationwide youth assemblies, teenagers are challenged for Christ's sake to wait, to reserve sex to the confines of marriage, to practice voluntary abstinence. As hundreds of us prayed that afternoon, it struck me that the same question should be put before the whole church. Why wait? In other words, why pray? Why prepare? Why should we wait on God for revival?

152

The answer is parallel. *God is calling the church to a form of "voluntary abstinence,"* to put aside our own ambitions, desires, and attempts to do God's work through our strength and resources—to wait for him to reproduce his reviving work for us in his time and his way. We wait for him to conceive revival in his people so that what is birthed is legitimate and can fulfill his purposes.

As any unmarried young person will tell you, voluntary abstinence can be painful. Delaying gratification may cause one to feel empty and inadequate. Or it may invite the scorn of one's peers. Those determined to make God their only hope for revival and to seek him for it until he grants it must be willing to sacrifice in similar ways.

To wait, however, is to suffer in a most unique sense, to suffer in *anticipation* of what lies ahead. The groanings of Christ on the cross are matched, according to Romans 8, by the groanings of creation, of the redeemed saints, and even of the Holy Spirit. All are groaning for the full will of God to be accomplished and for the delays to be over. Our suffering is in the hope of what he has promised for the final revival and, by implication, for every other revival. As Proverbs 13:12 tells us, when hope is deferred, it makes the heart sick.

But a seeker's sufferings may also rise from another source. Those ambitions for revival become immediately vulnerable to the "antiforces," not just human but demonic. Satan fears nothing more than a coalition of determined people who have anchored themselves in the promises of God for revival, set their sights on that and nothing less, and prepared accordingly. The enemy knows that as revival comes, the darkness will be pushed back further, his usurpations will be exposed, and multitudes of captives will be set free. So, determined people, expect retaliation!

This truth was illustrated for me at a Concert of Prayer held in a large civic center comprised of two auditoriums. In one an exhibition boxing match with George Foreman was scheduled. On the same night in our auditorium, Christians from scores of churches were gathered to pray for revival. To prevent confusion, the managers placed a sign at the civic center entrance with two large arrows pointing in opposite directions. One arrow said, "Boxing." The other, "Prayer." As I entered, it struck me, *What a unique decision to place before the citizens of this city as they attend the night's events. Will it be boxing or prayer?*

153

Further reflection made me realize this was the decision God sets before all Christians all of the time! We must choose whether to be in the boxing match or in the "wrestling match." By wrestling match I refer, of course, to that image of prayer portrayed in Genesis 32 where Jacob wrestles with God's angel all night, not letting go until God puts on him a blessing to empower him to fulfill the next day's mission in the Promised Land. As a result of his all-night encounter with God, Jacob was painfully disfigured for the rest of his life. It cost him. But he also, in wrestling, saw the face of God and received a new name. This was his personal revival! The next day when he confronted Esau and four hundred armed men, not only did God intervene to bring about peace, but Jacob was able to say of Esau and his band, "To see you is to see the face of God." Jacob had been so awakened to a fresh revelation of God's glory the night before that even before his enemies his ministry was forever transformed. The price he paid to wrestle with God at the Jabbok river was to be desired over what he would have suffered from his enemy without it.

If we stay in the wrestling match—if we remain determined pursuers of a spiritual awakening to Christ in the church no matter how costly it feels—then victory is sure. In the end we will not only be delivered from all enemies, but we will be sufficiently revived to move out in fullness of power to fulfill God's mission to the ends of the earth.

Determined seekers automatically open up to extraordinary times of dying. At the core of their being is a willingness to pay any price at any time and go anywhere in order that world revival might come. As Jesus begins to bring about the answer to our prayers for revival, our destiny is sealed even more with the destiny of his kingdom. For those who seek it, the coming revival will cost everything. But we are willing because we understand that our only hope to fulfill Christ's global cause is his manifest presence throughout the church. And further, those who share his sufferings will also share his glory (Rom. 8:17), including the glory that shines forth in world revival.

Extraordinary Receiving

Seekers become receivers. Determined people see themselves not only as people with a destiny, but people of a destiny. In their daily pursuit of revival they are increasingly putting themselves in a position before God to be the primary receivers of revival, for their sakes and the sake of many, many others. They fully expect to receive, knowing (in the words of A. W. Tozer) "Our pursuit of God is successful just because he is forever seeking to manifest himself to us."[8]

There are two ways to describe how this receiving happens. From one perspective, Olaf Hallesby in his classic book *Prayer* concludes that all intercession is simply a matter of "opening the door and inviting Jesus to come in." This is true, he says, whether we pray for our own lives, our churches, our city, or for world revival. Our prayers open the door to receive the entrance of the Lord to do his full work among us. So when we pray extraordinary prayers, we need to expect to receive extraordinary answers.

However, we are given a different picture by Richard Foster in *Prayer: Finding the Heart's True Home*. He suggests that God answers our prayers by opening the door of his heart and inviting us to come in, so that we may explore all the "rooms" in his heart. He wants us to know him for all that he is. This is his greatest gift to us in answer to our prayers. In this case, extraordinary prayers introduce us into extraordinary revelations of the heart of God. In both examples, however, we see how determined seekers receive something extraordinary that will not disappoint them and that will open new possibilities for many others.

One of the first things we must prepare to receive is a multiplication of ourselves in other determined people whom God raises up in answer to our prayers. As God used John the Baptist, so God uses us to prepare the way for the Lord in the lives of others—raising up valleys, pulling down mountains, making straight highways—so that multitudes can join us in the pursuit of world revival.

Every determined person is a gift from God. Their pursuit of God does not rise out of the flesh; nothing in us naturally wants to do it. Instead it is a work of *grace*. It is grace that calls into question the status quo. It is grace that confronts the idols on which we have depended. It is grace that reassures us of divine intervention, that stirs up the hope for so much more, that sustains us in the times of waiting, that ultimately answers our prayers for revival by giving approximations of the consummation and centering us fully on Christ alone. And if grace can do all of that for us, it can do that for anyone else as well!

That's why seekers must remain on the lookout for other seekers whom God "creates" by grace. Joined with us, these newly discovered determined people are the greatest hope we have that God will answer our pursuit of revival. As we saw in the last chapter, God is bringing to fullness the number of seekers and receivers that need to be in place for him to pour out a massive revival on this generation. (In the next chapter we will study how to find these people and mobilize them for the pursuit of revival.)

A short time ago I was on a flight out of Nairobi, Kenya, to New Delhi, India. Sitting all around me was a band of African missionaries who were going to minister among Hindus in India. About a half hour outside the New Delhi airport, just as the sun was breaking over the horizon, this group of thirty evangelists suddenly removed their seat belts, stood up at the same moment, turned around, got down on their knees, and began to pray. They remained in that position until just minutes before landing.

The whole scene remains a colorful parable for me of all the determined people I've known. Seeing the desperate needs of the world, they are ready to give their lives to Christ for his mission to the nations. But they also recognize there is so much more God wants to do to empower his church for this ministry. From their "superspective" position, they've caught the sunrise of a coming revival. Full of hope that it is not far off, they now give themselves with determination to pursue that revival, to seek and prepare for it in the full light of its expected impact, and to mobilize others to rise up and seek it with them.

Determined people are anchored in a hope based on a confidence that is sustained by these realities:

- the Decisive Person
- the Divine Pattern
- the Dark Prospects
- the Disturbing Paralysis
- the Dramatic Preparations
- the Distinctive Praying
- other Determined People

Do you want to join them? If so, the next chapter will give you practical ways to get started.

156

Part 3

Preparing the Way

11 Pacesetters for World Revival: Getting Started

Promoters of Revival?

At the start of the Indianapolis 500, a pace car circles the track slightly ahead of the others with the responsibility of bringing the whole field up to speed and into the race. People don't usually reward the driver of the pace car, but you can't have a race without one.

Similarly you can't have a movement toward national and world revival without pacesetters—men and women abounding in confidence about what is coming, who ignite and sustain an effort to pray and prepare for revival. The world belongs to those who offer it hope. For us that means it belongs to those who set the pace for the church toward the hope of full-orbed spiritual awakening to Christ.

This final segment of the book was written for one reason: *If any of us pry into the subject of a twenty-first century revival without intending to respond to that hope here and now, we fall far short of what God intended. In fact our delay in beginning to pray and prepare for revival now and to mobilize others with us may be the deadliest form of denying its truth.*

Jonathan Edwards championed appropriate efforts in promotion and preparation for revival. This is evidenced in the title of his little volume encouraging concerts of prayer in the mid 1700s, which began, *An Humble Attempt to Promote Explicit Agreement and Visible Union . . .* Edwards understood that the promotion of revival—embodied for him in preaching and organizing prayer for revival—was absolutely crucial to the final realization of God's gracious work.

159

Of course, in all revival God is sovereign. Just as faith is a gift of God, so prayer is a gift of God, praying people are a gift of God, and a movement of prayer is God's gift to his church. Therefore he alone receives the credit from beginning to end. But history is replete with stories of revival pacesetters who prayed and promoted preparations for revival, and who in many cases lived to see it break forth.

Recently I met with two hundred such pacesetters from throughout New England, representing almost fifty cities and communities. We gathered for a twenty-four-hour Pacesetters Retreat in which we worked with each other to define our vision for revival and to design a strategy for serving it. The retreat was held in a white clapboard church in Hopkinton, Massachusetts, just across the street from the Hopkinton Commons, launch point every year of the world famous Boston Marathon. At the conclusion of the retreat I took these leaders with me over to the Commons where we regrouped on its grassy knoll. There, about to enter our own marathon, we recommissioned each other to go forth to set the pace for many other seekers of world revival. And we committed ourselves to do so with our eyes fixed on Christ, who models preeminently the work of pacesetting for all of us (Heb. 12:1–2) and who gives us assurance that he will bring all our endeavors to success.

A Movement of Multipliers

What are some goals of pacesetters? One important one is a desire to multiply themselves. They understand how essential it is to expand the base of seekers of revival as fully as possible. Since what is coming is so extensive, there must be a sufficiently broad-based number of seekers in place to receive it. Therefore the most strategic thing revival-minded Christians can do is to grow as advocates of revival before God and before others and to mobilize others with them into a movement of seekers determined to settle for nothing less.

Clearly such multiplication does imply the development of a "movement," a word I've regularly used in these chapters. Pacesetters call people to *move* with them. What does this mean? In a university sociology textbook *People, Power, and Change: Movements of Social Transformation*, authors Gerlach and Hine define a *movement,* based on a number of diverse case studies:

160

A movement is a group of people who are organized for, ideologically motivated by, and committed to a purpose which implements some form of personal or social change; who are actively engaged in the recruitment of others; and whose influence is spreading an opposition to the established order within which it originated.[1]

It would be hard to produce a better definition for a movement of Christians toward a massive spiritual awakening to Christ. Take a look. We also have a purpose that is grand enough to focus all of our energies: national and world revival. We, too, are organized for and committed to this work of God so fully that we are willing to make whatever personal or corporate changes are needed. In addition we become active in recruiting others to seek and prepare with us in our pursuit of revival. Finally, everything pacesetters do is obviously in opposition to the established order. It is because of the condition of that order—both inside and outside the church—that we need revival, and it is that order which will be radically transformed when true revival comes.

Now you see why we must call the current crescendo of revival concern a "movement"!

The First Four Steps

Over the years I have trained thousands of pacesetters. I have seen how pacesetters for revival are God's special gift to the church. And I've become aware of four important steps that most have taken at the outset of their obedience to God in this vision. Thinking through these four steps is a useful starting point for evaluating your own call from God to set the pace in a movement toward national and world revival.

1. Embrace the Vision

As I've said, pacesetters not only believe in the coming revival and are getting set for it, they are also compelled to bring many others with them into the hope of spiritual awakening.

Has God given *you* the willingness to be such a pacesetter, to live with a burden for revival, and to mobilize others to that vision no matter what the cost? If not you, who? If not now, when? If not here,

161

where? If not this, what else? In other words, are you so convinced that God has called you to be a pacesetter that you have seized the vision as your permanent platform?

2. Build the Vision

Pacesetters read about revivals. They build for themselves a biblical foundation on the topic. In addition they are constantly seeking out communication networks that will keep them informed of broader developments in revival throughout their city, their nation, and the world. They seek out the "pools of renewal" in churches and organizations, nearby and elsewhere identifying individuals and groups who are pursuing revival. Whenever possible they attempt to visit places where prayer movements are flourishing and talk to those who may be experiencing the first tastes of revival.

Are *you* willing to continue expanding your own horizons as you set the pace for others? You can begin as you take time to meditate on the kinds of confidence-building reasons discussed in this book, attempting to learn more about each area, and making that information fuel for your prayers, obedience, and influence on others.

3. Integrate the Vision

Pacesetters also seek to develop an approach to their own daily discipleship that is consistent with their hope for revival.

Would *your* way of life convince others that you seriously expect national and world revival? Are you actively integrating your vision for revival into everything else you do in following Christ? Are you willing to live so as to end each day convinced it has counted strategically for the coming revival and for the sake of those whom you are pointing toward that vision?

4. Share the Vision

Pacesetters do not try to carry out their calling alone. They know they need to be banded with other committed pacesetters. Most have become a part of a small group of friends and associates who not only share their vision for revival but also their desire to promote that cause throughout the churches.

Are *you* willing to enter into a relationship with a team of people who encourage each other and hold each other accountable in this way? Are you open to being a part of a group that strategizes together on how to most effectively mobilize others into seekers of revival?

You Are Not Alone

If this is your desire—to seek and prepare for spiritual awakening and to bring others with you—be encouraged. You are not alone! There are many others actively setting the pace already. *And there are millions more waiting to be mobilized.* God is at work giving people the gift of hope. He is stirring multitudes with desire for world revival.

In all your efforts to be a pacesetter, you can work in the secure knowledge that God has *preceded* you. He is bringing about a "second conversion" in the church, converting nonseekers into seekers, converting those who have left the world to join Christ to now move with Christ into the acceleration of his global cause. He is making significant numbers of Christians restless, causing them to question the status quo, to challenge the idols of their counterfeit hopes, and to fix their eyes on the promises of his Word regarding revival.

A pacesetter's primary job is to find out what direction God is moving, to find those in whom he is working, and then to move with him in serving them. The pools of renewal have already been dug in churches and fellowships all through the body of Christ. Now pacesetters have the privilege of "digging the trenches" between these pools of renewal, so they flow together to form reservoirs of renewal, and ultimately rivers of renewal for the whole earth.

A Survey to Find Seekers

How do we uncover these people, and how do we bring them together? One way I have found helpful is through the use of a survey. I've provided a model at the end of this chapter. It is a six-part questionnaire that has been used successfully to uncover seekers and mobilize pacesetters. These are six questions most Christians have never been asked.

The questions follow a logical sequence. They help people under-stand and then express what God is already putting on their hearts. Because most Christians have never been asked these questions be-fore, leaders are amazed to find how many give positive responses. They learn that God has already prepared many to be a part of his movement toward revival.

The questions begin by identifying an individual's sense of the need for revival and what he or she considers to be the strategic role of prayer especially. And then the questionnaire goes on to help a per-son define the degree of hope he or she has about what God is get-ting ready to do, as well as his or her own readiness to get involved. From our experience in using the survey, I would not be surprised to find thousands in churches within your own community whom God is calling right now to seek and prepare for world revival.

Here is a short form of the survey. An expanded version is at the end of this chapter. When you design your own survey, feel free to substitute wording that would be meaningful to your people.

1. Is the church in need of revival?
   Circle one: no   maybe   yes

2. Will revival have an impact on the world?
   Circle one: no   maybe   yes

3. Must we pursue revival by united prayer?
   Circle one: no   maybe   yes

4. Is God ready to give us revival?
   Circle one: no   maybe   yes

5. Is God ready to help us pray as we should?
   Circle one: no   maybe   yes

6. Am I ready to be involved?
   Circle one: no   maybe   yes

Here are two ways this survey can be used.

First, *use it in a Sunday worship service as a bulletin insert.* For five minutes a pastor may guide his congregation through the six ques-tions. That provides an excellent opportunity to expose the congre-gation to a new way of thinking about what God is up to. That in it-self makes the questionnaire worthwhile. But it also helps the pastor get a reading on his congregation's thinking about revival. (Incidentally, do not require people to give their names. That way they all will be fully candid. But tabulate the responses between Sundays to bring back the encouraging report the following Sunday.)

In most congregations a majority will identify themselves toward the right side of each continuum. It is a tremendous experience for a local church to have its pastor report the following Sunday that half of the congregation (or more) are not only convinced of the need for and impendingness of revival, but also of their willingness to pray and prepare for it personally. Once those results have been made known, the church will act with renewed confidence to foster revival vision among its people.

A second approach is to *involve a number of churches within a community who give the survey on the same Sunday*. In the intervening week, the pastors not only tabulate results for their own congregations but pool the responses of all participating congregations. The findings are reported the following Sunday to each congregation. It is a revelation both to pastors and churches to discover that (possibly) thousands of others throughout the local body of Christ feel the same about a coming revival. This in turn instills a new level of comraderie among the churches to seek and prepare for revival together, beginning most logically in a movement of united prayer.

"Get Them to Me"

Now I want to explore with you a little of my role as a pacesetter. I have functioned this way for over fifteen years. But much more recently, in a time of crisis, I finally discovered the real "bottom line" of a pacesetter's minstry. Let me tell you what happened to me.

Having promoted united prayer across the world, I began to sense a growing dissatisfaction with what seemed to me to be (and these are the words that came to me) an "insignificant ministry of simply leading prayer." I reasoned that there was so much else that needed to be done, things that I was gifted to do, things that might be far more practical. What about the poor? What about the unevangelized? What about the moral free fall of my own nation?

I started asking God if there wasn't something more productive for me, something more important, more strategic, more effective for the advance of Christ's kingdom. One night I awakened at 2 A.M. with an answer ringing in my ears. I will never forget what seemed to be God's response to me that night: *David, get them to me, just get them to me—and I will take them from there.* I knew he was right. That's my job description!

If we can get God's people united together before his throne, seeking his face for the work of revival that's so deep on his heart, he will not fail to take them from there. He will take them on to Christ and the hope at hand, and then on into being a part of the answer to our prayers. How can any pacesetter assume a more vital role than to get Christians together before God in prayer so that he can "take them from there," especially when we know so many are waiting to be led? Especially when we know their destination is a spiritual awakening to Christ?

A Job Description for Pacesetters

With this as the great objective, I can boil down my job description over the years into three words: *Incite. Unite. Invite.* These three objectives provide any pacesetter solid tracks to run on.

Objective One: Incite God's People

Incite God's people to pursue him wholeheartedly for the hope of revival. This objective can be accomplished by at least five approaches: by Scripture, through stories and reports, by logical reasoning, through networking, and by dreaming.

1. Incite People through the Word of God

We must keep people's expectations for national and world revival (which includes personal and congregational revival) in line with the promises of Scripture, so they are looking for nothing more and nothing less than what God has ordained. I recently worked through my Bible from Genesis to Revelation, marking with a yellow highlighting pen all the passages that deal with how much more God has for us, particularly his promises for revival. Almost half of my Bible turned yellow! The Scriptures are full of messages that can incite people to faith and hope.

Of course, we must present the biblical vision with balance—emphasizing the three dimensions to revival that have been explored in this book: focus, fullness, fulfillment (see chapter 4, especially). They're like a sailboat, which can only move if there is a sail, a boat, and the wind. The fuller focus on Christ in revival is like the wind. The sails catching that wind with all of its empowerment are like God giving the fullness of Christ's life to his church in revival. And the vessel itself, which takes us from one side of the lake to the other, is God leading his church through revival into the fulfillment of Christ's mission to the nations. All that we teach from Scripture, therefore, must keep this same balance, as we give emphasis to this threefold theme. Only then can we properly incite a movement toward biblical revival.

In sermons or small group Bible studies, we can help people appreciate more fully great revival passages (the verses marked yellow) if we help them answer questions like these:

- What is the hope this passage sets before us (either regarding the consummation or any approximation of the consummation)?
- How does that hope relate to the overarching theme of revival (either the final revival or some intermediate experience of revival)?
- Specifically how does this text encourage us to pray and prepare for a stronger focus on Christ's glory in revival? Or for the fullness of the life of Christ in his church through revival? Or for the fulfillment of the mission of Christ among the nations out of revival? Or for all three?
- How do these findings apply to issues touching the dark prospects in the world or the disturbing paralysis in the church?
- What obedience is required of us as a movement of seekers based on our discoveries in this text?

(For more help with biblical texts that can be used to inspire vision for revival, see my *Biblical Agendas for Concerts of Prayer*.)[2]

2. Incite People through Stories and Reports

Compelling stories can be gleaned from church history, out of the Scriptures, and from current movements toward revival around the world. Tell stories that show why we need revival, how God works in revival, and the growing signs of a coming revival. Church historians point out that stories on revival may be the single most important human factor in the promotion of revival in past spiritual awakenings. (See appendices 3 and 4 to get you started.)

3. Equip Yourself to Present Arguments for Revival

This book provides a basis for such persuasion. Consider taking a group of people through this book, using *The Hope at Hand: A Small Group Study/Discussion Guide* (available through the offices of Concerts of Prayer International).[3]

4. Help People Network with Others Pursuing Revival

Perhaps the most exciting way this can be done is through the development of a citywide movement of prayer in your own community. Or two churches can adopt each other, praying for revival in each other's congregation and circulating regular reports of evidences of answered prayer. On another level, city prayer movements have actually adopted each other, praying for each other and reporting preliminary activities of God in revival within each city, to encourage each other. Other means of networking include newsletters published by revival-minded ministries or special 800 numbers that provide regular updates by phone on the acceleration in revival across the country and around the world. Groups like the National Prayer Committee, International Prayer Summits, the Denominational Prayer Leaders Network, the National Youth Leaders' Prayer Forum, and Mission America 2000 can help you.

5. Incite People by Showing What God Intends

People will be moved when they see the contrast between the status quo and what God intends. Help them come to grips with both the "dark prospects" and the "disturbing paralysis." A vision for revival can electrify people if we help them grasp what revival accomplishes to reverse and displace our desperate needs.

We need to help people gain a personal vision of what revival might look like in their own lives, in their churches, and cities within this generation. *Revival dreaming*, we might call it. Their vision should be

168

as unique and colorful as possible in light of who they are, in light of their present and past, and most of all in light of God's Word on revival. Our goal is to gain consensus and excitement about the coming revival so that people will be compelled to seek it together until it comes.

Revival dreaming can be facilitated in a number of ways. Here is an example. Take key revival passages of Scripture (such as Isa. 54, Jer. 33, Acts 1 and 2, or any of the great passages on the final revival, such as Isa. 60 or Rev. 21). Ask people to outline the basic characteristics of the revival described, either of an intermediate revival or of the consummation itself. Ask them to dream about how such revival might impact individual Christians, communities of Christians, and beyond. Then ask them to imagine what it would be like for an approximation of those principles to be worked out in their own setting.

Have people brainstorm in small groups on this series of questions:

- If Christ and his kingdom were to become the focus of attention in our city, in answer to our prayers for revival, what might this look like?
- What might be the impact of this work of God on four key areas:

  1. On the daily walk of individual Christians?
  2. On the churches in our city, both inside the churches and among the churches?
  3. On the needs and challenges of the city as a whole?
  4. And ultimately on the nations of the world?

Then have people report back, placing their answers in four columns based on the four areas discussed. I have used this approach with many groups, and as people begin to dream along these lines it brings dramatic results. In fact, you can use these four columns to develop your own "concert of prayer." Plan for an hour of prayer and divide it into six, ten-minute segments: an opening ten minutes of worship and praise, then ten minutes each to pray through the issues in the four columns, and finally ten minutes for the reconsecration of lives to be a part of the answer and for worship.

169

Objective Two: Unite God's People

Once incited to hope (and growing in faith as a result), God's people must unite to pray concertedly for world revival. In Hong Kong, when *With Concerts of Prayer* was translated into Chinese, they could not employ the idea of a concert when inviting people to pray. In their culture a reference to concerts might remind Christians of extravagant musical events only attended by the wealthy. My translators were afraid that Hong Kong believers would interpret "concert of prayer" as referring to a prayer meeting for the upper class! Instead, translators chose Chinese characters that literally mean "united-in-heart-and-soul kind of praying." And that's perfect! It is exactly what a revival pacesetter wants to promote.

To unite people in concerted prayer we need to keep the balance. The primary agenda for prayer is *focus, fullness, fulfillment*. These are the three dimensions of revival and thus of all revival praying. Pacesetters should help people pray through these three agendas every time they gather.

In addition, we must help people pray on three different levels: personal, local, and global. We fall short of God's intention if we concentrate on any one of these to the neglect of the other two. The emphasis on world revival means we're pursuing a spiritual awakening of such a magnitude that it touches every other level as well. Accordingly our prayers must do the same.

Putting the six together (the three agendas and the three levels) results in the following grid:

	Focus	Fullness	Fulfillment
Personal			
Local			
Global			

Each of the boxes represents one of nine facets of prayer for revival. For example, we should pray for a greater focus on Christ not only for ourselves but for our local churches and for the body of Christ worldwide. We should pray for the fulfillment of Christ's mission out of revival not only through our own ministry or the ministry of churches in our communities but also among unreached peoples. This simple grid can help prayer groups stay on target. (For further help in leading exciting prayer gatherings, contact Concerts of Prayer International for the video "How to Lead a Concert of Prayer." The address is at the beginning of this book.)

What all of this means is that we can achieve significant unity in prayer because we are agreed on the basic vision we are praying for.

Now, *when it comes to mobilizing united prayer, we need to work at two major fronts: the integration front and the intensification front.*

1. The Integration Front

First we should help people integrate revival prayer into their daily walk with Christ. I suggest as a starting point *a fifteen-minute "daily discipline"* in which every Christian can participate. Try it for a month. The minutes are divided into seven areas:

- *Rejoice* (one minute)—Praise God for what he has done, is doing, and is getting ready to do in local, national, and global revival.
- *Review* (five minutes)—Dip into books, magazines, other literature, and most of all the Scriptures to learn the nature of revival and of the coming world revival. What is discovered during these five minutes makes the remaining nine minutes more meaningful.
- *Repent* (one minute)—Confess to God on your behalf and on behalf of the whole church the specific ways in which we are hindering revival.
- *Resist* (one minute)—Target in prayer those points where Satan is attempting to undermine the life and mission of the church in order to diminish the potential for revival.
- *Request* (five minutes)—Intercede for full revival in the church, using the preceding chart as a guide.
- *Recommit* (one minute)—Reflect on all you have learned from the Lord and all you have said to him, and commit yourself back to him to be used in answer to your prayers, whatever the cost. Recommit yourself to set the pace for others to pray with you in the same directions.

171

- *Record* (one minute)—In a journal, record whatever you sense God has given you in the previous fourteen minutes. What new understanding has he shared with you on revival? What new directions has he given for prayer? What new steps of obedience has he called you to take as a result of praying? How has he encouraged you to set the pace for others? Over time this journal will provide a tremendous encouragement not only about your praying but about how God is working in response to your prayers.

If a Christian would commit to this fifteen-minute daily discipline for twelve months, he or she would add *ninety hours* of revival praying to his or her life. All other things being equal, what difference might that make in that Christian's walk with Christ and in his or her personal preparation for revival? What difference might that make in how God accelerates the coming revival in answer to his or her prayers?

Or what if a church of two hundred adult members would commit themselves to the same daily discipline, holding one another accountable to it for a year? The result would be *eighteen thousand additional hours* focused on prayer for revival. All other things being equal, what impact might this have not only on the current spiritual climate of that one congregation but on preparing that church to enter into God's greater works in a revival of biblical proportions? (Not to mention that God answers prayer!)

Here's another way revival prayer can be integrated into church services, Sunday school classes, and small group meetings. For example, I ask pastors, "What if you would commit to ten minutes a week during Sunday morning worship to help your people pray for revival by praying your sermon back to God?"

Many pastors say they cannot get their people to attend church prayer meetings. What I'm suggesting is that we take the prayer meetings to the people! Sunday morning is when we have most of the people together. It's a perfect time to start uniting the church to pray concertedly toward the hope of world revival.

This brief time for prayer can easily be freed up if a pastor shortens his preaching by ten minutes and uses the extra time for prayer, knowing that such praying is actually a continuation of the message but through the interactive approach of group intercession. In addition, if a pastor's message provides, as a central focus, greater understanding of important issues in revival, the ten minutes of prayer could appropriately be called revival praying.

The ten-minute prayer response is simple to conduct. For example, if a pastor has a four-point outline in his message on revival, he simply helps the people pray those major concepts back to God, asking the Father to activate each one in the life of the congregation. One could shape this session the following way: one minute of opening praise (for all we've learned about Christ in the sermon), two minutes of intercession for each of the four points, and the final minute for a prayer of recommitment (or a minute of silence in order to listen to God). For the ten minutes of prayer, the people might be broken into cluster groups of five or six, or the church elders might come to the pulpit to pray through these points, using the same time frames. (For many exciting ways to lead people in corporate prayer, write to Concerts of Prayer International for my *Creative Approaches for Concerts of Prayer*.)

Suddenly your church will be united in prayer for the larger works of God in revival. This will impact a church in several ways.

First, *it will change the way the pastor preaches*. If a pastor knows that whatever he preaches on a given Sunday will be the specific issues his people ask God to give to their church, he will look at his sermon in an entirely different light. It will give him a new excitement about sermon preparation, as well as new ways to teach on a text.

Second, *it will change the way the people listen* to the message. If they know that immediately after the message is over they will pray it back to God, they will be much more attentive (perhaps even taking notes), so that they will be ready to pray as they ought.

Third, *it will actually change the church!* Why? Because God answers prayer! For the first time, on a consistent and informed basis, your church will be praying together in ways that give God an opportunity to work toward revival in a way he has not had before. He will not turn away the prayers of the saints. In addition, it will change the people's hearts Sunday by Sunday. Whenever we pray the Word of God back to the Father, it allows the Holy Spirit to take the message out of our minds and put it down into our hearts, where it revitalizes our daily obedience to Christ.

A church might try this on Sunday mornings as a two-month experiment. At the end of eight weeks the elders could meet to evaluate what difference the weekly prayer time has made, to see if God has given any indication that the church should proceed further, that this is his prayer strategy for the church (or that he wants them to develop an even more effective one).

We can take the integration approach to a more intimate level through *prayer partners* and *prayer triplets*. The idea is for two or three Christians to enter into a covenant to pray together on a regular basis for local and world revival. They may choose to meet together for ten minutes a week, perhaps between Sunday school and morning worship (and thereby avoid planning an extra meeting). Or they might pray together by phone (particularly if one of them has a phone with conference-call capabilities). Again they can use the guidelines above to orchestrate these times of prayer.

Finally, praying for revival can be integrated *every time* Christians pray together, even if it's only for a few moments at the dinner table, during family devotions, in a Bible study group, at the opening of a Sunday school class, or in personal devotions. In whatever form, a revival pacesetter wants to insure that revival praying takes place every time Christians pray together.

2. The Intensification Front

We also need to intensify revival prayer in the body of Christ. As we sense the impending nature of national and world revival and all that it is bringing, as we see the desperate need of the church and the world for such a revival to come, we will want to find ways to increase the work of revival prayer among God's people.

In my own city of New York we have seen the integration/intensification balance take a special form through two broad efforts. Prayer-Net attempts to network hundreds of regular prayer groups from churches throughout the city who are willing to integrate ten minutes of prayer for world revival every time they meet for prayer, no matter what other issues they may also address. They see themselves as part of a citywide coalition of prayer groups, praying the same issues back to God based on suggestions sent to them by a coordinating team. This is a form of integration. But on the intensification front we have scores of churches (involving hundreds of prayer groups) participating in *The Lord's Watch*. We just concluded a six-month Lord's Watch in which one or more churches were committed for one of 180 consecutive nights to pray for our region and for world revival. Each church brought together a group of people (sometimes the entire congregation) on their appointed night to form a "watch" for that night, interceding for revival on the basis of the guidelines we sent them. Afterward the leaders of that night's groups called the leaders of groups meeting the next night to pass the torch of prayer, encouraging them by sharing how God worked the previous evening. Our goal is to see The Lord's Watch functioning every night of the year.

Another way to intensify prayer is through large group events, such as *Concert of Prayer rallies*. In New York City not only are there large gatherings of pastors in prayer for revival, but on some weekends as many as ten Concerts of Prayer may be conducted simultaneously throughout the city, bringing together thousands of Christians. Similar efforts are under way in many cities across the nation.

Such a large event, though it involves extra time and commitment, has tremendous impact. It embellishes the idea of gathering together for prayer and worship, so that people rediscover the blessing of sustained corporate prayer, which they take back with them to their own congregations. Also, by sharing a brief message at a prayer rally on the coming revival, there's an opportunity for people to be built up in their faith, to be filled with hope. Further, in a large assembly, praying Christians find out how many of God's people throughout their community have the same growing burden for revival, which encourages everyone to stay faithful in the work of prayer at all times. In such events new pacesetters for revival will be raised up to serve the local churches. In fact, toward the end of a rally, leaders even make a call for commitment to become pacesetters. Those who desire to do so may come forward for special prayer by all of those at the rally. This might be followed up with prayer training events in the ensuing weeks to help train pacesetters to carry out their assignment in their own churches and/or in the city prayer movement.

Objective Three: Invite God's People

Beyond inciting the vision and uniting in prayer, we must encourage God's people to *prepare comprehensively* in the hope of spiritual awakening. Our preparations for impending revival are similar to changes Scripture challenges us to make whenever we contemplate the final revival. After all, all revivals are a "coming" of Christ to his people, a fresh manifestation of his presence by his Spirit, an approximation of his final and visible arrival. Should we not have the same attitude of watchful readiness—an eagerness to meet him, with no fear that we will pull back in shame? Should we not get set for revival with the same spirit by which we must prepare for his ultimate, glorious revelation? (See, for example, how 1 John 2:28 and 3:2–3 could also apply to readiness for revival.)

Although there are many ways to promote preparation among God's people, here are two of the most important steps:

1. Preparing by Repentance

In our invitation to the church to prepare for revival, one key emphasis by every pacesetter must be to foster a healthy spirit of repentance. There may be no single step more important than this. Repentance is the most dynamic inrush of the kingdom within ordinary history.[4] John the Baptist pictured repentance as lowering the mountains, raising up the valleys, straightening out the crooked ways so that God can reveal his glory to all flesh. If, as missionary leader Jack Miller says, "it is simply impossible for a man to meet the Lord of Glory in the full revelation of His Majesty and not be grieved by his particular sins and want to confess them," then it's equally true that any who anticipate a coming revelation of God's majesty in world revival will be grieved over everything in us that contradicts what is coming, or that hinders it. We will confess these things and turn from them in order to be prepared to receive what God is ready to give.

Repentance can be measured in a number of ways. It is measured against the character and ways of God revealed in his historical acts in Scripture. But it can also be measured against how God promises to reveal his character and his ways increasingly in the future, ultimately in the consummation itself. Repentance is the response that comes not only from seeing who God is but also what more he wants to do for us. Discerning where he is headed, we learn to take him as seriously as he takes himself.

176

Repentance is based not so much on what we are turning *from*, but rather on what we are turning *toward*. "Repent and believe" was the message of Jesus based on the fact that "the time has come, the kingdom is near" (Mark 1:15). Repentance therefore acts as a hinge that swings the church from what we are toward what is coming so that we make the necessary readjustments to receive it as it comes.

Of course in repentance there must be confession to God, sometimes with feelings of deep brokenness and tears. It comes out of our sense of solidarity both with the world and its dark prospects (because the human race is our race) as well as with the church and its disturbing paralysis (because we have helped to bring that paralysis on us and because it is in us all).

In the end, all of this actually points us *forward*. What we own up to and then confess and forsake, sharply defines what it is we want to seek from God in the coming revival. Repentance turns us with hope toward the future. Repentance is a heart broken in longing as much as in shame. We long for what God has promised but that is still waiting to appear, rather than just expressing regret over what could have been but never was.

In repentance *we identify anything that hinders our full enthusiasm for revival* and a decisive devotion to Christ to seek it. We identify everything within us and within the church that may be hindering, resisting, counterfeiting, ignoring, diminishing, or undermining God's new work in us to prepare us for revival. We acknowledge to him the ways we have been blinded to such revival, rebelled against it, hardened our hearts against it, or even fled from him in the fear of it.

Here's another reason repentance is a first step into comprehensive preparation for revival: Through repentance *we relinquish to God everything that revival must transform.* Sometimes these may be good things. But God asks us to do more than simply let them go. He wants us to give them over to him to be transformed in the outpouring of his Spirit. We must even be willing under his directives to actively dismantle in our own lives and in our congregations everything that may compete with or be a stronghold against revival. Again these may be good things—good programs, good plans, good agendas, good achievements, good experiences, good intentions. But if they compete with the greater glory God wants to reveal in his Son, they must go.

177

A good starting point for repentance may be a moratorium in our schedules, in which for a period of time we voluntarily set aside good things in our lives and ministries to give ourselves more fully to pray and prepare for God's very best: the coming revival. For example, the members of one of the fastest growing urban churches in America, with a plethora of ministries to the poor, to prostitutes, to drug addicts, to AIDS patients, and others, recently concluded that with all of these good activities they were merely making a dent in reaching their city for Christ. And so, they set aside eight weeks to give themselves to prayer every night. They canceled all church programs except for Sunday morning worship. And they prayed. Night after night, over one thousand gathered for prayer. And on Sunday they poured themselves out in intercession following the morning worship. Because they called this moratorium, they experienced a fresh touch of Christ in their lives—a foretaste of the coming revival—and were able to reenter the fray with new enthusiasm and greater power.

Whatever issues we choose to confess, *repentance must ultimately become a way of life* for any people who are concerned for revival. And it must be reflected in the practical ways we change our living to conform to our confessions.

If repentance is to prepare for revival, it must be more than a personal response; it must also be *corporate*. For whatever hinders revival in the church, we all share responsibility. The sooner we confess corporately, the more poised we will be for God to act. As we give God comprehensive corporate repentance (the approach to repentance most often called for in Scripture), we make preparation for a comprehensive corporate revival.

And what are some of the unique issues that must be dealt with, both individually and corporately, by Christians committed to preparing the way for God's visitation in revival? Here are a few suggestions, areas that we often don't think about when we think of repentance, but they must be addressed, especially if the hope of revival is at hand.

- Repent of a lesser view of Christ, which has led us to a lesser concern for his purposes, his presence, and his power.

- Repent of pursuits and priorities that are ungodly and that have robbed us of a vision for and enthusiasm for the final revival or any revival that precedes it.
- Repent of our tentative spirits regarding revival. We say to God "Show me, and then I'll believe." We need to say, "I believe, help my unbelief."
- Repent of unbelief that says our particular situation is hopeless and cannot be transformed, even by revival.
- Repent of our unwillingness to confess our frustrated and hopeless condition as a church, with no hope outside of revival.
- Repent of how our daily living advances the present order of things, instead of being a part of preparing the church for the in-breaking of God's kingdom in new ways through revival.
- Repent of our indifference and apathy. We are willing to be satisfied with much less than God has promised us and the nations.
- Repent of our "religious flesh," as we attempt to do God's work in our own strength. This is evidenced in our self-sufficiency, self-confidence, self-righteousness, and self-promotion.
- Repent of our counterfeit hopes that are centered on this life, on our church, in particular Christian leaders, or in our own programs and systems.
- Repent of our lack of prayer as a church. This reveals our hearts' hidden aversion to the living God and his purposes for all the earth.
- Repent of the fear that hesitates to seek revival, because we are afraid of what it might cost us.
- Repent of the disunity of the church, that makes it impossible for God to pour out a broad-based spiritual awakening. God's whole revival must come to the whole church, for the sake of the whole earth. We must repent of divisiveness caused by our denominationalism, traditionalism, competitiveness in ministry, and racism.

You may be able to identify other areas of repentance that need to be a part of how we prepare the way of the Lord.

2. Preparing by the Strategy of Silence

Of supreme importance, overarching all other preparations including repentance, we must practice what I call the "strategy of silence." This should not surprise us since one of the major impacts of revival when it comes will be silence—a sense of awe and the fear of God that make us prostrate in spirit before him (see Revelation 1:17 as an example).

We must take time to listen to God. We must remove all the clutter and static that keeps us from hearing his voice. This is possibly the greatest evidence that revival is near. As God's people are humbled before him, silence not only means we have a heart full of wonder but also a spirit of readiness to respond to the Lord no matter what revival requires of us.

Initially silence may simply mean asking God questions and giving him undistracted time to answer us. As you practice the strategy of silence and help others to do the same, here are some suggested questions you might ask:

- Has God given us a greater sense of hope and confidence about the coming world revival? And has our hunger for revival increased?
- As we seek to prepare for a national and world revival, in what ways is God calling us to obey him in response to our growing vision?
- Do we see any preliminary answers to our prayers for revival taking place right now?
- Are there ways we should give testimony to what God is teaching us or testimony to the ways he's beginning to answer? Are there ways we should begin challenging others to renewed confidence about the coming revival? Does God want us to set the pace in any new directions?

Finally, as we look at our own walk with Christ and our work to mobilize other believers for the coming revival, it demands that we evaluate and adjust the full scope of our discipleship on a regular basis. And we must wait in silence to hear God's answer.

Press On!

On a number of occasions I have led citywide revival prayer concerts in the Antelope Valley just north of Los Angeles, a short dis-
tance from the runway on which the space shuttle lands. I have often
thought as we prayed together and then went forth from those rallies to watch for the answers that it was as if we too were putting
down a runway, a runway for revival. We were preparing a way for
the Lord, for him to "land" among us with a fuller manifestation of
Christ and his kingdom. We were getting ready to receive him and
then to "take off" with him.

In light of the coming revival, life preparation is key, both personal
and corporate. We must constantly encourage each other to do everything we can to make room for God to act. We must "clear the decks"
for God's initiatives among us so that we might go forward into all
that world revival holds for the twenty-first century. True, revival is
God's work, it is his visitation. But we have a job to do as well. We
must be sure everything is in place for him to arrive!

So press on! Set the pace with confidence. You are simply uncovering what God has already begun to do among the people for whom
you are setting the pace. Don't despise the day of small beginnings.
Even if only a few seem to be ready to seek and prepare for revival,
be assured that God can and will work powerfully with that initial
few until ultimately he brings forth a great host who are ready to receive it.

Be patient with the process. Know that God is as committed to the
process leading toward revival as he is to the revival itself. The process
of seeking and preparing contains within it the seeds of the awakening toward which we are moving.

And set the pace with joy and enthusiasm. Hope is infectious—it's
caught, not just taught. Emphasize how much more God wants to
give us than we have yet experienced. At the same time help people
face up to the fears they have about revival and talk about them freely.
Help them come to grips with the radical nature of revival and help
them want it because nothing less will do. Let them feel the excitement in store for us as God takes us together through revival into advances of the kingdom we have not experienced before. Above all,
never be satisfied until they understand that all revival, plain and sim-

ple, is *Christ*. We are seeking and preparing for his manifest presence among us.

Pressing on means we must stay alert for the inevitable spiritual conflicts that lie ahead. Satan will try to undermine movements of seekers in every way he can. He'll attempt to divert us, distract us, discourage us, and divide us because he knows that the coming revival will cut his time shorter than ever. He will attack with fury all who have set themselves to mobilize the church to seek and prepare for this triumphant work of the Spirit.

So stay determined. Don't give up. Never be apologetic. You are not on a fool's errand. Sow the vision among others. Plant and water. And then press in on God to give you the increase. You will reap if you faint not. World revival *is* coming! The hope *is* at hand!

A Survey about Local and World Revival

Note: By means of this questionnaire, we wish to gauge the nature of your attitudes on issues related to a coming world revival. For each question below, there is a continuum provided for your response that allows you to indicate the intensity of your feelings. All answers are confidential. We will report back the results at a future date. The questions are given in summary form. The one administering this questionnaire will explain each question in more detail.

1. To what extent does the church worldwide (including our church) need a greater manifestation of all that Christ is for us, in us, and through us? To what degree are we in need of a true biblical revival?

1	2	3	4	5	6

It would be helpful, but not essential to our task.

Without it most churches (our own included) will languish, and we will fall short of God's purposes for us in this generation.

2. What impact would a world revival (as well as revival where we live) have on the worldwide advance of Christ's kingdom? To what degree is revival in the church the only hope for our city and for the nations?

1	2	3	4	5	6

It would be helpful, but not essential to our task.

We can never carry out the Great Commission task to the comprehensive degree that God has called us to in this generation, without a true biblical revival.

3. How strategic is it for the body of Christ (including our church) to work concertedly in prayer and preparation for a coming world revival?

1	2	3	4	5	6

It would be helpful, but not essential to revival.

God will only respond with a local and worldwide awakening in the church if we unite as a body to pray for it and to prepare for it together.

4. Is God willing, able, and *ready* to give world revival to this generation (and to us right here)?

1	2	3	4	5	6

Undoubtedly God is able. I'm not sure he wants to at this time.

Absolutely! God yearns to do such a thing right now. It is his highest priority for us in this generation.

5. Does God desire to fill his church (including our church) with confidence and hope about a coming revival and to enable us to seek it and prepare for it together?

1	2	3	4	5	6

I'm not sure.

Absolutely! Such a spirit of corporate hope and obedience is a gift of God.

6. Am I ready to get involved right now with other believers in new ways to seek and prepare for local and world revival?

1	2	3	4	5	6

I'm not sure.

I want to make such involvement a number-one priority in my life, reflected in such things as my commitments of time, energy, resources, and prayer.

Epilogue: A Story about the Coming Revival

Surprised at Yale

It was the last of a week-long series of meetings scattered in cities throughout New England. A team of us had been visiting a number of the prayer movements in five states, encouraging and training leaders, meeting with pastors in various communities, holding evening citywide prayer rallies, and generally planting a vision for revival everywhere we went. Our trip concluded with a gathering of local leaders at the chapel of Yale University.

At the conclusion of the afternoon we united in prayer, seeking God for a greater work of his kingdom on that campus while asking him to seal our many other ministries for Christ during the previous week. Finally there came a time of absolute silence as the sense of God's presence came upon us. It was during that period that a passage of Scripture leaped into my mind, one I had not read for many years: 2 Samuel 5:1–12. I could vaguely remember the account, so I quietly slipped out my Bible and turned to read the passage in full. Before long I realized that God was providing me a most intriguing analysis of what he ultimately has in store for this generation throughout New England, and of what true revival always looks like when it fully comes.

Deciding to share my insights with the others, I rose to speak. But immediately I found myself in tears that flowed wave upon wave. The understanding that God gave me in those moments simply overwhelmed me. I saw the glories of the coming world revival captured in this one story. Since that afternoon, the text has become a major touchstone in my thinking on the hope at hand.

Dress Rehearsals of the Coronation

Throughout this book one way I have defined revival is as *an approximation of the consummation*. Scripture foretells that the consummation deals ultimately with the open, visible coronation of Christ by all heaven and earth—a cosmic coronation. Therefore it should come as no surprise that every approximation of that final revival will also carry a strong sense of *coronation*—a dress rehearsal of it.

For example, in the final revival the elders, who have already cast their crowns before the throne, fall down before the Lamb because he has redeemed people from every tongue, tribe, and nation to make them a kingdom and priests for God (Rev. 5). In a similar way, in every revival we taste of this preeminent coronation. Confronted with the manifest presence of Christ the King, the church in every revival surrenders afresh to him, renouncing our many other allegiances, abandoning them to give all of our devotion to the Lamb on the throne. In a sense we crown him with our prayers that pursue revival, and then we crown him with our obedient responses to revival when it comes.

It is this same drama that we witness in 2 Samuel 5 when David was finally anointed king by all of Israel. I'd like to conclude this book by describing some of the parallels between David's coronation and the coming revival for the twenty-first century—when Christ will assume more openly by the outpouring of the Spirit his role as Lord of the church and hope of the nations.

Pictures from 2 Samuel 5:1–12

All the tribes of Israel came to David at Hebron and said, "We are your own flesh and blood. In the past, while Saul was king over us, you were the one who led Israel on their military campaigns. And the LORD said to you, 'You will shepherd my people Israel, and you will become their ruler.'"

When all the elders of Israel had come to King David at Hebron, the king made a compact with them at Hebron before the LORD, and they anointed David king over Israel. . . .

The king and his men marched to Jerusalem to attack the Jebusites, who lived there. The Jebusites said to David, "You will not get in here; even the blind and lame can ward you off." They thought, "David cannot get in here." Nevertheless, David captured the fortress of Zion, the City of David.

On that day, David said, "Anyone who conquers the Jebusites will have to use the water shaft to reach those 'lame and blind' who are David's enemies." That is why they say, "The 'blind and lame' will not enter the palace."

David then took up residence in the fortress and called it the City of David. He built up the area around it, from the supporting terraces inward. And he became more and more powerful, because the LORD God Almighty was with him. . . .

And David knew that the LORD had established him as king over Israel and had exalted his kingdom for the sake of his people Israel.

I see in this coronation event the following characteristics of all true revivals:

1. *They had to come to the end of themselves.* The tribes of Israel had tried everything else to bring forth God's purposes for the nation. They were at a crossroads. The nation was disintegrating. Everything looked hopeless. They were defeated. It was time for a new beginning. Is not the church in general at such a point of need in this hour? Are we not in the thick of dark prospects on the outside and disturbing paralyses on the inside that render us helpless in so many ways?

2. *They pursued the one hope they had, and they did so in unity.* They knew that the national revival David could give them would come only as he assumed leadership for all the tribes—for the whole people of God. Whatever future there was for the entire nation, it was for all of them together. No tribe would survive long by itself. In the same way, we must seek Christ together as our only hope in the full expectation that when revival comes, it will bring blessing upon the whole body of Christ and lead us as his people into the mission he can only fulfill as he rules over us together.

3. *The leaders led the way.* It was the leaders who needed to take the initiative. Only as they came to their senses, embraced the hope David held out to them, and set the pace in the pursuit of his manifest kingship among them would the rest of the nation be rallied to David in readiness for the answers. This is how it must ultimately be in every revival. Determined people who see the hope at hand become pacesetters who incite, unite, and invite. But the elders and

spiritual leaders at all levels of the churches must comprise the front-line advance by their prayers and by how they proclaim the hope toward which we are praying. To God's glory we see today a groundswell of such leadership.

4. *Their focus was on David alone.* They were hopeful that David would be sufficient under God to reverse their fortunes as a nation—to heal the divisions and to lead them triumphantly against their enemies. They had nowhere else to turn. He was their only hope, their only life. He was, they said, "bone of our bones and flesh of our flesh." They reflected on what David had been for them in the past, the ways he had given them victory in other times. And they longed to see it happen again, but in an even more comprehensive way. And so it is in all true revival: There must be a singular focus of God's people on the One who is our Leader, who is bone of our bone, our life, our health, our hope. The centrality of Christ in revival as well as in the pursuit of revival is nonnegotiable. He and he alone is the answer to all of our cries for a worldwide spiritual awakening.

5. *The Word of God was the basis of their faith.* They knew what God had spoken previously about the role David was to play, and they would settle for nothing less. Even so, in all revival God's Word must be proclaimed throughout the body of Christ, particularly the message of who Christ is in our midst, as the hope of all the glorious things to come (Col. 1:27). Only then will a vision be stirred in us that is sufficiently compelling to drive people to pray and prepare for revival with confident expectation and perseverance.

6. *They called on David to fulfill one purpose and one alone: to be ruler over them.* They were ready to submit to the full scope of his lordship, whatever that would mean. As the Scottish reformer Samuel Rutherford described his prayer for revival, they were saying, "Come and conquer us!" Then they waited for his response. They consecrated themselves to him as king, even going so far as to enter into covenant with him. In essence they said if he would come and rule over them, uniting them and leading them to victory, they were willing to follow him wherever he may lead and whatever it might cost. They put their lives on the line and they said so, boldly.

Then came the coronation. They anointed him with oil. Even more, they anointed him with their longings toward him, with their love for him, and with their faith in what God would do through him. They confirmed him king as they threw open the doors of their hearts and of their individual tribes, inviting him to take center stage for the whole nation. And he did so. He assumed his full right and role as king, manifesting himself to them as the focal point for the future of the nation. In fact, the very covenant that was made was at the *king's* initiative. And this may be the most vivid application of this passage to all spiritual awakenings: It is only when the King sovereignly initiates a new relationship with his people that revival comes upon us.

Of course, every one of the other steps are equally true when revival comes. We precede revival by prayers that call upon the Father to have Christ reign over us in new and more powerful ways. Those very prayers are actually an anointing of our King. Have you ever thought of that? Our lives poured out in prayer are a very special way in which we crown him King of Kings. So are all the answers God gives to our prayers for revival. As we seek his face, God draws us into covenant with his Son to be fully his in the revival that is coming and in all of its implications for the nations.

7. *They were no longer paralyzed before their enemies.* Immediately God began to answer their many other needs. They marched forth to fulfill God's purposes for their generation. They were no longer on the defensive. They were no longer intimidated by the jeers of the enemy. They were on the offensive, and they attacked the situation with boldness and courage. All because David was king in their midst, uniting them, filling them with his presence, and going before them into battle. The parallels to revival are obvious: In true revival God liberates and galvanizes his people for nothing less than the fulfillment of the Great Commission.

8. *Destroyed were the strongholds the enemy had raised up against the work of God.* The fortress of Zion was so thoroughly divested of the dark forces that had held it captive that its name was changed in honor of the king who had brought these victories to pass. Even so, revival is the greatest act of spiritual warfare the world can ever witness! Through the manifest presence of Christ in his church, God breaks down the strongholds that have been exalted against the knowledge of Christ and brings many thoughts (as well as institutions and peoples) into captivity to Christ.

9. *The city (and ultimately the nation) began to be transformed.* It was built up to be what God intended in the first place. It was restored; it too was revived. David took up permanent residence within the city, manifesting his presence throughout the entire population in such a way that Zion came to be known as the "City of David," that is, the city where David dwells, where he is active, where he is the central issue.

God has the same desire for our communities, that Christ would become such a focus of attention in answer to our prayers that his coronation by revival would literally transform our cities to become the places where Christ dwells, acts, and prevails.

10. *God vindicated the coronation before nations.* God worked through King David to expand his kingdom throughout all the land and beyond. Pagan powers submitted to him, honored him, joined him. This foreshadows the many ways that Christ's kingdom has triumphed worldwide in the great revivals of the past, especially through the launching of renewed missionary endeavors and through social reforms. God has no less in mind for our generation—in fact, many feel the mission thrust that is coming may be the final advance.

Awake and Crown Him King

Every one of these steps in the coronation of David has parallel applications to the kind of coronation that takes place in all true revivals. It is exactly what we are waiting for in this hour, with longing and anticipation. This is the hope at hand.

Let us determine in our hearts that we will settle for nothing less than a reenactment of the coronation of David—and beyond that an approximation of the coronation of Revelation 5. May world revival for the twenty-first century be such a dynamic dress rehearsal of the ultimate coronation, by the power of the Holy Spirit, that it mobilizes leaders with new resolve to lead out in the cause of Christ. May it unite the body of Christ in oneness of devotion and purpose. May it bring us to full consecration and obedience to the Lord, worshiping and serving him with one heart and one voice. And may it give us new marching orders in the mission of Christ, tearing down the strongholds of darkness, manifesting the presence of Christ in our cities and throughout the nations, and bringing the testimony of his saving work before all peoples. Together let us sing:

> Crown Him with many crowns, the Lamb upon His throne;
> Hark! how the heavenly anthem drowns all music but its own!
> *Awake*, my soul, and sing of Him who died for thee,
> And hail Him as thy matchless King through all eternity.

Appendices

Hope Alert!

Peter writes, "Always be prepared to give an answer to everyone who asks you to give the reason for the hope that you have" (1 Peter 3:15). The following appendices help to support the claims for hope for a coming national and world revival, explored in confidence builders 3, 4, 5, and 6 in chapters 6–9.[1] You can use them in a number of ways:

- To fill in each chapter with insightful and often exciting practical illustrations.
- To provide you with new focus in your praying.
- To share with others your reason for anticipating revival, explaining the impact it might have.
- To use during group discussions, especially as you lead a group through this book using the *Small Group Study/Discussion Guide* available from Concerts of Prayer International.

Appendix 1
From Chapter 6:
The Dark Prospects

Global Prospects Overshadowing the Twenty-first Century

Premise: God loves the world and longs to see his Son exalted among all earth's peoples. But he knows the world is currently facing extraordinary crises and challenges beyond its own resources. He also knows humankind is under the dominion of dark spiritual powers. Deliverance for the nations rests once again in God's sovereign intervention to reveal his glory, to push back the darkness, and to release his solutions in Christ—in a revival equal to the desperate needs of our times. In fact, revival in the church is the only hope he holds out for the earth's peoples. Therefore we pray and prepare for a coming world revival with confidence.

This appendix contains a sampling of trends that offer potentially dark prospects for life in the twenty-first century. *For each heading ask yourself these questions:* 1. In view of these challenges, in what sense is revival in the church the only hope for the nations? 2. What difference might a world revival make for each prospect? 3. How should this affect the way we pray and prepare for the coming world revival?

Many of these trends and challenges overlap one another. For example, almost every trend from technology to religion also has political implications. The attempt has been made, however, to place various global issues under the categories in which they most logically fit.

Religious Prospects

1. There is an advance of secularism: the denouncing of supernaturalism and promotion of nonreligious/antireligious biases. There is a growing intolerance toward Christian things in many parts of the world. In the West, God is often denied, ridiculed, and trivialized. In the godless orientation of our culture, God is nothing more than a mere notion for many.
2. There is a secularization of many societies at all levels.
3. There is an increase in the philosophy of religious relativism worldwide.
4. There is an advance of naturalism: viewing the universe as a closed system based on cause-and-effect relationships without any overarching purpose.
5. An increase of the "new paganism" proclaims no fixed truth, no final good, no ultimate meaning or purpose. It sees a personal God as a primitive illusion. It promotes mysticism, occult forces and powers, communion with nature, suspicion of authority, discrediting of the concept of sin, and the worship of self over God.
6. There is rise of the New Age movement and the invasion of the West by Eastern philosophy.
7. There is an "openness to indifference" in the West—accepting anything and indifferent to everything.
8. There is the transformation of the West from a Christian culture into a post-Christian culture (sometimes called the "desacrilization" of society).
9. We find many "Ignostics": secularized people who have no Christian background—no Christian memory, vocabulary, or assumptions.
10. There is a sense of moral and cultural bankruptcy in the West, the loss of fixed standards of moral values. Seventy percent of those in the West reject moral absolutes.
11. The sanctity-of-life ethic has been replaced by quality-of-life ethic in many nations worldwide.
12. Affluence and hedonism in the West are dulling spiritual sensitivities. There is a growing "poverty of spirit" in the West.

13. Disillusionment over organized Christianity is causing a steep decline in church attendance and financial giving to the church in the West.
14. There is politicization of religious beliefs: transferring religious impulses from God to the nation, from God to traditions, from God to culture and art, from God to the political process.
15. There is a revival of major world religions (such as Hinduism, Islam, Buddhism, Shintoism), including widespread proselytism.
16. There is an invasion of historic world religions into the Christian West. For example, in the United States there are now more Muslims than Presbyterians, more Buddhists than Assemblies of God members, and almost as many Hindus as Episcopalians.
17. There is a rise of religious zealotry and an increase of religious-based terrorism.
18. There is growth of "millennial fever": increased expectations and preparations regarding an impending, cataclysmic, transcendental shift in the world community.

Technological Prospects

1. We see a proliferation of technological innovations, such as genetic engineering, with accompanying ethical dilemmas.
2. There is a trend toward dehumanization through technology, such as abortion, fetal-tissue experimentation, euthanasia.
3. There is the influence of robotics and the shifting of work and responsibility to robots.
4. There is an information explosion (knowledge doubles every ten years). The advances in communications and information systems are dividing the world into two classes of people: the "knows" and the "know nots," the information rich and the information poor.
5. There is a coming age of "global access," when no part of the world will be inaccessible to media. Popular media often portrays simplistic, violent solutions to human dilemmas. It can create a seductive, often flippant, condoning of immoral conduct. It often portrays religious convictions as bigotry.
6. The temptation to lust for power through technological mastery is always present.

7. There are environmental policies that promote conquest in consumerism.
8. There is pollution, both air and water.
9. There are toxic waste sites and nuclear dumps (with threat to health and environment).
10. There is global warming and the depletion of the ozone layer, with repercussions such as increased skin cancer.
11. We find damaging deforestation, such as the exploitation of tropical rainforests, and desertification, such as the southward movement of the Sahara in Africa.
12. There is the rise in the number of societies that believe human needs should be met and solved immediately. Impatience is aggravated by the dazzling promises of technological advances and by mass media and advertising that often fuel compulsive consumerism.

Economic Prospects

1. World population is exploding: The world's population will double to 10.2 billion in the next one hundred years. Currently 2.5 million babies are born each week.
2. Between now and the year 2025, 3.2 billion people will be added to the world's population. Of those, 95 percent will be born in poor countries. Population growth is outstripping economic growth and food productions in thirty-four nations of the Two-Thirds World.
3. There is an increase in earthquakes, famines, and plagues (with an increase in the number of poor affected by them).
4. One billion currently suffer from disease, poor health, malnutrition.
5. There is potential for megafamines and pandemics, especially in the crowded megacities of the Two-Thirds World.
6. There is a health-care crisis worldwide, magnified by the devastation of AIDS.
7. There are widespread fears of resource scarcity and material shortages.
8. There is hunger, famine, undernourishment.
9. There is the erosion of the middle class.

10. There is the fall in real wages in the West.
11. There are long-range prospects of scarcity and downward mobility within previously affluent nations of the West.
12. There is inflation, recession, fear of depression.
13. There is mounting foreign debt in many nations.
14. There are fears of international monetary collapse.
15. Debt-accumulating lifestyles prevail in westernized nations.
16. There is the culture in the West of the "never satisfied," created by economic prosperity, affluence, and consumerism. Consumer societies could actually be called "coveter societies"—a vicious cycle of desire, production and consumption, and greed.
17. There are the underemployed (those working well below skill level, in part-time jobs, or at poverty-level wages).
18. Increased welfare dependency often undermines human responsibility.
19. Almost one billion people live in extreme poverty. One-half billion live on the brink of starvation.
20. There is the growth of the urban poor.
21. There are slum or squatter settlements (housing approximately 25 percent of world population).
22. There is chronic unemployment by the hundreds of millions.
23. There is a massive increase of homelessness worldwide (the UN classifies one hundred million as refugees).
24. There is a growing gulf between the rich and poor, and the emergence of a sizeable "underclass."
25. Countries in the Southern Hemisphere are moving more and more into permanent economic bondage to countries in the Northern Hemisphere.
26. Ours is a world of interdependent communities with a world economy: We stand or fall together.
27. There is the AIDS pandemic: One million will die of AIDS by the year 2000 in Africa alone. In India, six cases of HIV positive were reported in 1986, today there are over one million. It is estimated that ten million will be infected in the next decade with the disease, with one million additional Indians suffering the full-blown disease. It is estimated that the death toll will be in the tens of millions by the year 2000. This has obvious eco-

nomic ramifications, but also impacts social, political, and religious concerns.

Political Prospects

1. There is the dismantling of the Soviet empire and the Communist world, with all the ensuing destabilizations that this creates.
2. There is the rise of "people power," especially in the Third World and Eastern Europe.
3. There is the realignment of ethnic national identities and the propagation of ethnic nationalist movements.
4. There are civil wars within many nations. Today, fewer than 10 percent of the 186 countries on earth are ethnically homogeneous. Unresolved hot spots: Central America, Ireland, Lebanon, South Africa, Israel, Bosnia, Somalia, Liberia, and others.
5. There is a large influx of immigrants from many Two-Thirds World nations into nations in the West, with the accompanying struggle to maintain cultural cohesion, as seen in places like Germany and Britain.
6. There is the growth of multinational corporations that can supersede many national governments in terms of both political and economic clout.
7. Continued proliferation of nuclear fuel and arms as well as poison gases and toxins for biological warfare is accompanied by defense cutbacks in many nations in the West.
8. There are extensive global human rights abuses and political oppressions. Many governments restrain the freedom of worship and the freedom to propagate the faith. More than 60 percent of all Christians live in countries where they are restricted in the practice of their faith by discrimination, torture, imprisonment, and even martyrdom.
9. There is instability in the future of nations like North Korea and China, including the reverting of the city-state of Hong Kong back to China in 1997.
10. Unresolved Middle-East crises include Iran and Iraq and Israel with its neighbors.
11. Democracy is struggling to find a new foundation of moral consensus in many nations, especially the U.S.

Social Prospects

1. There are shifting demographics: The world is becoming both younger and older. Youth population is increasing in the Two-Thirds World, while the entire population of North America and Europe is aging.
2. Increased polarization, such as between rich and poor, young and old, north and south threaten stability.
3. There is the growth in the West of the baby boomer generation, with its obsession with self-fulfillment.
4. Fifty-five percent of the world's population is under twenty years of age. There will be 2.4 billion children by the year 2000.
5. There are 2.5 million runaway kids and an additional 2.5 million "throwaway kids."
6. Each year 600,000 teenagers commit suicide, and another 500,000 try.
7. There is an increase in violent crime, especially among youth in the West.
8. There is an increase in life-controlling problems and addictions (drugs, alcoholism, tobacco, sex), especially among youth.
9. There is global traffic in illicit drugs. Drug addicts number more than seventy million.
10. There is the increase in "dysfunctional" families, including an increase in child abuse, spouse abuse, and senior abuse.
11. There is a revolution in traditional values, including a radical redefinition of family values in many modernizing cultures. There is a rapid destabilization of families, communities, and entire societies as traditional cultures give way to modernization. This can be seen in the upsurge of divorce worldwide.
12. There is a redefinition of the roles of men and women in many nations, particularly those that are being westernized.
13. Claims and counterclaims (and litigations) over personal rights clog the streets and the courts.
14. There is increased crime and the growth of prisons.
15. There is increased promiscuity and concern for "safe sex" (especially in light of the global AIDS epidemic).

16. There is an increase in global prostitution. At least thirty million women have been sold into prostitution worldwide in the past twenty years. There are two million prostitutes in Thailand alone, and 100,000 German businessmen go on sex tours to Thailand every year. Of the tens of thousands of prostitutes in Bombay, one-third are HIV-positive.
17. Child prostitution worldwide is staggering: 800,000 in Thailand; 400,000 in India; 250,000 in Brazil; 60,000 in the Philippines; somewhere between 90,000 and 300,000 in the U.S.
18. There is a frantic pace of life in westernized nations, with an accompanying rise in hypertension, heart disease, psychological disabilities.
19. There is the rise of 300 megacities. By the year 2000 over 500 cities will have populations of one million or more. Currently there are 7,000 metropolises with population over 50,000.
20. There is the possibility of "urban apocalypses" because Two-Thirds World cities don't have the infrastructure to sustain the level of population growth. The megacities of the world will determine the future, either as places of collapse or places of regeneration for the whole world.
21. There is a crisis in education, especially in the urban centers of the world.
22. There is an increased sense of loneliness and alienation, particularly in urban centers.
23. There is the globalization of the planet (examples: CNN, global economy, one billion air passengers a year, the spread of English).
24. There is an acceleration of nationalism and the rise of ethnicity and ethnic pride. The rise of nationalistic hate groups who kill "outsiders" along political, tribal, and religious lines.
25. There are vast migrations and millions of refugees. By the year 2000, it is projected that there will be one hundred million refugees on the earth, half of whom will be children.
26. There will be a projected 1.8 billion disabled persons (33 percent being children) by the year 2000.
27. Racism, ageism, sexism, and other forms of discrimination are much more prevalent than ever.

National Prospects Overshadowing the Twenty-first Century

Most of the trends and developments listed in the previous section at the global level can also be found within the American experience. However, there are other challenges our nation will uniquely face as it enters the twenty-first century. Again, *the questions before us are* 1. What difference would revival make in each area? 2. In view of these challenges, is there any other ultimate hope for our nation apart from revival in the church?

1. Church-state clashes occur on many fronts, such as the expulsion of the Bible and religious discussion from most American classrooms.
2. There is the conflict of Hollywood vs. America: the media's war on traditional, religious-based values. Some call it a "cultural civil war."
3. The American educational system at times promotes an atmosphere of hostile skepticism about any access to truth or even its existence. It may also promote disdain for traditional moral values. Alan Bloom calls this the "closing of the American mind"— an increasingly relativistic view of truth.
4. Tolerance has been elevated as a supreme virtue, leading to a smorgasbord of morally equivalent lifestyles and undermining any sense of moral absolutes.
5. There is increased job insecurity in the American workplace, putting millions in turmoil.
6. Incomes of U.S. workers have declined 13 percent over the past two decades.
7. There is the financial gap between white households and African American and Hispanic households.
8. There are fifty million urban poor in North America (most of whom also remain unchurched).
9. There is the economic erosion of the middle class, which is downscaling to the lower class.
10. There is an erosion of trust toward national and local political leaders, a growing disillusionment with government and bureaucracy.

11. Tens of thousands of elderly people will spend their last years abandoned, frail, lonely, and underserved.
12. There is the "coloring of America": The United States ethnic/cultural panorama includes 120 ethnic groups speaking over one hundred different languages. The shifting ethnic mix in America makes Hispanics the largest minority group in the 1990s. All of this presents a tremendous challenge to maintaining a national cultural cohesion, a shared political and social vision, and a national moral consensus.
13. Some project "coming race wars": The reality of racism, urban violence, and marginalization among African Americans and other races is dominating the American agenda more and more.
14. America is graying: Over half of all Americans in history who have lived over the age of sixty-five are alive today.
15. There are forty-three million disabled people.
16. There is a wide spectrum of human rights movements: civil rights, women's rights, children's rights, disabled rights, gay rights.
17. There has been an acceleration of divorce: Approximately 50 percent of marriages in the U.S. end in divorce. Since 1960 there has been a quadrupling of divorce rates.
18. One in four children in the U.S. is born out of wedlock.
19. There is the dissolution of the African American family: By the year 2000, 70 percent of black families will be single-parent households.
20. Currently there are thirteen separate types of households represented in our population, and they are rapidly eclipsing the conventional family patterns. Since 1960 there has been a tripling of the percentage of children living in single-parent homes.
21. There has been a rapid increase of dysfunctional families with resulting negative self-images, distrust of authority, pent-up anger, fears of intimacy, and increased inability to establish and maintain enduring relationships. Much of this is experienced by today's children, who will give shape to the next generation of families.

22. There has been a 58 percent drop in personal contact time between parents and children over the past twenty years.
23. There are 333,000 homeless children.
24. Twelve million children have little access to health care.
25. Twelve million American kids suffer from chronic hunger every day.
26. About one-quarter of the nation's teens are dropping out of high school.
27. The average score on SAT college entrance exams has dropped seventy-three points over twenty-three years.
28. Every day in school at least 100,000 students carry guns. Forty are hurt or killed by firearms; 6,250 teachers are threatened with bodily injury, and 260 are physically assaulted; and 160,000 children skip classes because they fear physical harm.
29. The number of teens hospitalized for psychiatric treatment jumped from 16,000 in 1980 to 265,000 in 1990.
30. There is increased teen sexual activity. According to a 1993 *Time*/CNN survey of teenagers, 19 percent of those age thirteen to fifteen had already had sexual intercourse, and 55 percent of those age sixteen to seventeen had. Of those who had had sex, 23 percent did so under the age of fourteen.
31. Substance abuse is the number one cause of death among youth, accounting for ten thousand a year.
32. Teen pregnancy has increased 621 percent since 1940.
33. Murder is the leading cause of death among youth age fifteen to nineteen. There has been a 222 percent increase of teens being murdered each year since 1950.
34. Teen suicide has increased 300 percent since 1940 and is now the second leading cause of death, with 5,000 a year, with 50 to 100 times as many trying to kill themselves but failing.
35. There is a high level of alcohol and other drug abuse among teens.
36. Juvenile arrests for crime are up fifteen-fold since 1950.
37. There are one million teenage pregnancies annually.
38. The crime rate in America has increased nearly 1,000 percent since 1950.

39. Since 1960, there has been a 560 percent increase in violent crime.
40. Over 100,000 rapes are actually reported every year.
41. One out of every 350 Americans is in prison—the highest rate in the world. There are 700,000 in federal and local prisons, a population that is growing ten times faster than the general population.
42. Fifteen million Americans use alcohol. As a result, nearly 20,000 are killed each year by drunk drivers. And 6.6 million children under eighteen live with an alcoholic parent.
43. Eighty million Americans have sought help from therapists over the past decade.
44. There is an increase of U.S. exports of unsafe and addictive products to other countries.
45. Twenty-three million Americans are illiterate.
46. Since 1960, there has been a 400 percent increase in illegitimate births.
47. One in three conceived children are actually aborted in the U.S. Over thirty-three million abortions have been performed over the past twenty years alone. Currently this one issue in the national debate has the potential of tearing the nation apart.
48. There is open sale of pornography and other obscene materials, and a rapid expansion of the market. We have become an eroticized society.
49. There is an explosion of litigation. The court systems are clogged.
50. America is choking on the steady diet of brutality in television, movies, and the media.
51. There is a growing "loss of conscience." Americans seem to be less and less ashamed of wicked behavior, both televised and personal. There appears to be a normalization of evil, particularly through the media.
52. The national debt is over six trillion now with an estimated 13.5 trillion by the twenty-first century. With this comes the fear of a major recession or depression.
53. An estimated four million personal bankruptcies a year are expected to be filed by the turn of the century.

Additional Dark Prospects in World Evangelization

Most of the issues highlighted in the previous two sections must be faced if we are to complete the task of world evangelization. For example, they help us define more accurately the wide spectrum of people groups that must be reached with the gospel and what it will take to reach them within the context of their own needs and struggles.

But there are still other overwhelming challenges that the church worldwide must confront if we are to fulfill the Great Commission. As we review these, *the questions before us remain:* 1. What impact would world revival make upon each one of these additional challenges? and 2. In light of such concerns, is there any other hope for the nations apart from world revival in the church?

1. There are 7,010 different language groups, 43 percent of which have yet to be reached with the gospel.
2. Illiteracy among many unreached peoples makes it impossible to reach them by print media.
3. Major world religions: 18 percent Muslim, 13 percent Hindu, 6 percent Buddhist, 17 percent non-religions (including one billion atheists), 13 percent other.
4. There are 908 million Muslims, projected to be 1.2 billion by the year 2000. Most of these Muslims live in over thirty nations, many of which are militantly opposed to the Christian faith.
5. There are 690 million Hindus, projected to be 859 million by the year 2000. They are to be found mostly in 3,000 Hindu castes, only 150 of which have any viable Christian witness.
6. There are 320 million Buddhists, projected to be 359 million by the year 2000. Many of these are in China, where there are fifty separate people groups who have no resident witness for Christ.
7. There are nineteen million Jews, projected to be twenty million by the end of the decade.
8. There are 5,000 tribal groups worldwide who have no church or Bible in their language.
9. There are nearly one billion nominal Christians around the world. In addition, there is an incalculable number of "hard-

ened people" who are not unreached or unevangelized but rather who are hardened to the gospel.

10. There are between 9,000 and 12,000 different unreached people groups worldwide, incorporating nearly two billion people who have no resident witness of Christ.

11. In over twenty countries 98 percent of the population is non-Christian.

12. In Asia, only 5 percent of the people are Christian. And there are evidences of renewed hostility against Christianity in countries controlled by Hindu, Muslim, and Buddhist majorities.

13. A major contest between Islam and Christianity is being waged in Africa right now, and the outcome is not certain.

14. There are 300 megacities worldwide, most of which have little significant witness for Christ to the multitude of people groups and social needs within them.

15. Twenty-five percent of the world population live in slum or squatter settlements. There are currently 10,000 urban slum population groups with little or no witness for Christ.

16. Fifty-five percent of the world is under twenty years of age. There are 1.8 billion teenagers, the vast majority of whom have yet to hear of Christ. And their numbers are increasing rapidly.

17. There are 3,000 major university campuses and 20,000 tertiary level schools, with sixty million students. The majority of these students have not yet been confronted with the gospel of Christ.

18. There is a critical shortage of missionaries. Although Hindus, Muslims, and Chinese make up 75 percent of the non-Christian world, only 5 percent of today's missionaries live and witness among them.

19. Six million new churches will be needed among non-Christians by the year 2000 if the Great Commission is to be completed.

20. This will require at least an additional 600,000 intercultural workers.

21. There will be an increase in persecution and martyrdom. It is projected that 500,000 Christians will be martyred each year by the turn of the twenty-first century because of numerous totalitarian regimes and continuous church-state clashes.

22. Increasing encounters with powers of darkness and an intensified conflict between the two kingdoms will take place as the
light of the gospel moves into previously uncontested territo-
ries and peoples. We still face major satanic strongholds arrayed
systematically against the gospel. Demonic forces blind and en-
slave multitudes through strongholds such as nationalism, mil-
itarism, traditionalism, technocracy, racism, scientism, secularism, and materialism, as well as a whole host of ancient cultural
religions that are beginning to reassert themselves within vast
people movements of the world. For example, recently Shintoism—the worship of the sun goddess—has taken center stage
once more in the life of the seemingly materialistic Japanese peoples, as seen in the royal wedding ceremonies in 1993.

Appendix 2
From Chapter 7:
The Disturbing Paralysis

Premise: God loves the church and intends to bring glory to his Son among the nations primarily through his people. But he also sees that the desperate condition of the world is largely due to the church's struggles with its own spiritual powerlessness, brokenness, dullness, and sin. His love for us and his calling for us in Christ cannot leave us indefinitely in this unrevived state. Since he is committed to the welfare of Christ's body, he must deliver us. He must awaken us to a fuller manifestation of his Son. He knows such revival is the only hope for the restoration and liberation of the church. Our paralysis is not the last word. It should, like the dark prospects around us, drive us toward our hope in God. We can pray and prepare with confidence.

Predisposition toward the *Status Quo*: Forms It May Take

Following is a list of some of the reasons why we try to preserve the status quo, and some of the ways we do so. Such predispositions not only rise from our disturbing paralysis of unbelief but actually help to feed that paralysis. *For each entry ask yourself the following four questions:* 1. Without a comprehensive revival, is there any other way we can be delivered from such forms of disturbing paralysis in the church? 2. What difference can we expect the coming world revival to make for each form of a predisposition toward the status quo? 3. What does each form tell us about our need for repentance if revival is to come, and how would such repentance be expressed both in prayer and in obedience? 4. In what other ways do we manifest a predisposition toward the status quo?

1. We may fear *supernatural intervention* because we've heard such interventions encourage religious fanaticism, or because we resist being in a situation where we are out of control, or because we recoil at the sacrifices such changes may require of us both individually and corporately should revival come, or because we fear greater intimacy with God.
2. We may act as *custodians of religious and cultural heritages*, seeking simply to provide the necessary ceremonies and services to keep the traditions alive.
3. We may be preoccupied, as *beneficiaries of the status quo*, with conserving what we have, which makes us uneasy about taking risks to seek something more and something beyond.
4. We may have *vested interests* that resist any changes that might diminish our ministry reputations, our denominational distinctives, or our seeming rights, privileges, and rewards.
5. We may have a *survival mentality* bent on maintaining our current condition, expecting little growth or changed lives or impact on society. We have become a "chaplaincy to the rat race" as we seek to do little more than help people hold their lives together in a fast-paced society.
6. We may be *blind to the spiritual jeopardy of the world*, either by choice or ignorance, and therefore blind to the desperate need for change in the church if Christ's kingdom is to impact earth's peoples.
7. We may be *ignorant of the battle* in which we find ourselves. We refuse to take Satan seriously and thus lose a sense of need for divine intervention to unleash Christ's victories in our generation through a newly empowered church.
8. We may be guilty of *parochialism*, which comes from living in religious ghettos where we only see other Christians and, more specifically, Christians like ourselves.
9. We may be *cocooning* in an insulated, self-contained, evangelical subculture that is seemingly able to exist on its own without significant reference to outside challenges or resources to

guarantee our survival and the prosperity of our own churchly operations.

10. We may have a *tourist mentality*, which has forsaken the pilgrim's role in Christian living with its sense of destiny toward the consummation. Instead we have become more and more distracted and embroiled in the allurements of our affluent society.

11. We may harbor a *smugness* that says our present boundaries of understanding of the ways of God are the permanent boundaries of his readiness to reveal himself.

12. We may have *a self-indulgent complacency*. We choose to come to Christ only as far as *we* need to go to get our own needs met, and no more.

13. We may be *indifferent* because we are only concerned about that which impinges on our own lives and happiness.

14. We may be *mentally lazy*, unwilling to take the time and hard work demanded if we are to understand the future and how we can advance Christ's kingdom in the twenty-first century.

15. We may be guilty of *cynicism*, which is the way of less energy since it is easier to be opposed to progress and to expect things to get worse than to plan and act with the conviction that things will get better.

16. We may *lack passion* because our goals are no larger than our own physical comforts and the pursuit of personally fulfilling relationships with others who are just like us.

17. We may *lack urgency* because we have decided that no matter what could happen if revival comes, if it doesn't we can live quite happily with what we have.

18. We may have *compassion fatigue*, numbness to the human condition, as a result of trying to make a difference in the face of overwhelming odds but doing so depending upon our own strength and ingenuity.

19. We may harbor *despair* because we feel that nothing we are doing is making any significant difference in terms of the needs of the world or the cause of Christ.

20. We may be prey to a *theology of failure* that springs from the conclusion that world and community needs are too intractable to

213

ever be changed. Our only hope is for the survival of a remnant "until Jesus comes."

21. We may have a *siege mentality*. We feel victimized by the desperate needs of our society and the nations as a whole and choose therefore to retreat into a position of protectionism and isolationism.

22. We may suffer a *suffocation of spiritual ambition and vitality* due to high levels of affluence in lifestyle or maintenance activities in the church. Such things consume the human resources of middle class evangelical churches—resources that could bless the nations.

23. We may experience *burnout* because our resources, time, and talents have been depleted in churchly activities. "Expectations became exploitations" as church programs capitalized on our original zeal for Christ, co-opting us to sustain existing systems but leaving us empty, unfulfilled, and disillusioned.

24. We may take a *reactive rather than proactive stance* as our major coping strategy for bearing up under the weight of responsibilities, opportunities, demands, and causes that evangelicalism often lays upon us.

25. We may be *frustrated by gridlock*, having so many clashing activities, agendas, and causes that we become too embroiled in trying to sort it all through to ever set out toward exploring new horizons.

26. We may attend a *fragmented and disunited church* that becomes like a black hole, drawing away all our ambitions for change because we are demotivated by the brokenness of relationships inside the body of Christ.

27. We may be hurt by the *polarizations among Christians and churches*. Our vision and energy is consumed over secondary biblical interpretations and doctrines that become the reason for divisiveness and party spirits; over the shape and form of Christian mission; over the right approach to church-state relations, political involvements, justice issues, or ministry among the poor; over the competitive use of mass media in evangelism.

In the end, the evangelical church as a whole appears to be too overwhelmed—overloaded, oversold, overextended, overactive, and overfed—to effectively serve Christ in radical transformations of the status quo or to even seek from him the great transformation called revival. It should come as no surprise that we battle with a disturbing paralysis that leaves us imprisoned within the status quo.

Predisposition toward *Idolatry*: Forms It May Take

Many of the areas listed in the previous section also point toward a distorted view of God and toward various forms of idolatry. This can be seen in responses of smugness, parochialism, self-indulgence, or various fears based on false notions of who God is. What follows is a list of additional idolatries: seductions, misplaced methodologies, works of "religious flesh." In the end, all idolatry is spiritual adultery. It seriously grieves and quenches the work of the Holy Spirit. As you study this list, *ask yourself the same four questions:* 1. Without revival, is there any other hope that we can be delivered from such forms of disturbing paralysis in the church? 2. What difference can we expect the coming revival to make for each manifestation of our predisposition toward idolatry? 3. What does each form tell us about our need for repentance if revival is to come, and how should such repentance be expressed both in prayer and obedience? 4. In what other ways do we express our predisposition toward idolatry?

1. We may be seduced by the spirit of *naturalism*. For all practical purposes we act as if we live in a closed system in which progress can happen only through cause and effect, without an overriding purpose that will make any difference on a daily basis. We have become "practical agnostics."
2. We may be seduced by the spirit of *humanism*. We are obsessed to find the most rational and efficient ways to get God's work done for him, and it is on this we focus rather than on Christ.
3. We may be seduced by the spirit of *narcissism*. Even in spiritual matters we primarily seek self-potential, self-fulfillment, self-veneration, leading to self-affirmation—rather than the glory and promotion of Christ and his kingdom.
4. We may be serving *mammon*. We have come into bondage to our financial resources, so readily available to the church in the

U.S. We have fallen into the sins of accumulation and affluence and so have become a church that is "consumed by its own consumption."

5. We may be guilty of *worldliness*. Our false trust in the powerful claims of the world's approaches and institutions and our ensuing pursuit of the world's measure of success is also idolatry.

6. We may live for our many *Christianly activities*, which often can be a cover we use to avoid intimacy with God, to avoid engaging him on a direct and personal basis.

7. We may be guilty of *inordinate affections*. We prize something good and Christianly so much (such as fellowship, music, or gifted leaders) that in the end we love it above Christ himself.

8. We may worship the "*god of the quick fix*," looking to Christianly products or organizations to get us out of physical and spiritual adversity as quickly as possible. All this is a mirror of the general worldview of a technologically conditioned society.

9. We may *depend on methods*. When we look primarily to state-of-the-art techniques for motivating people spiritually, organizing God's work, or recruiting and fund-raising (and the like), this too is idolatry.

10. We may *depend on market-driven approaches*. When we succumb to business models for ministry, where the bottom line is not so much glorifying God as it is "potential customers," and as we make this the motivating and controlling factor for how we conduct Christian ministry, we commit idolatry.

11. We may be guilty of the *commercialization of religion* as we make Christ and his kingdom a product we seek to market to the world. "The church has become a harlot because her religion has become an industry. It is itself big business" (John White).

12. We may *depend on super-leaders,* looking to those who are popular and attractive in their Christian ministries, even living vicariously through their experiences and successes. Instead of following Christ, we end up following those who can best meet our needs and fulfill our dreams.

13. We may *depend on political leveraging* to change the moral climate of our nation rather than depending on divine interventions and, more specifically, the work of Christ in revival.

14. We may *rely on the past*—past successes, methodologies, organizations, common traditions—instead of the God who worked the past and goes with us from the present into the future.

15. We may worship the *idol of autonomy*. We've produced a do-it-yourself religion that leaves us self-satisfied, with an impression of self-sufficiency, and with little sense of our need of heavenly resources.

16. We may have a *consumer mentality*. God's main reason for existence, we think, is to meet our wants and needs.

17. We may be guilty of the *privatization of Christianity*. Our Christianity is centered primarily on ourselves, our needs, our dreams, and our preferences, rather than on Christ and his global cause.

18. We may be *hoarding* all that we have rather than seeking ways to share God's material and spiritual blessings with others. One estimate says 80 percent of the Christian resources of the world and 70 percent of the Christian laborers are concentrated in the United States.

19. We may be guilty of *spiritual schizophrenia*. We take Christ for what he can do for us, while we try to avoid any serious engagement in the mission he wants to fulfill through us.

20. We may seek to *manipulate Christ*, coming to him to the degree that we have needs and for nothing more. We have made him our "mascot," to whom we turn to be cheered on in the game of life but whom we relegate to the sidelines as we seek most victories in our own strength.

21. We may be guilty of *dead orthodoxy*. We put God in a box as we pursue habitual traditions, selective religious doctrines, and churchly purity in place of pursuing him.

22. We may be *empire builders* as opposed to kingdom seekers. We want the praise of others more than the praise of God. We promote our own reputations, our own agendas, and our own ministries.

23. We may succumb to *religious flesh*. Our affections and allegiances are diverted away from the person of Christ and toward the systems, creeds, organizations, leaders, and causes upon which we have put the name of Christ. We seek to fulfill whatever vision

we have for serving Christ in our own strength and to enhance the reputation of ourselves and our churches.

24. We may *depend on dead works* based on self-sufficiency, self-confidence, and self-righteousness. We become presumptuous, believing we are adequate to solve our problems ourselves, even to the place that we become self-congratulatory.

As J. B. Phillips put it three decades ago, "Your God is too small." Or to say it another way, our gods are too small. We desperately need a visitation of God's Spirit on the church, reviving in us a comprehensive revelation of Jesus Christ—a spiritual awakening that will shatter these deficient substitutes and break the paralysis of unbelief. *It is our only hope!*

Appendix 3
From Chapter 8:
The Dramatic Preparations

World Revival: Encouraging Highlights

Premise: Contemporary church attempts to fulfill the Great Commission form nothing less than a prelude to revival. The great increase in local churches among the nations, in potential resources and workers, in the comprehensive strategies for world evangelization, in the cooperation among Christians to complete the task—all cry out for the empowerment that revival brings. Clearly God is setting the stage worldwide for a new advance of Christ's kingdom. If this is his work of preparation, he will not fail to bring it about. We can seek revival with confidence that it is coming.

This list introduces a few of the stories of what God is doing both in general preparations among the nations as well as within the church to get our generation ready for world revival. *As you survey these amazing facts, ask yourself these questions:* 1. In what sense are such highlights clear evidence that world revival cannot be far off? 2. In the coming world revival, how will preparations like these insure that such revival can have the greatest possible impact for Christ's global cause? 3. In what practical ways should these preparations help to shape how each of us prays and prepares for world revival, both individually and as churches?

General Preparations among the Nations

1. A universal urban culture, broadly used trade languages, international communications, and mass transportation systems

are setting the stage for everyone on earth to see and hear the message of Christ.

2. There appears to be a growing sense that everyone is a part of a global community. This is greatly enhanced by the growing, widespread use of English, by our interdependent economies, by the massive movement of people around the world (one billion air passengers each year alone), and by global media (such as CNN).

3. There appears to be a much greater receptivity worldwide to new ideas (including the gospel) due to many sweeping changes internationally. There are growing signs of global concern for compassion (whether dealing with natural disasters or world hunger), a passion for justice (whether concerning discrimination, apartheid, or human rights), and a desire for a "new world order" (such as the international community's effort to arbitrate civil wars or to maintain surveillance on nuclear weapons).

4. Today at their own expense, vast numbers of people are flocking into every city of the world. The potential for a twenty-first century Pentecost is unmistakable.

5. When there are wars or struggles for justice, when natural disasters occur, it is a time of "creative instability." Such upheavals help move mankind toward the ultimate answers in Jesus Christ and his indestructible kingdom if the church engages those situations with declared purpose, clear goals, and the gospel.

6. There is an awakened spiritual hunger among many of the 2.5 billion unreached peoples, such as Muslims, Chinese, Hindus, Buddhists. Many are searching for meaning in their lives, whether they be refugees, university students, cultural revolutionaries, or those seeking justice and deliverance from oppression. Many long for a place of belonging (such as Palestinians or those caught up in urban migrations), while others are seeking the transcendent in new ways. All of this makes religions of all kinds much more attractive.

7. It is predicted that the next age of Christianity will be an "age of global access," with no part of the world inaccessible at least to media, and well over 90 percent of the nations of the world are even now open to Christian workers to come in one capacity or another.

General Preparations within the Church

1. About 70 percent of all progress toward completing the Great Commission has taken place since 1900. Of that, 70 percent has occurred since World War II. And 70 percent of that has come about since 1992.
2. Missionary statesman Ralph Winter says, "We have before us the brightest set of hope-filled resources, the most extensive global network of eager believers in thousands of prayer cells and strategizing committees. We have never ever had as many competent, sold-out soldiers for Jesus Christ. The job to be done is now dramatically smaller *in terms of our resources* than ever before."
3. Christians can be found in 22,000 denominational groups worldwide, each of which has special ways of reflecting the grace and power of Christ before the nations.
4. Worldwide there are 2.5 million "worship centers" waiting to be fully empowered by the Holy Spirit to become bases of operations for Christ's kingdom among all nations.
5. Currently there are seven million evangelical, Bible-believing congregations in the world that can focus on the remaining 9,000 unreached people groups.
6. While church growth in the United States continues to stagnate in many ways, there is an explosion of spiritual harvest around the world that is unprecedented in history.
7. There has been a dramatic shift of the center of Christendom to the Two-Thirds World. Sixty percent of the church will be found there by the year 2000. Much of this growth is among the poor, with whom God often does his mightiest works.
8. Of the 500 million active Christians worldwide, 300 million have experienced the Charismatic renewal.
9. The charismatic family alone accounts for 14,000 denominations spread across 8,000 ethnolinguistic cultures and 7,000 languages. It is increasing by 54,000 new members per day and nineteen million members per year. It is active in 80 percent of the over 3,000 largest cities of the world.
10. The Charismatic renewal has also surged through the Catholic church worldwide for twenty-five years. At least 7 percent of the world's 700 million Catholics have been a part of this. One

of the impacts of such renewal is that currently the "Evange-lization 2000" offices in the Vatican have set as their goal that 51 percent of humanity will profess allegiance to Jesus Christ by the year 2000.

11. One billion nominal Christians worldwide provide the Holy Spirit a "starting place" as revival comes because they already have some exposure to and understanding of the gospel.

12. In the hands of over four million full-time Christian workers, there are forty-two million computers, fifty million Bibles, and billions of dollars in uncommitted tithes to support them. Money, manpower, and technology are available to the cause of Christ as never before.

13. There are 2,520 Christian radio/TV stations around the world. About 4.6 billion of the world's population receive gospel radio broadcasts in their own tongue.

14. In 1992, 67,440 new Christian book titles were published world-wide.

15. Christian periodicals published worldwide in 1992 were over 26,000.

16. Over the past twenty-five years an inclusive, global evangelical network has been forming. It includes such groupings as the Lausanne Committee for World Evangelization; the A.D. 2000 and Beyond movement; International Charismatic Congress on World Evangelization; and The World Evangelical Fellowship.

17. There is a growing sense of the potential for closure in fulfilling the Great Commission. Some speak of this as the "final frontiers," or Christ's victory among the "last of the giants." There is a spon-taneous networking of plans worldwide focused on the year 2000. In fact, currently there are as many as seventy international strate-gies in motion, each of which is focused on total world evange-lization by the early part of the twenty-first century.

18. There are currently fifty-six "Great Commission global networks" that bring together ministries concentrated on more than two hundred countries, seeking the fulfillment of the Great Com-mission.

19. Five hundred million of the world's Christians are intentionally committed to help fulfill the Great Commission. This number

is growing by 6.9 percent a year, which is six times faster than the population generally.

20. There are 3,970 mission agencies (1,000 of them in the Two-Thirds World), 285,250 career missionaries, 180,000 short-term missionaries, and 400 Great Commission research centers worldwide.

21. The non-Western missions movement is growing five times faster than the Western.

22. Currently there are 49,000 Two-Thirds World missionaries, 35.5 percent of the total Protestant missionary force worldwide. It is expected that by the year 2000, the number of Two-Thirds World missionaries will surpass those of Western nations.

23. In the past twenty-five years there has been an unprecedented explosion of Christian service organizations worldwide, forming many multinational ministries.

24. In the United States alone, 350 new mission agencies have been established since 1950.

25. With the great increase of youth mission movements worldwide, we are seeing more than 100,000 young people involved in short-term missions each year.

26. Worldwide, Christians have a total annual personal income of about eight trillion dollars. However, Christians spend only 1.5 percent or 130 billion per year on their churches and home ministries. Only 0.1 percent goes to foreign missions. There is massive untapped financial potential for fulfilling the Great Commission.

27. If the blood of the saints is the seed of the church, then the great increase in martyrdom should encourage us. No sixty years in all history since the crucifixion has seen so many men and women martyred for their faith. It will reach an estimated 500,000 a year by 2000.

Illustrations from Asia

1. A mass movement into organized Christianity began to get under way in East Asia in 1980. That year there were only sixteen million Christians in all of East Asia. In less than ten years there were eighty million.

2. In Thailand recently nearly two million people indicated decisions to trust Christ, with 4,000 being trained to share their faith and over 3,000 new churches planted. By the most conservative estimates, church growth there has been over 600 percent in fourteen years.

3. In Laos the church has grown from 5,000 to 20,000 in five years. To overcome government opposition, many believers are fasting, some electing to eat only on weekends.

4. Nagaland, India once considered 90 percent Christian, is now claiming to be 100 percent Christian.

5. Missouram, in Northeast India, has seen such church growth that they are now planning to send off 3,000 missionaries by the year 2000.

6. A recent seminar in Calcutta on unreached people groups spawned 400 prayer groups that have established new ministries among sixteen people groups.

7. It is estimated that there are 15,000 Christian baptisms per week in Hindu India, and nearly 80 percent are responding to Christ through some kind of supernatural encounter.

8. In India a recent survey indicated that 25 percent of the people would like to be Christians if they could stay within their family groupings.

9. In Indonesia the percentage of Christians is so high the government is afraid to print it.

10. The church in Korea is praying and preparing to send out 3,000 missionaries into China alone, once the door is open for such an exchange.

11. In Japan, three major prayer movements have arisen and are beginning to work together with a common focus on full revival in the church and the total evangelization of their nation (which currently is less than 1 percent Christian). Hundreds of thousands of Japanese Christians are being drawn into these movements.

12. The church in Taiwan has united in the A.D. 2000 gospel movement to organize prayer, resources, manpower, and full cooperation for the total evangelization of Taiwan by the year 2000, including the sending out of at least 200 cross-cultural mis-

sionaries to reach non-Chinese-speaking, unreached people groups elsewhere.

13. There is a rapid rise in the number of Christians in Mongolia. In 1991 there were fifteen believers in a country of two million people. Today the number is at least 1,000 and growing, with many "worship centers" planted in major population centers.
14. In China an estimated 25,000 people a day are coming to Christ.
15. It is estimated that there may be as many as seventy million Christians in China today, which would be 5 percent of the population.
16. Even the three self-church movement (government supervised) churches in China have increased from 4,000 to 7,000 churches in just five years.
17. The Chinese government has permitted Bibles to be distributed to every Christian in China for the first time since 1949.
18. Currently a movement of prayer among Chinese churches throughout the Chinese world has thousands praying for revival in the churches of America.

Illustrations from Europe

1. Each night in Billy Graham's Pro-Christ '93 in united Germany, he brought the gospel to 1.8 million people of Europe—the largest audience ever addressed in a crusade.
2. In the Commonwealth of Independent States (former Soviet Union) after seven years of oppression, the Christian movement is 36 percent of the population (more than 100 million), which is five times the size the Communist Party ever reached. And now some believe that Russia particularly is entering into the greatest spiritual harvest in history.
3. A coalition of over fifteen Christian missions (called CoMission) is cooperating to work in a complementary way to assist Russian believers in the great harvest that is now taking place there.
4. In Albania just a few years ago, Christians were martyred for their faith. Now the government has revamped their entire educational system with major emphasis on training in biblical Christian values.
5. In Romania the "Army of the Lord" within the Romanian Orthodox church is working effectively toward personal and na-

225

tional, moral and spiritual renaissance, focused on the centrality of Christ.

6. Thousands of new house churches have begun in England within
   the past fifteen years despite dismal projections that we would
   see the rapid demise of Christianity in the British Isles within
   this generation.

7. In major cities in England and in capital cities across Europe,
   hundreds of thousands of Christians have become involved in
   "Marches for Jesus," which in the last couple of years have presented many Europeans with a dramatic public witness for
   Christ.

8. Norway is the largest missionary sending nation in the world,
   when comparing numbers of missionaries to population. It has
   inspired a standard for churches in every nation toward which
   we must pray and work.

Illustrations from Africa

1. It is estimated that there may be as many as 20,000 Africans
   coming to Christ every day and that 40 percent of the continent's population identifies now with Christianity in some
   form.

2. In 1992 probably the largest meeting of African pastors in history took place in Nigeria, with 11,000 pastors participating
   from 2,156 denominations in forty-five African countries. They
   committed themselves to the full evangelization of Africa by the
   year 2000.

3. After seventeen dark years of persecution at the hands of the
   Marxist dictatorship, thousands of Ethiopians are now coming
   to Christ. In one area more than 10,000 were baptized over a
   two-month period.

4. During a recent crusade under the cooperative efforts of charismatic and evangelical churches, the Central African Republic
   saw 200,000 people respond to the gospel in only six nights.

5. South Africa is on the brink of the dismantling of apartheid and
   the democratization of this multiracial country. Many believe
   this will open up the spiritual dynamic of the South African
   church (of all races) to impact the whole of Africa and the cause

of Christ worldwide as a result of what South African Christians have learned about the gospel of reconciliation in the crucible of oppression.

Illustrations from Latin America

1. The evangelical movement is growing three times faster than the population at large.
2. Altogether there are 150 Latin American mission agencies, sending out more than 3,000 missionaries.
3. Continent-wide congresses designed to set new goals for the role of Protestant churches in world evangelization have brought together thousands of leaders for prayer and planning over the past ten years.
4. In Argentina recently an estimated three million prayed to receive Christ following one television presentation of the gospel.
5. The Base Community movement that began in Latin America almost exclusively among the poor, with its strong emphasis on prayer for their families and their cities, "may be more pervasive than the Charismatic renewal worldwide," says Richard Lovelace. It is estimated that there may be five million small group base communities, modeled off those that have brought significant renewal throughout much of Latin America, distributed among the world of the desperately poor by A.D. 2000, enabling the poor (46 percent of the world) to be evangelizers in their own right.

Illustrations from Islam

1. Among many of the over 800 million Muslims, Jesus is increasingly revered more highly than Mohammed. And thousands of Muslims are turning to the Bible in East Africa.
2. More Muslims have come to Christ in the past decade than in the previous 1,000 years combined.
3. Recently as many as 25,000 people made personal decisions to follow Christ as a result of the effort of 150 churches to reach out in Egypt. Before that time there were only 15,000 registered believers in that one denomination.

227

4. In Iran there were only 2,700 evangelical Christians fifteen years ago. Now there are 12,000, with another 12,000 to be found scattered across the Western world.

Illustrations from the United States

1. People in the United States seem to be incorrigibly religious. The majority of American people believe that the values and attitudes that make America work are "divinely ordained" and that many national expressions are based on religious convictions.
2. Ninety-seven out of 100 say their lives have been touched by Christ.
3. There is a growing search for spiritual meaning in America. *Time* calls it a "generation of seekers." So does *Newsweek* in its cover article "A Time to Seek," discussing the return to religion among baby boomers. A recent Barna Research Group survey discovered that 90 percent pray to God, 61 percent make specific requests of God, 60 percent do so every day, and 46 percent listen silently for the answers. There is obviously an openness for the kind of breakthrough that comes in revival.
4. The evangelical movement in the United States is the most organized, populous, financially prosperous, strategic thinking, visible, mobile, culturally pervasive, and prolific of any genuine Christian movement in the history of the world.
5. There are 2,000 denominations with nearly 500,000 churches. Sixty percent of American people are in some faith community.
6. There is a string of over 1,000 Christian radio stations that currently blankets the country and can provide a significant resource of pulling the Christian community together in a time of revival.
7. The church is sophisticated in its use of all forms of mass media and highly attuned to its audience, helping to transform the popular Evangelical movement into the most dynamic sector of modern religion.
8. Churches are increasingly being saturated with small group fellowships and care groups to help bring lay people into the ministry of the church.

9. The church is highly innovative and entrepreneurial, with the ability to identify personal and social needs and then determine specific programs, projects, and ministries to meet those needs.
10. Evangelicals are leading the debate regarding abortion, morality and family issues, religion and education. At the same time, mainline activists are focused on civil rights, economic distribution, peace making, and environmental issues. As the two groups learn from each other and complement each other, they are able to give to the nation a more comprehensive display of the Lordship of Christ.
11. The number of Bible-believing congregations that can be launch points for Christ's transforming work throughout our society far outstrip the combined number of ACLU, Planned Parenthood, and NOW offices nationwide.
12. In the U.S. there is now tremendous opportunity for reaching blocks of unreached people groups that have settled in our own nation.
13. There is an increasing concern for evangelism within historic mainline denominations.
14. A widespread passion for the coming of the Holy Spirit today may have partially displaced passion for Christ's return tomorrow.
15. Evangelicals have virtually taken over the field of foreign missions. Fifty years ago evangelical agencies sponsored 40 percent of all American missionaries; today the figure is about 90 percent.
16. There is a growing consensus across the nation among spiritual leaders that the only hope for the nation is revival in the church and that the only hope for revival is a movement of united prayer. Accordingly many are leading the way into what has already become by many standards the greatest prayer movement for revival in the history of our nation.

Appendix 4
From Chapter 9:
The Distinctive Praying

Distinctive Praying: Inspiring Accounts!

Premise: God is stirring up his people to pray specifically, increasingly, and persistently for world revival. He is doing this by giving believers everywhere a common vision for the need for revival, a broad-based agreement on what the coming revival will look like, and a growing conviction that revival is at hand for those who seek it together. If God is stirring up the church to pray with this distinctive focus and consensus, he will not let us pray in vain. He has promised to hear and answer us fully. We can prepare for the answers with confidence.

The worldwide prayer movement is accelerating so rapidly that it is difficult to stay current on examples! As you read the following examples, keep asking yourself these questions: 1. If God is setting his people to pray in such an unprecedented way, to seek him for world revival, how should this affect the ways I pray day by day? 2. Am I confident God is ready to answer this global groundswell of intercession? If so, how should I begin to prepare for the answers even before they are fully revealed?

Stories from North America

1. Every year tens of thousands of Christians from thousands of churches and hundreds of denominations are uniting in mass prayer rallies in cities across the continent. Hundreds of thou-

sands of others are joined on a daily basis by radio broadcasts that lead the nation in prayer. In addition, 800 numbers offer immediate access to information on the rapidly growing prayer movement and on the ways God is answering with preliminary phases of revival.

2. Twenty-eight thousand Canadian Christians recently met in a sports stadium for a "Save the Nation" prayer rally, claiming the promise of 2 Chronicles 7:14. It was sponsored by three hundred churches and coupled with an evangelistic outreach afterward.

3. In some cities there have actually been traffic jams at the location of mass prayer rallies because so many Christians showed up for the prayer meeting. In one rally people literally had to be turned away from the prayer meeting at the largest auditorium in the city because there were no more seats or parking places.

4. Groups of seventy pastors each gathered in four different cities (in four regions of the nation) on the same week to pray for nationwide revival. Most of the groups prayed and fasted for twenty-four hours or longer. No one in any of the groups knew that similar pastors' gatherings were taking place simultaneously elsewhere. This is part of a growing phenomenon of pastors' prayer gatherings in many cities.

5. Hundreds of leaders of citywide prayer movements have met over a period of eight years in annual Consultations on United Prayer, to hear reports, to strategize together, and to hold days of intercession over their cities.

6. In 1993, 300 leaders, from 166 denominations and Christian ministries, from thirty-five states, representing almost half of the Protestant churches of North America, gathered for a National Consultation on United Prayer, issuing a national call to united prayer as a result. A few weeks later a three-day National Prayer Summit took place in Canada with 200 leaders from across the nation. A National Prayer Summit in the United States has called for a gathering of 600 leaders to spend four days of "prayer only" for revival in the nation.

7. In the Pacific Northwest where only 3 percent of the population claims any church membership, over recent months as

many as 3,000 from nearly 100 different communities have gathered together for Prayer Summits, involving thirty to forty pastors from a single community, spending four days of intercession for one another and for their cities. They have returned to mobilize their churches into citywide concerted prayer and have successfully mobilized nearly 100,000 in united prayer within a short time. (See Joe Aldrich's *Prayer Summits: Seeking God's Agenda for Your Community*. Portland: Multnomah Press, 1992.)

8. Some 800,000 Americans marched in more than 300 cities in all fifty states in a "traveling prayer movement" called Marches for Jesus. In places like Pittsburgh some 40,000 marchers turned out on this day to stand in the gap with praise and prayer for their cities and for the nations.

9. A significant groundswell of prayer among high school students is being registered in a number of ways. National conferences are taking place, involving thousands of high school students who come together for three days of nothing but prayer for revival on their campuses and throughout the nation. In recent years on the opening day of school in September, nearly two million high school students have gathered in early morning prayer groups around the flagpoles on tens of thousands of high school campuses, to begin the school year interceding for revival on their campuses. Many of these September gatherings have resulted in thousands of ongoing prayer groups throughout the year. Recently a nationwide evangelistic outreach to high schools through television was preceded by weeks of prayer concerts inaugurated and led by high school students in cities from coast to coast. As a result an estimated 75,000 students made commitments to Christ on the night of the evangelistic outreach, one of the largest responses ever among high school students in a single evangelistic event.

10. A similar movement is occurring among college students. At one university on the West Coast, 300–500 students meet every week to pray for revival. At a major student missions conference involving nearly 20,000 a whole night was recently given to intercede for the worldwide advance of the kingdom. And

233

college students have sponsored grassroots regional conferences to pray and train together for mobilizing revival prayer on their campuses.

11. Many "mass crusade" organizations are beginning to build crusade strategies that not only insure the success of the crusade itself, but also help launch ongoing movements of united prayer for spiritual awakening within the host cities long after the crusades are over.

12. Recently a "prayer tour" was set up for many cities in which major sporting events were scheduled, to work in partnership with the evangelistic outreach at the events and to motivate Christians within a city to draw together in mass prayer rallies for revival long after the outreach was over.

13. The leaders of some of the major Christian foundations in the United States convened to consider their responsibilities in undergirding the growing prayer movement as well as the ministries of prayer in many missionary organizations through the investments of their foundation monies.

14. For the last few years America's National Day of Prayer has seen a tremendous increase in the participation of millions of Americans who take the first Thursday of May to intercede for our country. They have done so through morning prayer breakfasts, evening Concerts of Prayer, twenty-four-hour prayer watches in churches, and prayer rallies at city hall. Recently tens of thousands gathered at municipal buildings to pray for America in more than 2,500 locations.

15. A number of national prayer networks have formed to help encourage and strengthen this prayer movement for revival. Among them: The Denominational Prayer Leaders Network links denominational leaders from over thirty denominations, who resource each other and pray and strategize together regarding wholesale denominational prayer strategies. The National Youth Leaders Prayer Forum links leaders of some sixty national youth ministries who share a common commitment to mobilize young people into united prayer for revival. America's National Prayer Committee has set the pace for this prayer movement and provided counsel and encouragement for over

fifteen years. The committee represents prayer leaders from a broad spectrum of ministries and denominations. The Spiritual Warfare Network is a unique prayer coalition bringing together the leaders of over thirty prayer ministries that are specifically focused on intercession to defeat the dark spiritual forces arrayed against revival in the church and the worldwide advance of the kingdom.

16. A number of denominations have devoted their annual denominational meetings to explore a denomination-wide call to united prayer for revival. In a number of cases a "year of prayer for revival" has resulted. Currently within one denomination, "solemn assemblies" are taking place within individual congregations and among congregations within specific regions. At the same time thousands of churches have been linked up in a prayer watch that covers every hour of every day and night of the entire year with prayer by intercessory groups within one or more churches. Another denomination that sought to mobilize 1,000 retired pastors to give one hour a day in prayer for revival have found themselves overwhelmed with commitments by some 5,000 pastors.

17. Members of one of the fastest growing urban churches in America (it grew from 500 to 5,000 in five years) recently shut down all church activities but Sunday morning worship to give themselves for a period of weeks to pray for revival. Every night they saw thousands of their people coming together in prayer; they sustained the thrust for over eight weeks. In another city a Lutheran church has taken on a full-time pastor of prayer and has seen 2,000 of their members turning out once a week for united prayer. Many churches are experiencing similar enthusiastic responses.

18. A seminary professor in New England has guided a daily noontime prayer meeting on his campus, praying for revival and missions, for almost eighteen years. Out of these gatherings God has salted the whole region with pastors and Christian workers who have made concerted prayer a hallmark of their ministries.

19. In New England a prayer movement is growing on many levels in a five-state area. Some region-wide prayer rallies have at-

tracted thousands of participants in a region of the country that is one of the least churched.

20. In another city 300 churches have formed an ongoing prayer movement focused on praying for revival throughout the Christian community, so that they may have a strategic impact on hundreds of thousands of international visitors who will be involved in international sporting events within their city over a four-year period.

21. In another city a movement of hundreds of women in prayer has adopted 1,000 of the pastors of that city, so that each one is prayed for daily by at least two intercessors.

22. In an underevangelized city on the East Coast, a prayer movement developed, primarily by pastoral leadership from scores of African American churches, with a focused consensus that if they would build a citywide prayer movement, God would pour out revival on the whole city. This movement was also directly linked with a mass evangelistic outreach.

23. In another urban center, hundreds of churches are pulling together for a "Lord's Watch" (from Isa. 62:6–7). Every evening of every day of the year is covered by one or more churches with intercession for spiritual awakening. The assigned churches for each night pass the torch along to the groups for the next night by a phone call of report and encouragement.

24. Church leaders in one of America's largest cities have scheduled certain weekends for Concerts of Prayer in ten or more different regions of the city simultaneously. These have involved thousands of people being led by hundreds of pastors from all kinds of denominational and ethnic backgrounds.

25. In one of the most dangerous sections of a major city hundreds of pastors took the "risk" to gather together in a church that was guarded by armed police in order to spend a half day interceding for revival in that section of the city as well as in the whole city.

26. One citywide prayer movement made up of 300 churches has set its sights on a seven-year commitment, involving both pastors' prayer gatherings and citywide prayer rallies as well as local church prayer gatherings, to pray unrelentingly for revival until it comes.

27. A prayer movement in a large city in the Midwest that has been brewing for almost nine years has now broken forth into 6,000–7,000 person prayer rallies, involving over 300 congregations, plus rallies involving thousands of teenagers. All of this is focused on prayer for revival. And all of it is impacting the lives of pastors and local congregations on an ongoing basis.

28. In a recent prayer rally in the Midwest the participating pastors were invited to come forward for specific prayer for them and for their ministries and for revival in their congregations. As 200 walked to the front, the audience of 5,000 gave them a standing ovation and then extended their hands in prayer for God to bring spiritual renewal to each one.

29. In Southern California as many as 1,000 pastors at a time have gathered quarterly for three to four hours of united prayer for revival in their cities. They have also assembled their churches in prayer rallies of as many as 10,000. When urban race-riots took place, about 700 area pastors who had been united in this movement of prayer joined in prayer and ministry in the aftermath of the riots. Lloyd Ogilvie of Hollywood Presbyterian says, "Being part of this prayer movement has been a profoundly moving experience. The separateness, aloneness, and self-gratifying independence have been replaced by honest sharing of our needs, penetrating prayer for one another, and unified, shared discipleship and mission in our city." Dr. Benjamin F. Reid, a respected African American pastor says, "One of the greatest spiritual blessings to occur in our community is this movement of prayer. God initiated this interracial, cross-cultural, inter-church prayer gathering. And the Holy Spirit has honored it. I see it as a major spiritual force for good in the future as we continue to glorify Christ and to intercede for the deep spiritual needs of our city."

30. Plans are underway to bring one million men to the Mall in Washington, D.C., to repent before the nation on behalf of the church and to pray for a national revival.

Of course behind all of these illustrations (and there are hundreds more that could be given) are the countless prayer bands that

237

have persevered "underground" for almost a generation in their intercession for God to give a prayer awakening throughout North America.

International Stories

1. In 1984 the International Prayer Assembly for World Evangelization was held in Seoul, Korea, under the sponsorship of the Lausanne Committee for World Evangelization and the World Evangelical Fellowship. It brought together 3,000 prayer mobilizers from seventy nations. They not only prayed for world revival but strategized on how to mobilize citywide and nationwide movements of prayer. It was the first event of its kind in the history of the church.
2. For over ten years a formal, international network of national intercessory movements has brought together over sixty countries with sustained national prayer movements for revival.
3. Out of a 1989 International Congress for World Evangelization, a "global prayer strategy" was launched to mobilize millions of Christians worldwide into a commitment to spend the first five minutes of their day (as the sun is rising) to intercede for world revival. As the sun moves across each time zone, the torch of prayer is being passed around the clock, around the world. Intercessors from 180 countries are now involved. Everyone uses John 17 as his or her prayer agenda.
4. A multinational prayer committee recently sponsored an International Prayer Leaders Retreat, bringing together national prayer mobilizers from twenty-six nations to spend days in prayer and strategizing together.
5. Out of the increased burden worldwide for evangelism in this decade have arisen amazing prayer initiatives. In October of 1993 over three million intercessors, including at least one million Korean Christians, were enrolled to pray and fast for the major unreached people groups. As well, 240 teams of intercessors were deployed throughout various nations for on-site prayer meetings among the unreached peoples themselves. One international prayer leader concluded that up to that point, it was the most massive, focused prayer campaign in history.

6. In 1984 another worldwide prayer focus was planned. Called "A Day to Change the World," it was dubbed as the largest prayer meeting in history. The goal was 160 million, or 30 percent of the world's practicing Christians, to be linked up by satellite to intercede unitedly over a twenty-four-hour period for world revival. Concerts of Prayer and Marches for Jesus were planned for almost every capital city of the world that day as well as in thousands of other cities, involving an expected twenty-five million Christians. All of this came almost ten years to the day after the "unveiling" of God's worldwide prayer movement at the International Prayer Assembly.

7. In various church traditions there are efforts to mobilize prayer on a global scale, such as with the Moravian denomination. Increasingly since 1957, it has been the goal of the international church that the "hourly intercession" (known in some places as the "prayer watch"), first begun under the leadership of Zinzendorf in the early 1700s, should be restored worldwide. Now year after year each of the provinces of the Moravian church in many nations takes a block of time that it is responsible to divide among its congregations. After that, local members or families volunteer to cover a half or full hour sometime in the day or night to be in prayer for the stated needs of the church. Thus a chain of prayer is sustained. Devoted members become part of a corporate prayer experience across national and geographical lines. And remarkable spiritual growth has been reported.

8. Even Christians within the Catholic church have been called to a worldwide prayer campaign. Under the auspices of the New Evangelization 2000 offices in the Vatican, millions of Catholics are being mobilized to pray for world revival. In their official publication entitled *Prayer: Taking Hold of God's Power*, they write:

Without prayer, Evangelization becomes the effort of men doing what they are able to do. But evangelizers are meant to be instruments of what God can do, as He transforms us into nothing less than a "new humanity." Prayer goes with the evangelization the way air goes with breathing. There is no movement, no vitality and no power without it.

The "Worldwide Prayer Campaign" is an effort to generate the power needed for dynamic new evangelization in anticipation of the year

2000. We need to join forces in begging Almighty God in his mercy to move millions of human hearts to proclaim the Good News of salvation and other tens of millions to hear that proclamation. If God hears us praying together from one end of the globe to the other, he will give us the power for bringing the Good News to every nation. We must implore God to change each of us radically, to move us out of our fears and apathy, transforming us into courageous and inspired evangelizers, ready to carry the Gospel message boldly into the third Christian millennium.

9. One unique facet of prayer, found predominately in the Catholic church, is the base communities made up primarily of Christians among the poor in Latin America, Africa, and Asia. Currently millions are involved in these small prayer cells, focusing prayer on their families and their cities.
10. Prayer marches continue to grow both in numbers and participating cities. Nearly ten million were recently involved, in 1,000 cities, in forty-three countries. As Christians conduct these "traveling prayer meetings," they sing and pray through the streets at the center of their city, finally converging for a concluding concert of prayer to ask God to awaken their cities to Christ. As a result, new levels of prayer have also been initiated within individual congregations.

Stories from Europe

1. A number of prayer leaders from European nations have formed Prayer Link, so that they might coordinate continent-wide prayer thrusts.
2. In France, one of the most difficult mission fields in Europe, a national consultation on united prayer transpired to strengthen the growing prayer movement throughout that land.
3. Throughout Germany, Scandinavia, and other countries, a week of prayer for revival is conducted once a year.
4. In England the Evangelical Alliance has set up a prayer department with a full-time prayer secretary to work with the burgeoning prayer movement throughout the British Isles.

5. In 1987 the Soviet church called upon Christians around the world to pray for them. They cited lack of unity and other problems, but the unwritten request was for deliverance from seventy years of captivity (it was the seventieth anniversary of the Bolshevik Revolution). At least 100 prayer networks worldwide responded, making January a special month of prayer for that nation. The first working day of February, President Gorbachev released all religious prisoners, and that began a chain of events that has led to the spiritual revolution that we see today in the former Soviet Union. At the heart of that revolution is the continuation of united prayer across the body of Christ there as well as in parts of Eastern Europe.

Stories from Africa

1. In West Africa in countries like the Ivory Coast, Ghana, and Nigeria, God has raised up full-time prayer mobilization ministries that are not only ministering to local churches but sponsoring nationwide and region-wide congresses on united prayer for revival.
2. In South Africa interdenominational and multiracial prayer bands have been active for a number of years, and many believe they are the fountainhead of the social and spiritual transformations now taking place in South Africa. A center for guiding this prayer movement has been set up, calling itself after one of South Africa's greatest prayer leaders: The Andrew Murray Center for Prayer, Revival and Mission.
3. The president of Zambia joined 3,000 Christians for a prayer rally in this south central African nation, arranged by the Evangelical Fellowship of Zambia. The rally began with a march through the city's central streets and on to the local show grounds. After the service, the president invited a number of ministers to come to his house to spend hours more praying for the nation.
4. In Kenya expatriate missionaries have been assigned to work full-time in prayer mobilization, not only among the missionary communities but also in league with national Kenyan prayer leaders. In Nairobi at least 600 Christians gather once a month for all-night vigils of prayer for revival in their nation.

Stories from Asia

1. There are more than one million charismatic Catholics in India, many of them organized into over 10,000 prayer groups focused on praying for Muslims and Hindus to be won to Christ and undergirding mass preaching and healing crusades that sometimes attract crowds of up to 100,000.

2. In India dozens of national missionary societies have mobilized thousands of prayer cells to fast and pray on a weekly basis for revival and the full evangelization of their nation. Many of these prayer bands have sent out some of their own number as missionaries, so that currently hundreds are taking the gospel to unreached people groups within their nation because of this prayer movement.

3. Recently the largest congregation in Korea scheduled a prayer meeting that filled the Olympic Stadium in Seoul. They held it during working hours on Friday so the attendance would not go beyond the capacity of the stadium! At another time within the same summer months 700 college students gathered for training to mobilize concerted prayer on all the campuses of Korea, while 100,000 high school students gathered for three days and nights of prayer and praise in the Olympic Stadium, as did 500,000 in the Yoida Plaza in the center of the city for twelve hours of fasting and revival prayer.

4. In Japan three prayer movements have emerged simultaneously seeking revival in the churches of a nation where less than 1 percent have become Christians. One movement emphasizes worship and prayer for revival; one emphasizes evangelism and prayer for revival; and one emphasizes mobilization of revival prayer. This third movement was launched out of three nights of prayer with 60,000 participants convened in the largest baseball stadium in Japan.

5. In Taiwan a national, interdenominational movement to evangelize the whole nation by the twenty-first century has built all of its strategies on the back of a national prayer movement. Thousands have been trained and mobilized for this prayer effort, which also has its sights set on sending out hundreds of Chinese workers among other unreached people groups worldwide. Re-

cently in a city of 750,000 that has only 6,000 Christians total, nearly 1,000 came out every night for three nights to pray for revival. That was fully 16 percent of the total Christian population.

6. In Nepal, a predominately Hindu country, evangelism and discipleship are officially illegal; it is a criminal act to attempt to convert anyone. But even so, a national prayer movement has emerged, including national prayer assemblies, with a goal to establish 8,000 new churches by the twenty-first century. Many prayer groups have been mobilized in some of the remotest areas of the Himalayas.

Stories from the Middle East

1. A missiologist, upon returning from a research tour of the Middle East, found that the great breakthroughs in the Muslim world are taking place where missionary teams spend hours a day in intercession for the advance of Christ's kingdom.
2. A Christian woman from Pakistan has raised up hundreds of Middle Eastern women in a prayer movement for revival, with prayer bands to be found in most Middle Eastern countries.
3. Recently an international mission organization helped to mobilize 100,000 Christians from seventy missions, churches, and related groups into thirty days of prayer for Muslim evangelism. This thrust was held to coincide with Ramadan (the month in Islam when daytime fasting is observed annually).

Stories from Latin America

1. In Costa Rica 600 pastors gathered for a national congress on evangelization. They began with three days of focus on prayer mobilization for their nation, convinced that only in this way would any other plans succeed. Prayer committees were established for eighteen regions of the nation.
2. In Mexico City a revival prayer group of 120 became so effective in their prayers and were so threatening to the residents of that part of the city that one night their prayer meeting was broken up by 10,000 angry residents who chased them into the streets with clubs. The Christians acquired a restraining order

from the courts so that they could continue to pray for spiritual victories in their city.

3. One mission thrust that is focusing on the evangelization of the major cities of Latin America has taken as its primary agenda the targeting of every home in a city for prayer. These groups raise up intercessors for those homes not only within the body of Christ in that city or nation but also from Christians in many other parts of the world who receive maps of particular neighborhoods with homes identified. This way they can focus their prayers not only for revival in the churches of that city but for unreached families as well.

4. In Argentina a similar evangelistic plan has set as its goal the establishing of 2,000 "prayer houses" or family groups who will systematically cover their neighborhoods house by house with intercession. In addition, frequent prayer vigils take place uniting all the intercessors of the city for all night intercession. This is combined with visitation to each home at least three different times, plus the proclamation of the gospel through television, radio, crusades, and social projects. The pastors of the city are also meeting twice a month in prayer retreats and vigils.

Notes

Introduction: Is There Any Hope?

1. Jeffrey C. Sheler, "Spiritual America" in *U.S. News and World Report*, April 4, 1994, 48–59.

2. Summarized and analyzed by Doug LeBlanc, "Read 'em and Weep" in *World*, March 27, 1993, 26–27.

3. Lance Morrow, "Video Warriors In Los Angeles" in *Time*, May 11, 1992, 68.

4. Referenced and analyzed by *New York Times* syndicated columnist Anthony Lewis in *Wisconsin State Journal*, March 9, 1994.

5. Chuck Colson, "Reaching the Pagan Mind" in *Christianity Today*, vol. 36, Nov. 9, 1992, 112.

6. Mark Bubeck, *The Satanic Revival*. San Bernardino, Calif.: Here's Life Publishers, 1991.

7. George Barna, *The Invisible Generation: Baby Busters*. Glendale, Calif.: Barna Research Group, Ltd., 1992, 44, 85, 89.

8. Dick Eastman, *The Jericho Hour*. Orlando, Fla.: Creation House Publishers, 1994, 14.

9. For example, forty prominent Roman Catholic and evangelical leaders signed an "unofficial" document agreeing to work together to "contend against all that opposes Christ and His cause." They also covenanted to strengthen societal structures such as the family, church, and charitable agencies. These included leaders such as Chuck Colson, Pat Robertson, J. I. Packer, John White, and John Richard Neuhaus, along with a number of Catholic archbishops. There has been subsequent concern expressed about the need for further theological refinement in the document that was produced. But most agree that the concerns and motivations that brought this historic convocation together are worthy of further exploration. At the very least, it is a harbinger of the increased determination among evangelical leaders to uncover biblical approaches for Christ-centered unity in the body of Christ around the issues of vision, prayer, and preparation for the coming world revival. Even as I write, I am working with the National Prayer Committee, the Denominational Prayer Leaders Network, the Lausanne Committee, and other coalitions to bring together a "Forum on National Revival," designed for national evangelical leaders, across the spectrum of the body of Christ, who have been given by God nationally recognized leadership. They will have opportunity to discuss the points at which we can reach consensus on the shape of biblical revival, and on what we believe God is getting ready to do for the rest of this decade.

10. Paul Johnson, *Modern Times: From the Twenties to the Nineties*. New York: Harper-Collins, 1991, 784.

Chapter 1: The Rising Hope for World Revival

1. William A. Henry III, "Ready Or Not, Here It Comes!" in *Beyond the Year 2000—What to Expect in the New Millennium,* Fall 1992, 34.

2. Lance Morrow, "A Cosmic Moment" in *Time,* Fall 1992, 6.

3. Morrow, "A Cosmic Moment," 6.

4. John Naisbitt, *Megatrends 2000.* New York: Manno, 1990.

5. David Briggs, "International Survey Finds Signs of Religious Revival" in *Wisconsin State Journal*, May 18, 1993.

6. Henry Gruenwald, "The Year 2000: Is It the End—or Just the Beginning?" in *Time*, March 30, 1992, 73–76.

7. Kant is quoted by W. P. Kaufmann, *The Faith of a Heretic.* New York: Doubleday Anchor, 1961, VII.

8. Jack Hayford, *A Passion for Fullness.* Dallas: Word Publishers, 1989, 2.

9. Timothy Jones, "Great Awakenings: Americans Are Becoming Fascinated with Prayer and Spirituality. Is It Time to Rejoice?" in *Christianity Today,* November 8, 1993, 23–25.

10. A saying originally attributed to Woody Allen.

11. David L. McKenna, *The Coming Great Awakening: New Hope for the Nineties.* Downers Grove, Ill.: InterVarsity Press, 1990; Matthew David, *Revive Us Again! Realistic Thinking on Revival.* Ferndale, Mich.: Harvest Time, 1990; Robert Coleman, *The Spark That Ignites: God's Promise to Revive the Church through You.* Minneapolis: World Wide Publications, 1989; Brian Mills, *Preparing for Revival.* Eastbourne, England: Kingsway Publications, 1990; Wesley Duewel, *Revival Fire.* Grand Rapids: Zondervan, 1975.

12. Billy Graham, "The King Is Coming" in *Let the Earth Hear His Voice: Congress on World Evangelization in Lausanne, Switzerland.* Edited by J. D. Douglas. Minneapolis: World Wide Publications, 1975, 1466.

13. Paul Cedar, quoted in *NAE Action,* March-April 1992, 55–56.

14. Don Argue, "America Needs Revival" in *Charisma,* June 1993, 18.

15. Published first in *World Wide Challenge,* March 1983, 29, but Bright has often stated this in my hearing on various occasions over the past few years.

16. John Perkins, "Is There Hope for Racial Reconciliation?" in *Urban Family,* Summer 1993, 17.

17. Mario Murillo, "Why We Need Fresh Fire" in *Charisma,* March 1993, 46.

18. Quoted by Jim Sire in a book review of *The American Hour* (Free Press, 1993) in *Christianity Today,* May 17, 1993, 51.

19. James Dobson, *Monthly Newsletter,* October 1991, 3. He has made similar pleas in subsequent newsletters.

20. Carl F. H. Henry, "Golden Opportunities Squandered" in *Christianity Today*, October 5, 1992, 34.

21 Jim Wallis, *Revive Us Again: A Sojourner's Story.* Nashville: Abingdon Press, 1983, 189.

22. William Abrahams, *The Coming Great Revival: Recovering the Full Evangelical Tradition.* San Francisco: Harper & Row, 1984, 112–13.

23. Roger Greenway, et. al., *Missions Now: This Generation.* Grand Rapids: Baker Book House, 1990.

24. Ibid.

25. Quoted in *AD 2000 and Beyond Handbook*. Edited by Luis Bush. Colorado Springs: A.D. 2000 and Beyond Movement, 1993, 19.

26. Richard Halverson, "Evangelicals' Subtle Infection" in *Christianity Today*, November 12, 1982, 47.

27. Dr. Orr shared this with me in personal conversation just weeks before he died. He often stated it publicly in lectures at Fuller Theological Seminary as well as at the Oxford Association for Revival. It was based on the words of Matthew Henry who said, "Whenever God is ready to show great mercies to His people, He always sets them a-praying."

28. David Barrett and Todd M. Johnson, *Our Globe and How to Reach It: Seeing the World Evangelized by A.D. 2000 and Beyond*. Birmingham, Ala.: New Hope, 1990, 27.

29. *Life*, "Why We Pray," vol. 17, March 1994, 54.

30. Richard Lovelace, "An Historical Look at the Cycles of Renewal" in Presbyterian and Reformed Ministry's *International Renewal News*, Spring 1993, 5–6.

31. John Naisbitt, *Megatrends*. New York: Warner Books, 1982, 252.

Chapter 2: People of Hope, People of Revival

1. Alain Baublil and Claude-Michel Schonberg, lyrics by Herbert Kretzmen, *Les Misérables*. Broadway premier, 1987.

2. Tom Sine, *Wild Hope: Crises Facing the Human Community on the Threshold of the Twenty-first Century*. Dallas: Word Publishing, 1991, 230.

3. J. I. Packer, "What Is Spiritual Renewal?" in Presbyterian and Reformed Ministry's *Renewal News*, Fall, 1991, 7.

4. Part of a response given by the executive director of the Prayer Summits, Terry Dirks, to *National and International Religion Report*, May 30, 1994, 4.

5. David Bryant, *In the Gap: What It Means to Be a World Christian*. Ventura, Calif.: Regal Books, 1986, 110.

6. David Bryant, *With Concerts of Prayer: Christians Joined for Spiritual Awakening and World Evangelization*. Ventura, Calif.: Regal Books, 1984.

7. J. Edwin Orr, *The Eager Feet: Evangelical Awakenings 1790–1830*. Chicago: Moody Press, 1975, 248.

8. J. I. Packer, *A Quest for Godliness: The Puritan Vision of the Christian Life*. Wheaton, Ill.: Crossway Books, 1990, 36.

9. Packer, *A Quest for Godliness*, 36.

10. Packer, *A Quest for Godliness*, 36.

11. Packer, *A Quest for Godliness*, 322.

12. George Eldon Ladd, *Theology of the New Testament*. Grand Rapids: Zondervan, 1974.

13. Donald G. Mostrom, *Christians Facing the Future*. New York: Diadem Communications, 1993, 86–87.

Chapter 3: Confidence Builders about the Hope at Hand

1. Robert Oscar Bakke, "The Concert of Prayer: Back to the Future" Doctoral diss., Gordon-Conwell Seminary, March, 1993.

2. Charles Finney, *Lectures on Revival*. New York: Fleming H. Revell, 1868, 294–99.

3. Attributed to Charles Spurgeon but source unknown.

4. A survey conducted by Focus on the Family in 1992 and reported to me by Dr. James Dobson in personal conversations at that time.

5. Bradley Baurain, "Urban Congress Urges 'New Visions' For City" in *Pulse,* June 24, 1994, 5.

6. Quoted by Michael Green in *I Believe in Satan's Downfall,* Grand Rapids: Eerdmans Publishing, 1981, 21.

7. Ed Silvoso, *That None May Perish: How to Reach Entire Cities for Christ through Prayer Evangelism.* Ventura, Calif.: Regal Books, 1994, 155.

8. From an interview with Desmond Tutu, "A Prisoner of Hope" in *Christianity Today,* October 5, 1992, 41.

Chapter 4: Confidence Builder 1: The Decisive Person

1. Robert Webber, *The Majestic Tapestry: How the Power of Early Christian Traditions Can Enrich Contemporary Faith.* Nashville: Thomas Nelson Publishers, 1986, 33.

2. Stephen Neill, *One Increasing Purpose: Lenten Meditations.* London: Bible Reading Fellowship, 1971.

3. David Mains, *Thy Kingship Come: A New Look At Christ's Kingdom Message.* Grand Rapids: Zondervan, 1989, 31.

4. Henri Nouwen, *With Open Hands.* Notre Dame, Ind.: Ave Maria Press, 1972.

5. Ian Murray, *The Puritan Hope.* Edinburgh: Banner of Truth Trust, 1979, 90.

6. I am deeply grateful to Richard Owen Roberts who first pointed out to me this concept developed by our spiritual forefathers.

7. Richard Owen Roberts, *Revival,* Wheaton, Ill.: Tyndale House Publishers, 1982, 107.

8. C. S. Lewis, *Chronicles of Narnia: The Lion, The Witch and The Wardrobe.* New York: Collier Books, 1950, 74–75.

Chapter 5: Confidence Builder 2: The Divine Pattern

1. D. Martyn Lloyd-Jones, *Joy Unspeakable.* Wheaton, Ill.: Harold Shaw Publishers, 275.

2. Elton Trueblood, *The Incendiary Fellowship.* New York: Harper & Row, 1978, 100.

3. Bryant, *With Concerts of Prayer.* See chapter 5, 95–106.

4. Walter Kaiser, *Quest for Renewal: Personal Revival in the Old Testament.* Chicago: Moody Press, 1986.

5. Lloyd-Jones, *Joy Unspeakable,* 100.

6. Lovelace, "Cycles of Renewal," 5.

7. J. Edwin Orr, *The Fervent Prayer: The Worldwide Impact of the Great Awakenings of 1858.* Chicago: Moody Press, 1974, 193.

8. Timothy Smith, *Revivalism and Social Reform: In Mid-Nineteenth Century America.* New York: Abingdon Press, 1955.

9. J. Edwin Orr, "Potent Answers to Persistent Prayers" in *The Rebirth of America.* Philadelphia: Arthur S. DeMos Foundation, 1986, 63–64.

10. James Burns, *The Laws of Revival.* Edited by Tom Phillips. Minneapolis: Billy Graham Evangelistic Association, 1992, 33.

11. Burns, *The Laws of Revival,* 34.

12. Burns, *The Laws of Revival,* 49–50.

13. Andrew Murray, *Key to the Missionary Problem.* Fort Washington, Pa.: Christian Literature Crusade, 1984.

14. Andrew Murray, *The State of the Church.* Fort Washington, Pa.: Christian Literature Crusade, 1983.

15. Lance Morrow, "Old Paradigm, New Paradigm" in *Time*, January 14, 1991, 66.

Chapter 6: Confidence Builder 3: The Dark Prospects

1. Rodney Clapp, "Overdosing on the Apocalypse" in *Christianity Today,* October 28, 1991, 26.

2. Paul Kennedy, *Preparing for the Twenty-first Century,* quoted in Nita Lelyveld, "Future Problems Overwhelming" in *Wisconsin State Journal,* April 27, 1993.

3. Quoted in Sine, *Wild Hope,* 217.

4. Sine, *Wild Hope,* 2.

5. George Friedman and Meredith LeBard, *The Coming War with Japan.* New York: St. Martin's Press, 1991.

6. Terry E. Figgie, *The Coming Collapse of America and How to Stop It.* New York: Little, Brown and Co., 1993.

7. Larry Burkett, *The Coming Economic Earthquake.* Chicago: Moody Press, 1991.

8. Quoted in Larry Burkett, "America's Debt Crisis" in *Intercessors for America Newsletter,* 4.

9. William Pannell, *The Coming Race War?* Grand Rapids: Zondervan, 1992.

10. Quoted in David Broder, "Campaign Platitudes Won't Save Our Cities" in *The Newark State Ledger,* April 5, 1992.

11. Quoted in Anastasia Toufexis, "Losing the Next Generation" in *Time,* March 23, 1992, 41.

12. Claude Lewis, "Americans Choking on a Steady Diet of Brutality" in *Wisconsin State Journal,* November 25, 1992.

13. See for example James Davison Hunter, *Culture Wars: The Struggle to Define America,* Basic Books, 1991.

14. Michael Medved, *Hollywood vs. America: Popular Culture and the War on Traditional Values.* San Francisco: HarperCollins, 1992. Quoted in Michael Cromartie, "The Triumph of Perversity" in *World,* November 7, 1992, 11.

15. Carl F. H. Henry, *Twilight of a Great Civilization: The Drift Toward Neo-Paganism.* Westchester, Ill.: Crossway Books, 1988.

16. Charles Colson quoted in George W. Cornell, "Fellowship Founder: U.S. Losing Religion" in *Wisconsin State Journal,* August 3, 1993.

17. From a talk given by George Hunter in September 1992 to a National Association of Evangelicals sponsored event on church planting toward the year 2000. Similar themes are addressed in his book *How to Reach Secular People,* Abingdon Press, 1992.

18. From class lectures on "The Spiritual Dynamics of Church Growth" given at Fuller Theological Seminary, 1975. I have heard Dr. Orr state a similar idea in subsequent talks.

19. From a poll conducted by the National Association of Evangelicals in preparation for the fiftieth anniversary celebrations in 1992.

20. Bryant Myers, "The Changing Shape of World Mission" in the MARC newsletter, March, 1994, 6.

21. Aleksandr Solzhenitsyn, "Men Have Forgotten God," reprinted in *Pastoral Renewal,* April, 1984, 116.

22. Olaf Hallesby, *Prayer.* Minneapolis: Augsburg Press, 1931, 77–78.

Chapter 7: Confidence Builder 4: The Disturbing Paralysis

1. John R. W. Stott, *Decisive Issues Facing Christians Today.* Grand Rapids: Fleming H. Revell, 1990. Stott is quoted in "Wake-Up Call for the Church," in *Eakin* magazine, May 1993, 40.

2. George H. Gallup Jr. and Timothy Jones, *The Saints Among Us: How the Spiritually Committed Are Changing Our World.* Richfield, Conn.: Morehouse Publishers, 1992, 12.

3. These statistics appear to originate with George Barna and have been quoted in various sources such as his *What Americans Believe.* Ventura, Calif.: Regal Books, 1991.

4. An analysis based on research presented by the executive director of ACMC, Bill Waldrop, and quoted in *Pulse* (Evangelical Missions Information Service), February 1993, 1.

5. Cal Thomas, "A Revolution Is Needed to Revive the Churches" in *Wisconsin State Journal,* May 10, 1991.

6. Murillo, "Why We Need Fresh Fire," 46.

7. Sine, *Wild Hope,* 180–87.

8. Chuck Colson, "With Custer's Lieutenants at Little Big Horn" in *Christianity Today,* October 5, 1992, 23.

9. Os Guinness, *No God but God.* Dallas: Word Publishers, 1992, 183.

10. A. W. Tozer, *The Pursuit of God.* Harrisburg, Pa.: Christian Publications, 1948, 17.

11. James Reapsome, "Our Grand Assumptions" in *Pulse* magazine (Evangelical Missions Information Service), September 11, 1992, 8.

12. Tom Sine, *Wild Hope,* 201.

13. Clinton Arnold, *Powers of Darkness: Principalities and Powers in Paul's Letters.* Downers Grove, Ill.: InterVarsity Press, 1992, 191.

Chapter 8: Confidence Builder 5: The Dramatic Preparations

1. George Otis Jr., *The Last of the Giants.* Grand Rapids: Chosen Books, 1991, 144–46.

2. E. Stanley Jones, *The Unshakable Kingdom and the Unchanging Person.* Nashville: Abingdon Press, 1972.

3. Richard Lovelace, *Dynamics of Spiritual Life: An Evangelical Theology of Renewal.* Downers Grove, Ill.: InterVarsity Press, 1979, 151, 424.

4. John Dawson, *Taking Our Cities for God.* Lake Mary, Fla.: Creation House, 1989, 63.

5 Expressed in personal conversations during a meeting with New York City leaders in January 1994.

6. From an interview entitled "Martyrdom: The Most Potent Factor in World Evangelization" in *Pulse* magazine, (Evangelical Missions Information Service), July 7, 1989, vol. 24 no. 13, 5.

7. Barrett, *Our Globe,* 37.

8. In lectures given to a leadership retreat in New Jersey, May 1992.

Chapter 9: Confidence Builder 6: The Distinctive Praying

1. Bryant, *With Concerts of Prayer,* 24–26.

2. Jean Seligmann, "Talking to God" in *Newsweek,* January 6, 1992, 38.

3. George Gallup, interviewed in "George Gallup Looks at Religion in America" in *Reformed Theological Seminary Journal,* 11, 1991.

4. Alvin VanderGriend, *The Praying Church Sourcebook.* Grand Rapids: Christian Reformed Publishers, 1992.

5. These ideas are discussed in depth in C. Peter Wagner's *Your Church Can Pray!* Ventura, Calif.: Regal Books, 1993.

6. All published by Regal Books, Ventura, Calif. in 1992 and 1993.

7. J. Edwin Orr, *Campus Aflame.* Chicago: Moody Press, 1972.

8. See further from Joe Aldrich, *Prayer Summits: Seeking God's Agenda for Your Community.* Portland, Ore.: Multnomah Press, 1992.

9. Richard Foster, *Prayer: Finding the Heart's True Home.* San Francisco: Harper Publishers, 1992.

10. Donald Bloesch, *The Struggle of Prayer.* Colorado Springs: Helmers & Howard, 1988.

Chapter 10: Confidence Builder 7: The Determined People

1. The term *seekers,* as I use it here, should be distinguished from the way the term is used by the Willow Creek Community Church and other similar models of Christian outreach. For them, the term is often used in the phrase "being seeker sensitive." By this is meant developing an approach to or style of evangelism that is sensitive to the needs of any nonbeliever with a growing desire to know God. What I mean by the term carries this principle to much greater depths. From the beginning of conversion onward, God wants all of us to *remain* seekers, all the time. In the Scriptures, the believers who received the highest commendations from God were those whose lifestyles marked them as constant, persistent, determined, and eager seekers of everything God had for them. Furthermore, every great revival has come to the church when God has ignited a "critical mass" of Christians who are determined to look to God for revival, and nowhere else, and to do so until revival comes. In a sense, you could say that *God* is "seeker sensitive" because he gladly rewards those who diligently seek him for such an outpouring of his Spirit (Heb. 11:6).

2. Lewis A. Drummond, *The Awakening That Must Come.* Nashville: Broadman Press, 1978, 136–37.

3. Samuel Shoemaker, *With the Holy Spirit and with Fire.* New York: Harper & Brothers Publ., 1960, 119.

4. I am grateful for this insight and for the term itself to theologian Vernard Eller.

5. John Piper, *Desiring God.* Portland: Multnomah Press, 1986, 113.

6. Roberts, *Revival,* 68–69.

7. Martyn Lloyd-Jones, *Joy Unspeakable: Power and Renewal in the Holy Spirit.* Wheaton, Ill.: Harold Shaw Publishers, 1984, 224.

8. Tozer, *The Pursuit of God,* 65.

Chapter 11: Pacesetters for World Revival: Getting Started

1. Fulton P. Gerlach and Virginia H. Hine, *People, Power, and Change: Movements of Social Transformation*. New York: Bobs-Merrill Company, Inc., 1970, xvi.

2. David Bryant, *Biblical Agendas for Concerts of Prayer*. Wheaton, Ill.: Concerts of Prayer International, P.O. Box 1399, 1993.

3. David Bryant, *The Hope at Hand: A Small Group Study/Discussion Guide*. Wheaton, Ill.: Concerts of Prayer International, P.O. Box 1399, 1995.

4. An observation frequently stated by historian Richard Lovelace.

Appendices

1. The statistics and observations in the four appendices have been gleaned from many different scholars, demographers, and missiologists. It would be impossible to document every one. The resources on which I have relied heavily include the following:

Patrick Johnstone, *Operation World*. Grand Rapids: Zondervan, 1993.

Tom Houston, *Scenario 2000: A Personal Forecast on the Prospects for World Evangelization*. Monrovia, Calif.: World Vision International, 1991.

George Barna, *Barna Reports,* for 1990, 1991, 1992, 1993. Ventura, Calif.: Regal Books.

Leith Anderson, *Decade of Volatility: Ten Powerful Trends Facing the Church*. National and International Religion Report, Special Report, 1990.

World Evangelization, a publication of the Lausanne Committee for World Evangelization. I've drawn from research published in issues for 1988 through 1991.

Frank Caleb Janzen, General Editor, *Target Earth*. Pasadena, Calif.: Global Mapping International, 1989.

David Barrett, who has published in various journals and periodicals including *World Evangelization* and the *International Missionary Bulletin*. Many of his basic findings were documented in the *World Christian Encyclopedia: A Comparative Study of Churches and Religions in the Modern World,* A.D. *1900–2000*. New York: Oxford University Press, 1982.

George H. Gallup Jr., whose research and statistics are published and quoted widely in current periodicals and newspapers, both secular and Christian.